Gender and Power in Families

Behind the systems approach to the family lie the hidden assumptions that men and women are equal within the family structure, and that women and men are treated equally in clinical practice. *Gender and Power in Families* challenges these assumptions, presenting both a conceptual discussion of the subject and a review of the clinical practice.

The contributors, all experienced therapists who work with women in a variety of public health and social service settings, re-examine the position of women and men in families and in family therapy. Drawing on their work with women from varied social and ethnic backgrounds, the authors look at the issues as they relate to women who have suffered sexual abuse as children, and women struggling to bring up children alone, or with partners with whom they are in perpetual conflict. They also explore the problems of women who are deemed mentally handicapped; women who are first-generation immigrants; and black women, who are marginalized and oppressed by race and class combined with gender.

Gender and Power in Families looks closely at the family in its wider social context, arguing that the issues of gender and power are central to family therapy training and practice. This new approach makes the book essential reading for students and practitioners in family therapy, social work, psychology, psychiatry, and psychotherapy.

Gender and Power in Families

Edited by

Rosine Jozef Perelberg

and

Ann C. Miller

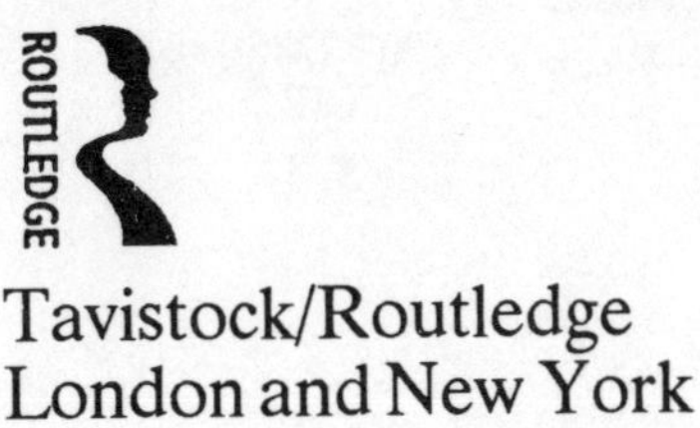

Tavistock/Routledge
London and New York

First published 1990
by Routledge
11 New Fetter Lane, London EC4P 4EE

Simultaneously published in the USA and Canada
by Routledge
a division of Routledge, Chapman and Hall, Inc.
29 West 35th Street, New York, NY 10001

Reprinted 1992

Typeset by
NWL Editorial Services, Langport, Somerset TA10 9DG

Printed and bound in Great Britain by
Mackays of Chatham PLC, Chatham, Kent

British Library Cataloguing in Publication Data
Perelberg, Rosine Jozef
Gender and power in families. 1.Medicine. Family therapy
I. Title
II. Miller, Ann C. 616.89156

Library of Congress Cataloging in Publication Data
Gender and power in families/edited by Rosine Jozef
Perelberg & Ann C. Miller
p. cm.
Includes bibliographical references.
1. Sex role. 2. Family psychotherapy. 3. Feminism.
4. Sex differences (Psychology)
I. Perelberg, Rosine Jozef. II. Miller, Ann C.
HQ1075.G46 1990 90-32385
305.42–dc20 CIP

ISBN 0–415–05207–6
0–415–04911–3 (pbk)

To my mother, to whom this book would have offered inspiration.

AM

To Sergio and Daniel.

RJP

Contents

Contributors

Charlotte Burck holds an M.Sc. in Social Work and qualified in Family Therapy at the Tavistock Clinic in London where she is a Clinical Lecturer in Social Work. She also teaches at the Institute of Family Therapy. She has published papers with the Family Studies Group at the Great Ormond Street Hospital for Sick Children.

Maureen Clark gained a BA (Hons) in Sociology, and a Post-graduate Diploma in Applied Social Studies and a Certificate of Qualified Social Worker (CQSW) at the University of London. She works in the Social Services Department of Essex County Council.

Gwyn Daniel completed an M.Sc. in Social Work and the two-year advanced course in Family Therapy at the Tavistock Clinic in London. She is Director for Training at the Institute of Family Therapy, London and Co-Director of the Oxford Family Institute. She is currently involved in a joint Families at Risk and Essex University project on growing up in step-families.

Jane Dutton-Conn is a qualified teacher and social worker and accredited Family Therapist with an M.Phil. in Social Work. She has worked in a variety of local authority social work settings as a practitioner and manager, is a Senior Lecturer at Middlesex Polytechnic and is also a trainer and consultant in the field of family and organizational systems.

Gill Gorell Barnes was among the founders of the Institute of Family Therapy, London, where she was the Director for Training. After gaining an M.Sc. in Social Work, she worked for many years with Robin Skynner at the Woodberry Down Child and Family Clinic. She is a Senior Social Worker in the Department for Children and

Parents at the Tavistock Clinic, and a tutor at Brunel University and Birkbeck College, University of London. She teaches widely both in the UK and abroad and is the author of *Working with Families*.

Ann Heavey trained in Family Therapy at the Institute of Family Therapy, London and in Psychiatry at the Maudsley and St George's Hospitals in London, gaining an M.Phil. in Psychiatry from the University of London. She is a Consultant Psychiatrist with the St Helier NHS Trust, Carshalton, Surrey and is Honorary Senior Lecturer in Psychiatry at St George's Medical School, London. She has published in the areas of anorexia nervosa, psychotherapy and medical communication.

Sue Holland trained in Clinical Psychology and Psychotherapy. She has been involved in mental-health work for twenty-five years, setting up programmes for working-class black and national minority groups. Sue runs a neighbourhood women's mental-health project for Hammersmith and Fulham Social Services Department in London.

Elsa Jones trained in Clinical Psychology in South Africa and was a Sheldon Fellow of the Family Therapy Programme at the Tavistock Clinic, London. She is a Family Therapist and trainer at the Family Institute in Cardiff, where she organizes the Advanced Diploma in Family Therapy. She is also book review editor of *The Journal of Family Therapy* and author of the forthcoming books: *Working with Adult Survivors of Childhood Abuse* and *Family Systems Therapy: developments in the systematic therapies*. She is also a free-lance therapist and trainer.

Annette Kilworth qualified as an Art Teacher and then did a Certificate of Social Work. She is a Social Worker in a Child Guidance Clinic in Essex.

Barry Mason is a qualified social worker. He trained as a Family Therapist at the Institute of Family Therapy in London, where he is a Clinical Supervisor. He is also a Family Therapist at the Family Institute in Cardiff.

Ed Mason is a qualified social worker. Prior to qualifying, he worked with adolescents, both in a psychiatric unit and a day centre. He is now a Team Leader for the National Society for the Prevention of Cruelty to Children in Rochdale.

Ann C. Miller trained in Clinical Psychology at the University of

Melbourne. She is Principal Clinical Psychologist at the Marlborough Family Service (Parkside Health Authority), and Honorary Research Fellow at the Academic Department of Psychology, University College, London, where she is Course Organizer of the Diploma in Family Therapy. She is Honorary Teaching Fellow at Birbeck College, London, Member of the Institute of Family Therapy, London, and teaches abroad as well as in the UK.

Margaret O'Brien holds a Ph.D. in Social Psychology. She is a Principal Lecturer in Psychology at the Department of Sociology at North East London Polytechnic and a Clinical Psychologist with Bloomsbury Health authority, London. She is the co-editor of *The Father Figure* and *Reassessing Fatherhood* and has published numerous papers.

Rosine Jozef Perelberg gained a Ph.D. in Social Anthropology at the London School of Economics. She is Honorary Research Fellow in the Academic Department of Psychology, University College, London. She worked at the Maudsley Hospital as a psychotherapist, is Senior Psychotherapist/Family Therapist at the Marlborough Family Service, Parkside Health Authority, London and works as a Psychoanalyst in private practice. She is a Member of the Institute of Family Therapy and an Associate Member of the British Psycho-Analytical Society. She is an Associate Editor of *The New Library of Psychoanalysis*.

Cas Schneider gained an M.Sc. in Clinical Psychology at Exeter University. She is a Clinical Psychologist, and Family and Individual Psychotherapist with Plymouth Health Authority.

Annie Turner gained a BA (Hons) and a Postgraduate Diploma in Applied Social Studies and a Certificate of Qualification in Social Work at the University of Hull. She is also an accredited Family Therapist. She has worked in local authority settings as a practitioner and manager and is currently a Regional Services Officer with RELATE. She is a trainer and consultant in the field of family and organizational systems.

Amy Urry trained as a social worker at Exeter University and later spent some time in the Training Programme in Family Therapy in the Washington Family Therapy Practice Center with Marianne Walters. She is a Family Therapist with Exeter Health Authority and also works in private practice.

Practice Center in Washington, DC. During and since her tenure as Executive Director of the Training Center at the Philadelphia Child Guidance Clinic, she has held faculty positions at several schools of social work and departments of psychiatry in the USA. She is on the editorial board of *Contemporary Family Therapy*, and is co-author of *The Invisible Web: Gender Patterns in Family Relationships.*

Acknowledgements

To the women, sisters, friends, and colleagues who have helped form my thinking about gender and power, in particular my sister Zoe Joyce, Angela Foster, Win Roberts, and Rosine J. Perelberg, my co-editor. To the men who have worked with me and struggled with these issues, particularly Chris Iveson.

AM

So many people played a part in the creation of this book that I will only be able to acknowledge a few of them. My special thanks go to: Jean La Fontaine, an important source of intellectual inspiration; Chris Dare, whose spirit of research has been a source of great stimulation over the years; my other colleagues and friends at the Institute of Psychiatry, especially Catherine Crowther; my colleagues at the Marlborough Family Service, particularly Alan Cooklin, whose conviction created the first Family Therapy post in the National Health Service; Ann Miller, my co-editor and an important presence in my work at the Marlborough; my patients – individuals, couples and families – who have taught me how to be a therapist; Bella and Georges Jozef, for their example of dedication to intellectual work.

RJP

To the participants in the Second Conference on Feminism and Family Therapy and all the contributors to this book for their trust that it would eventually be published. We would also like to extend our thanks to the South-East Association of Family Therapy for their support towards the cost of the conference; and to the Association of Family Therapy Education Trust for a grant towards the cost of the book.

To Judith Perle, our literary editor, whose clear thinking and skills with language have helped immeasurably in the production of this book.

To Maureen Hearn, Carole Frost, and Julia Constable, for their help in the completion of the final manuscript.

RJP and AM

Introduction I

Rosine Jozef Perelberg

Throughout history the genders have been perceived in a polarized way, although both have also been regarded as possessing contradictory attributes. Women have been seen as the source of all goodness, as the origin of knowledge, wisdom, or life itself; they have also been seen as dangerous, morally and sexually polluted, superstitious, and capricious. Men have been perceived in opposition to each of these categories, either as a force that must be tamed by the gentle control of women, or themselves as the source of wisdom and knowledge.

Medicine, literature, anthropology, and sociology abound in examples of these dichotomies, and indicate how men and women have been understood in terms of their opposition to each other. At the same time, these various areas of knowledge have themselves played a role in reinforcing gender categories. Examples taken from the western cultural baggage illustrate some of these perceptions.

In Aegean civilization, there was a belief that in the beginning there was a goddess. She was the Great Goddess, the Universal Mother, in whom all the functions of divinity were united. She symbolized fertility and the universal; she was immortal and omnipotent (Graves 1959).

Myths of the original power of women are also present in the first Marxist analyses of the origins of society which put forward the hypothesis that in the beginning there was Matriarchy. Such myths have flourished in many groups studied by social anthropologists. In indigenous societies from Latin America, for instance, myths such as the 'Myth of the Sacred Flute' and 'The Village of Women' tell of a time when matriarchy was supposed to have existed. Once upon a time the women took over the powers that belonged to men, who were allocated the roles which had up to then belonged to the women (Franchetto *et al.* 1980). We now understand that myths are stories which attempt to find a solution for contradictory propositions in the social system, sometimes trying to redress an imbalance in society by presenting an inversion of the prevailing social order.

The combined attributes encountered in each gender are sometimes explicitly indicated. It has been said about one of the main western symbols of femininity, *The Mona Lisa*:

> The lady smiled in regal calm: her instincts . . . to seduce and to ensnare, the charm of deceit, the kindness that conceals a cruel purpose – all this appeared and disappeared by turns behind the laughing veil and buried itself in the poem of her smile. Good and wicked, cruel and compassionate, graceful and feline, she laughed.
>
> (in Freud 1910: 109)

Women have been reproached as the cause of general malaise and unhappiness in many major literary works, paradigmatic of western culture. Shakespeare's *Hamlet* is a case in point. Both Hamlet and his father are united in reproaching Gertrude, Hamlet's mother, for her sexual weakness. One of the threads of the play stresses Gertrude's responsibility for the tragedy (for a further discussion see Rose 1986):

> Frailty, thy name is woman
> ...
> She married – O most wicked speed! To post
> with such dexterity to incestuous sheets!
> It is not, nor it cannot come to good.
>
> (Act I, Sc. II, V. 146; 155–8)

Mozart's opera *The Magic Flute* emphasizes a polarized perception of the genders. In the story, there is a battle between good and evil, light and darkness, a struggle between a patrilineal lineage (Sarastro and Tamino) and a matriarchal one (the Queen of the Night) (Hiatt 1979; Jordanova 1980). Sarastro rules the Temple of Wisdom and a constant theme throughout the opera is the need for the ignorance of women to be combatted by the reason and wisdom of men. Male reason is emphasized as good and women are reminded of their inferior position.

In culture, therefore, a number of contradictory images of women exist. The counterpart of the devoted, altruistic mother is the cruel, sadistic stepmother of fairy tales; the innocent virgin is also the source of tragedy; the protective and nurturing woman is contrasted with the witch and the seducer. *Mother, Madonna, Whore* is the evocative title of a recent book (Welldon 1988).

In many societies, women have been perceived as polluted and dangerous. Especially at certain periods of the month, they have to be avoided or excluded from major ritual ceremonies. They have been identified with the 'in-between', liminal state of rites of passage (so that they are neither here nor there), and are not perceived as complete social persons. In some contemporary societies, for example, they are considered to bring bad luck to certain kinds of ships, such as those going to war; in Brazil they must be avoided in the important 'concentration' ceremony in the days preceding a major football match.

Simone de Beauvoir has pointed out the importance of such images in both expressing and reproducing perceptions of women. One must stress, however, that there is no one-to-one correlation between ideology and the material conditions in which the genders exist; stereotyped images carry on being reproduced when the economic infrastructure may have already been transformed. There are discontinuities between the two, contradictions which exist side by side.

This book will look at therapeutic work with women in many different situations. There is a complex variation in the ways in which women exist, which cannot be subsumed by stereotypical characterizations of women. The challenge is to look at the ways in which images of women such as those described here have been incorporated into the fabric of society and have thus profoundly influenced the way in which both men and women are perceived and thus treated in the clinic.

The family and the State in England

A few words about the relationship between the family and the State in England will help to place family therapy in its wider context.

The nineteenth century witnessed an impressive proliferation of charities in England. In London alone, it was estimated that during the second half of the century, some 640 religious and secular charitable institutions maintained charity schools, hospitals, dispensaries, asylums, orphanages, reformatories, and penitential homes for prostitutes. Many of the most famous English charities, including the Salvation Army, the YMCA, and Dr Barnardo's, date from this period.

Several authors (for example, Fraser 1973) have pointed out that it was fear of social revolution, together with a desire to improve the moral state of the poor, that lay at the root of these charities. It has also been emphasized that their main function was to act as agents of social control, attempting to inculcate middle-class values among the working class. Stedman-Jones suggests that the absence of direct economic links between the upper and lower classes largely explains the particular importance of charitable activity in London, both as a mode of interpreting the behaviour of the poor and as a means of attempting to control them (Stedman-Jones 1971: 240).

These charities, therefore, appeared neither because of the 'failure' of the family itself to cope with its internal social roles, nor because of interpersonal conflicts. Explanations must be sought elsewhere, and can be divided into three main groups:

(1) The development of the capitalist mode of production, the social and political consequences of which created a need to control great masses of the population;
(2) Philanthropic organizations represented attempts to 'normalize' this stratum of the population by trying to impose certain norms derived from elsewhere in society;
(3) The issue of morality lying at the root of the various philanthropic movements.

In keeping with the moral character of these charities, their members assumed that poverty was the result of personal failing. The Metropolitan Visiting and Relief Association, for instance, declared that its goal was the 'removal of the moral causes which create or aggravate want; to encourage prudence, industry and cleanliness' (in Fraser 1973: 119). William Booth similarly perceived the Salvation Army as part of the fight against 'the evils which lie at the root of all miseries of modern life' (Booth 1890: 17). He aimed to 'change the man when it is his character and conduct which constitute the reasons for his failure in the battle of life' (ibid.: 85).

Donzelot termed these agencies the 'tutorial complex' (1977: 91) and viewed them as representing preliminary laboratories for the development of ideas and social practices from which various techniques of social control were subsequently derived (ibid.: 135). The argument suggests that these functions were progressively taken over by the State through medico-psychological schemes, as part of a process which reduces the socio-historical dimension to a problematic localized in the individual.

Despite the proliferation of philanthropic organizations in England in the late nineteenth century, they all tended to wait for individual clients to approach them for help. It was only through the establishment of the Charity Organization Society in 1869 that a visiting system, based on a rigorous enquiry into the lives of the people for whom help was provided, was initiated. This system was, in fact, a precursor of that adopted by social services in the mid twentieth century.

Legislation dealing with the family during the late nineteenth century was mainly directed towards children and this approach was shared by many charities. The moral content of the NSPCC (the National Society for the Prevention of Cruelty to Children), established in 1895, is clearly evident in their belief that the need for infant welfare services was due to a failure in motherhood. The declared aim of the NSPCC was to reform the character of working-class mothers (Lewis 1981; see also Perelberg 1983).

A major step in the growth of government concern with childhood problems was the Children's Act of 1848 which addressed the care of deprived children and set up children's committees to establish a secure family environment for children in care. Family policy was at that time mainly concerned with child care, although neither the problems encountered by working mothers nor the redistribution of roles within the family were included within its brief (Steiner 1981: 184).

The turn of the century witnessed the increasing intervention of the State in areas previously covered solely by philanthropic organizations. The Labour Party was founded in 1900 and in 1905 public work schemes were instituted by the government in order to relieve unemployment. The Education Act of 1906 legalized medical inspections and the provision of meals in schools, and the Children's Act of 1908 made parental neglect of a child's health a legal offence. Thus, the State gradually claimed responsibility for the hungry, the unemployed, and the sick.[1]

In 1915 the Women's Co-operative Guild published a collection of letters written by working-class mothers in which they pointed out that lack of food, overwork, and exhaustion were the prime causes for still births at the time. Although Herbert Samuel's preface to the book supported the women, it still spoke in terms of 'bad environment'. He stated:

> It is the duty of the community, so far as it can, to relieve motherhood of its burden, to spread the knowledge of mothercraft that is so often lacking, to make medical aid available when it is needed ... The infant cannot, indeed, be saved by the State. It can only be saved by the mother. But the mother can be helped and can be taught by the State.
>
> (in Llewelyn Davies 1978, preface)

From the nineteenth century onwards, the State's preoccupation with the family was primarily focused on the child and the mother. The paradoxical aspect of the progressive intervention of the various professionals on the family throughout the twentieth century, however, lies in the fact that the mother has become both an ally of those professionals and the person whom they must reform. The promotion of the educational role of women as mothers and of their support of medical knowledge became embedded in the way Family Planning Clinics, Health Centres, and Child Benefit schemes presuppose the co-operation of mothers. In direct contrast, theories linking bad motherhood and mental illness have abounded in the second half of the twentieth century.

The penetration of outside agencies into the family domain is an integral part of the history of the poor in England since at least the last century. Donzelot (1977: 58) pointed out that one effect of 'morally uplifting the poor', their normalization and surveillance, adopted by the philanthropists is to reduce familial autonomy. It thus becomes a form of violence against the family.

In the late 1970s, my field-work as a social anthropologist in a deprived area of London gave me insight into a more complex picture. Having started with a framework rooted in the anti-psychiatry movement and an anti social-control standpoint, my qualitative study of families showed me how they did not want 'less intervention', but more appropriate forms of intervention. The families who were at the receiving end of the services actually did want help, but they felt they had been insufficiently involved in the process of deciding what kind of help they needed. They wanted more participation in the delimitation of boundaries between their own responsibility and that of the agencies; they wanted support in their negotiations with these agencies. However, on many occasions, these agencies attempted to impose a specific 'shape' upon the families.

Against this background family therapy has made its appearance in England, first in the 1960s, with the anti-psychiatry movement, then in the 1970s, with systems thinking. Although family therapy has challenged the manicheistic way in which the relationship between mental illness and the family has been perceived, it has not challenged the way professionals have approached the genders in the clinic. More specifically, it has not taken on board the paradoxical role which has been allocated to women, as both the professional's main ally and their main target for change.

It is against this complex background that this book must be seen.

Note

1. Gough (1979) distinguishes between two types of theories that attempt to explain the origins of the British welfare state – the functionalist and the action theories. The first perceive the welfare state as a functional

response to the needs of capital; the latter sees it as the fruit of working-class struggles. Gough suggests that whereas the former objectify history, the latter subjectify it. He stresses the contradictory character of the welfare state as it has to be envisaged both as functional to the needs of capitalist development and as the result of the political struggle of the organized working class.

References

Booth, W. General (1890) *In Darkest England and the Way Out*, London: International Headquarters of the Salvation Army.

Donzelot, J. (1977) *La Police des Familles*, Paris: Éditions de Minuit.

Franchetto, B., Cavalcanti, M.L.V.C. and Heieborn, M.L. (1980) 'Antropologia e feminismo', in B. Franchetto, M.L.V.C. Cavalcanti and M.L. Heieborn (eds.) *Perspectivas Antropológicas da Mulher*, Rio de Janeiro: Zahar.

Fraser, D. (1973) *The Evolution of the British Welfare State*, London: Macmillan Press.

Freud, S. (1910/1981) 'Leonardo da Vinci and a memory of his childhood', *Standard Edition of the Complete Psychological Works of Sigmund Freud, Vol. XI*, London: Hogarth Press, p. 109.

Gough, I. (1979) *The Political Economy of the Welfare State*, London: Macmillan.

Graves, R. (1959) *The Greek Myths*, Vol. 1, Harmondsworth: Penguin.

Hamlet (1982) London: Methuen.

Hiatt, L.R. (1979) 'Queen of the night, mother-right, and secret male cults', in R.A. Hook (ed.) *Fantasy and Symbol: Studies in Anthropological Interpretation*, London: Academic Press.

Jordanova, L.J. (1980) 'Natural facts: a historical perspective on science and sexuality', in C. MacCormack and M. Strathern (eds.) *Nature, Culture and Gender*, Cambridge: Cambridge University Press.

Lewis, J. (1981) *The Politics of Motherhood*, London: Croom Helm.

Llewelyn Davies, M. (ed.) (1978) *Maternity: Letters from Working Women*, London: Virago.

Mozart, W.A. (1981) *Die Zauberflöte*, London: Cassell.

Perelberg, R.J. (1983) 'Family and mental illness in a London borough', unpublished Ph.D. thesis, University of London.

Rose, J. (1986) *Sexuality in the Field of Vision*, London: Verso.

Stedman-Jones, G. (1971) *Outcast London: A Study of the Relationship between Classes in Victorian Society*, Oxford: Clarendon Press.

Steiner, G.Y. (1981) *The Futility of Family Policy*, Massachussets: Brookings Institution.

Welldon, Estela V. (1988) *Mother, Madonna, Whore: The Idealization and Denigration of Motherhood*, London: Free Association.

Introduction II

Ann C. Miller

If one agrees to take the establishment of the first family-therapy training course in 1973[1] as the birth of family therapy in this country, then in 1989, it has reached the age of consent. It therefore seems very appropriate that the first book on gender and power in family therapy to appear in Britain should be published now, since the consent of women, as therapists and clients, to family-therapy practice may yet be in the balance. Family therapy itself has been subversive of much in established modes of clinical practice. It has challenged the idea of individual pathology and the positivist models prevailing in psychiatry and psychology. It has stressed the importance of context in the development and maintenance of the problems which people present and its practice has engaged directly in contextual change. It has progressively widened its thinking about context to include professional networks which impinge on the family, so that family therapists have addressed the ways in which professional interventions, in attempting to solve problems, become part of those problems. It has also been subversive of professional and bureaucratic boundaries by questioning modes of service delivery in Health and the Social Services which 'cut up the ecology' by creating specialists to see adults in one place, adolescents in another, and children in yet another.

Family therapists were proud of the revolution in thinking and practice that family therapy appeared to have represented. In recent years, however, especially since 1982 and the Women's Project in Family Therapy conference in London, a different voice has been heard. Relatively quiet at first, it is becoming more insistent. American women therapists Marianne Walters, Betty Carter, Olga Silverstein, Peggy Papp, Rachel Hare-Mustin, Virginia Goldner, and others have been publishing challenges to the hidden assumption, prevailing in the systems approach to the family, that there is equality of power between men and women. Despite this the issue remains still a relatively marginalized one. We hope that this book will go some way towards rectifying that situation, and provide an impetus for making the issues of gender and power central to family-therapy training and practice.

The contributors to this volume do not offer a unified conceptual position about the relationship between feminism and family therapy, although they all share a strong commitment to examine the issues involved in that relationship. They all work, or have worked, in the public sector and many are involved in training. Some (Gill Gorell Barnes, Elsa Jones) are very well known as trainers and writers in the field. Others (Rosine Jozef Perelberg, Margaret O'Brien) have published in closely related fields (anthropology, sociology). Sue Holland is widely known for her pioneering work with black women in inner London. While she is not strictly speaking a family therapist, we have included her work for the inspiration it provides and the challenge it represents to established practices. Amy Urry and Cas Schneider are part of a group of women therapists (the Southwest Women's Group) specifically focusing on gender issues. Several are publishing for the first time.

The range of issues addressed in these papers relates to women from a variety of social and ethnic backgrounds and includes women struggling with bringing up children alone, or with partners with whom they are in conflict or whom they protect; women involved with the power of the State directly intervening in their family lives by removing their children; women who have survived sexual abuse as children; women who are deemed mentally handicapped; women who as first-generation immigrants are negotiating between two cultures; middle-class women balancing the world of work and the world of home; black women for whom race and class combine with gender in the mix that marginalizes and oppresses them.

We have also included two chapters specifically about men, both as clients and as therapists, for if women in families are not to be further disempowered by their experiences of therapy then the role of the male therapist is also in urgent need of exploration. For family therapists, the examination of gender and power is well overdue.

©1990 Ann C. Miller

Note

1. Family and Marital Therapy Course, Institute of Group Analysis, London.

Part one

Conceptual Frameworks

Chapter one

A feminist perspective in family therapy

Marianne Walters

There is no therapy, including family therapy, that can adequately reflect the range of human experience and conditions without including a feminist perspective. Yet a feminist perspective can never be monolithic or homogeneous as it will reflect the diversity of the complex social relations it addresses. A feminist perspective in family therapy is not limited to any particular methodology or technique, but rather is committed to exploring and elaborating the *context* and the *process* in the formation and transformation of any human experience.

Any feminist perspective in therapy has, I believe, four major components, each of which will be elaborated within a variety of theoretical and methodological frameworks. These components are (1) the conscious inclusion, in both theory and practice, of the experience of women growing up; developing; relating to each other, to men, and to social institutions; raising families; working; and growing old in a culture largely shaped and defined by male experience; (2) a critique of therapy practices, and the theoretical constructs on which they are based, that lend themselves to a devaluing of women, and of the particular social and familial roles of women – in other words, a critique of those practices and ideas commonly identified as sexist; (3) the integration of feminist theory, and the information derived from women's studies, into the knowledge base of psychological theory, as well as of methodological – and even pedagogical – framework; and (4) the use of female modes and models in the continuing expansion and development of theory and practice in the field.

What *do* women want?

This plaintive question has haunted such profound thinkers as Freud, to such mundane pundits as David Stockman. I would imagine Socrates himself pondering this dilemma as he framed yet another deductive question; or Nero dreaming of some answer to be found in the flickering flames of a burning Rome. Yet despite the best efforts of men to answer this question, it has remained largely a source of confusion, and perhaps concern, but certainly not resolution – partly, of course, because different women want different things, much as men do. But the answer is ultimately to be found in the construction of a society that equally represents the interests and aspirations and values of both sexes. To accomplish this task would mean rearranging power and privilege in our society – a difficult, if not for many an unwelcome, task. Yet, as a relatively enlightened microcosm of our society, it would seem that attempts at some rearrangement of that tiny piece of turf on which we therapists cavort would be welcome. Or so I thought when I first became interested in exploring with my family-therapy colleagues the relevance of feminism to family therapy, and my own experiences as a woman therapist. What I learned (or perhaps already knew but chose to deny in order to get up the nerve to forge ahead) was that even in a field committed to change, and to representing the interest of the family and its members – both female and male – the subordination and devaluing of women were so strongly ingrained that even the wisest in the field had trouble broadening their vision.

Family therapists who have pioneered a feminist critique of the field have encountered all of the usual responses, everything from 'We're all human, aren't we?' to 'I've always loved women', to 'But, I've always thought women were better than men!' Some therapists thought feminist family therapists should not be allowed to do family therapy because they would lecture and harangue their clients; others argued that a feminist theory was the antithesis of the 'neutrality' and 'objectivity' of systems theory. And there were those whose understanding of the issues could encompass nothing deeper than the tired notions of the 'battle between the sexes'. Some of our movers and shakers embraced the new ideas with benign neglect; others trivialized it by exploring the 'complementary' plight of men. But perhaps more disappointing than the querulousness, or the opposition, was the tendency of the field to engage with the new ideas that feminist thinkers espoused, and then quickly assign them the significance of one, among many, issues in the field – which is precisely the problem. Although feminism raises issues for and about women, such as equal pay, child care, and maternity leave, its significance rests on its conceptual departure from a traditional, male-dominated perspective. Feminism, particularly in the field of family systems and family relations, suggests a fundamental rethinking of beliefs, principles, and practices. It suggests a search for new information, a conceptual dialogue, self-criticism. It is not about an issue, a symptom, or a segment of our society; it is about that society and the relationship of the two genders that compose it. As such, the feminist perspective challenges the field to restructure some of its practice and reconsider some of its assumptions. Such change is no easier for us than it is for our clients.

As a social worker, I learned a lot about human growth and development, about social systems and conditions, and some about the helping process. As my profession was mostly peopled by women (and never showed a profit), it was not highly valued by our society and was low in the hierarchical pecking order of the service delivery systems within which we worked, particularly those dominated by the medical profession, such as mental health. In this context, I often felt helpless and unclear about how to create change most effectively. And as the profession was often derivative – that is, flowing from and defined by professions higher in the hierarchy and with more power – social work did not evolve a distinct methodology of its own, separate from the roles and functions assigned by the prevailing power structures. Even within our profession, we tended to devalue much of what we know and many of our tenets of practice – such as the ways in which process is used to inform and to convey a message; or that behaviour is contextual and interactional; or that much of one's emotional development occurs within the family. Being devalued, women lacking power, and thus devaluing ourselves, we internalized the negative social and professional attitudes that surrounded our work lives. We did not lay claim to a distinct methodology, and we shied away from explicit and direct techniques of intervention. Like many social workers, when I encountered family therapy, I embraced it eagerly and lovingly – and pretty uncritically. Here were methods, explicit and direct techniques for change, ways to work, ways to think. It had a conceptual framework – systems theory – a structure from which to view behaviour and to tackle symptoms. And it did not take for ever to see change occur. For the first time I felt truly instrumental in my professional functioning. Now I was not 'merely' a social worker – I was a family therapist. It had a more authoritative ring to it.

When one feels instrumental and powerful, it is difficult to question some of the assumptions on which that instrumentality is based, or to understand that my own process of professional evolution mirrors the experience of women at every level in society and, of course, within families. Being in a woman's profession that was devalued and derivative, I was defined by others and began to devalue my own expertise. My roles and functions were prescribed within a male hierarchy. Unsureness, fed by a lack of power, undermined my effectiveness and self-esteem. Given the opportunity for instrumental functioning, I embraced that end without questioning the means by which it was achieved. I had forgotten that the ends seldom justify the means, that change without 'due process' can indeed diminish the human endeavour.

What *do* women want? Perhaps the question can best be addressed through the process of asking them and listening to their answers.

Women's experience

At this stage in the development of the women's movement and of feminist consciousness, and considering the changes that have already improved the status of women, it seems almost redundant to discuss the continuing need to include the experience of women in our understanding of family dynamics and in the practices of family therapy. Yet perhaps in our field, more than any other of the social sciences and helping professions, it is necessary to emphasize this point. Systems theory and systemic modalities unfortunately have functioned to discount gender socialization and to blur gender differences. Systemic equations treat the *parts* as interchangeable, depending only on their configuration within the system for definition and explanation of their motivation and behaviour. The fact that such configurations must have origins in larger contexts is acknowledged but goes largely unattended and unexplored. Systemic equations and formulations conjure up the illusion of an objectivity that obscures the value-laden reality that they are meant to represent. It goes without saying that representations of reality will reflect the prevailing order of things, the accepted hierarchy, the socially approved values – unless these are challenged and uncovered to reveal the subtext. And so our systemic formulations and interventions will represent – indeed, will reproduce – patriarchal social, relational, and attitudinal structures unless the different, and often hidden, experience and reality of women in society, and in our families, are entered into the equation.

What is this experience? It is the everyday fall-out – subliminal, explicit, and covert; direct and indirect; conscious and unconscious; accidental and purposeful; humorous and serious – of life for women in a male-dominated culture.

> She attends a wedding and hears jokes about entrapment and how *now* he will have to get rid of his sexy secretary. She leaves the wedding and goes to a bar where one of the drinks offered, along with the Singapore Sling and White Russian, is 'the dreaded mother-in-law'. She returns home and opens a magazine and learns that

the best gift a woman can receive is a new Electrolux vacuum that will allow her to reach into the corners of the house she will clean. She reads an advertisement that tells her how easily she can be deceived if she gets something she wants in the end: 'Promise her anything, but give her Arpege'. She watches television and discovers that the only way a woman can get on the crew of a 'love boat' is as cruise director, attending to the pleasures of the 'family' of passengers – or failing that, as the daughter of the captain. She reads a popular novel and learns that success in the world of business is achieved by women who are bitchy. She turns to a history book where humans are referred to as mankind, work is described in terms of manpower, and the products of labour as man-made. Leaders are called chairmen and a skilled craftsman is called master (even when said expert is a woman). She calls a friend who describes a 'cat fight' in the office, evoking images of people clawing at each other rather than landing a direct punch.

She goes to a synagogue and sees that the most sacred, holiest of rituals there requires the services of ten men. She enters a church and hears the words of the prophet Martin Luther: 'If a woman dies in childbirth it matters not, because it was for this that she was created by God.' She attends a dinner party with her husband where the women talk of children and schools and the men exchange information about their enterprises. As a girl, she is told the boys won't like her if she is too smart ('Men won't make passes at girls who wear glasses'). As a young woman, she is told she won't attract a man if she is too fat. As a wife, she is told she won't keep her man if she doesn't defer to his needs. She will be an old maid if she does not marry; but if she graduates from college, she will get a bachelor's degree as her reward. When her children marry, she becomes the stuff from which a whole genre of jokes are fashioned. Paintings will depict her goddess-like qualities when she is coupled with her infant child; journal articles will describe her as smothering and hanging on when coupled with her adolescent child. She speaks of 'a rule of thumb' only to discover that this expression derives from an old English law that denied men the right to beat their wives with a stick larger than the circumference of their thumb!

Does the cumulative effect of such messages constitute a kind of psychological onslaught that shapes the way women experience themselves and each other? Do such messages affect the emotional and intellectual well-being of women? Of course they do; how could it be otherwise? These are the questions a feminist perspective will seek to address. Feminist family therapists have enlarged the theory of family functioning to include gender as a significant, if not fundamental, ingredient in the construction of family structures and interpersonal transactions. This challenges the idea that the family as a system is governed by its own internal regulatory mechanism within which all interpersonal transactions can be understood.

Women's experience is to be found not only in their encounter with the messages of a male culture and language, but within familial social institutions and structures. The institution of marriage, for instance, dramatically exemplifies the ways in which patriarchy, both implicitly and explicitly, organizes our lives. Marriage begins with the tradition of father handing his daughter over to another man whose name she will take, forsaking her own. (Of course, in a historical context, this quaint tradition would seem quite benign as it does not include purchasing a bride, a dowry, or some other form of economic barter, and the consent of the bride is almost always required!) The rituals of the marriage ceremony reflect the expected structure of the liaison to follow. The daughter is brought to her husband-to-be on the arm of her father while her mother quite literally stands to the side. The bride's face is often covered by a veil, suggesting humility. She wears white, symbolizing chastity. (And how does the groom demonstrate his humility and virginity?) In today's world, the bride may choose to keep her surname, but her formal social classification will change from Miss to Mrs (his remains Mr) and her person becomes, at least publicly, identified with her mate. Her new career as a wife will be organized by roles and functions primarily identified with the *internal* life of the family.

Early life decisions for the newly married couple, such as where and under what circumstances they will live, will largely depend on the man's work or career. This begins to construct the context and rules for later decision making between them. A process is set in motion that will identify this wife, and later their family, by association with the work or career, the choice, the social and economic conditions of the husband, the man, the head of the household. (Women have head-of-household status only when there is no husband present.) This process, in which the life of one adult person is largely organized by, and identified with, the life and person of another, is at the very core of the institution of marriage and the structure of family life. In the life cycle of women, power is, for the most part, derivative: as daughter, father entitles; as wife, husband bestows.

How is it possible to conduct therapy with families, with couples in and out of marriage, with women, without understanding how this process constructs many of the problems, relationships, and conflicts that we encounter in our offices? How can we make *therapeutic* interventions – interventions that will create change without damaging self-esteem – and not be sensitive to the profoundly different meanings our words, tasks, and metaphors will have for men and for women as a result of their gender experiences? And how can we not but be aware that in a patriarchal culture life experience will be defined largely within a male frame of reference? These questions are not merely rhetorical. In fact, such questions, and the concerns that provoke them, surround the experience of women both as family members and as care givers within institutionalized frameworks.

Women and service delivery systems

Women are at both ends of service delivery systems, as consumers and as providers. As gatekeepers of the family, it is women who are largely responsible for seeking the services attendant to the general welfare of the family. Yet when seeking these services, women become both dependent on other women and in opposition to them. For instance, the working mother seeking day care for her child will feel both grateful to and displaced by the day care worker (over 90 per cent of whom are women). In turn the day-care worker, while providing care for the child, will feel both commonality and conflict with the mother whose parenting needs often interfere with her own job performance. And both are caught up in a system that is underfunded and devalued, where their services are much in demand and in short supply, and where neither of their efforts, as the caretakers of the children, are signified by the larger society through the accepted signs of signification – money, power, access to resources, or public attention.

Or let us take the hypothetical case of a grade-school teacher (over 90 per cent of whom are women) and a troubled young boy. His classroom behaviour is disruptive and his grades are dropping. He seems to show no interest in school or in his peers. His parents are asked to come in for a consultation. His mother comes in alone because his father is working. She works, too, but only part-time, so she is able to manage the appointment. As the teacher describes the problem, the mother begins to feel failed, responsible, and overwhelmed. She has two more children at home, a younger child who has temper tantrums, and a teenager who has been acting out of late. As the teacher enquires about family issues that might be affecting the boy's behaviour in school, the mother begins to get the message that she may be causing the problem. She becomes defensive; perhaps indulges in some denial. She's afraid her son might get known as a misfit or trouble-maker. She defends him and feels protective. She feels alone in this.

The teacher has thirty other children in her classroom and is a mother herself. She knows what this mother is going through, but she has her work to do and her job to protect. She begins to experience this child's mother as overprotective, defensive, even a bit resistant. The teacher recommends that the family seek help at a mental-health agency.

The mother makes the call. The intake worker (the majority of whom are women) suggests she bring her husband with her on their first visit. He refuses; he does not think his son needs therapy. The mother, son, and little sister arrive for the initial session feeling irritable with each other. The intake worker sees an overloaded mother, who projects on to others the problem with her son: the school, her husband, her own mother. The worker finds the mother overprotective and overinvolved with her children; perhaps there is marital conflict. She suggests that the mother encourage her husband to come to the next session. Since the mother had already asked him to come to this one, she wonders if the worker thinks it is her fault that he did not come. And thus a continuum is constructed along which women as caretakers, in a culture that devalues their services, begin to experience each other as adversaries.

Recently, at my training centre in Washington, DC, we worked with Lucy and her five children. They had been referred to us for family therapy by child-protective services following the disclosure by the oldest daughter, Rose, age 17, that her stepfather had been sexually abusing her for six years. Lucy, a waitress, had alerted the authorities and had her husband removed from the home; Rose had been put in temporary foster care. The four other children were all under the age of 12. One had cerebral palsy, and another a learning disability. With the removal from the home of Joe, the father, and Rose, the eldest daughter, Lucy was left with no child-care support. She borrowed money from a brother in Detroit for the down payment for legal fees, and filed for divorce and for custody of the children.

Joe filed a countersuit, claiming that she was negligent of the children and sexually promiscuous. Joe, who was in a sexual offenders' group and was being seen by a court psychiatrist, continued to harass Lucy and to force entry into the house where she and the children lived. Whenever she called the police, they would get him to leave, but there was nothing they could do about keeping him from trying again, as he owned the house in which the family lived.

The foster-care worker (a woman) received complaints from the foster mother that Lucy was inconsistent and demanding in making arrangements to visit her daughter Rose. When the foster-care worker saw Lucy and Rose together, she felt there was a lot of unresolved conflict between them. She supported Rose in expressing her anger at her mother for not protecting her from her stepfather. The protective service worker (a woman) needed to determine if Lucy could protect her daughter in the future, care for her other children, and provide financially for the family. The worker was concerned that Lucy's work as a waitress resulted in irregular times at home with her children, and that her child-care arrangements were haphazard. She thought that Lucy should arrange to stay at home more to be with her younger children. But Lucy also needed to demonstrate that she could provide financially for her family.

The court-appointed worker (a woman) was concerned about Joe's allegations, and worried about whether Lucy could provide a proper home for *any* of the children. In agency case conferences, discussion centred on Lucy's problems with being a responsible, consistent parent; on her immature, narcissistic, disorganized behaviours; and on her financial credibility. In this context, Lucy was referred to us with her children, for family therapy.

As a single parent, Lucy must provide for her children, but like many if not most women in our society, is untrained and poorly paid. Like most families of divorcing parents, the father's child support is either non-existent, unenforced, insufficient, or dependent on the vagaries of his financial situation. Lucy must work, but also provide adequate supervision for her children. The children must be cared for and nurtured. But public day-care facilities have long waiting lists, and private ones are too expensive. Lucy needs to protect her daughter, but does not herself have access to legal protection. She is expected to begin to restructure her own life, but if she does so she is in danger of neglecting her children.

These are some of the familiar contexts within which women are defined and from which they will internalize ideas and attitudes that shape their sense of self. Women do not need to undergo these specific experiences to have them as part of what Jung would have called their collective unconscious, and I would call a universal consciousness. (Not that I would presume to compete with Jung, but we family therapists do not like to talk about the unconscious!) Attitudes and messages that devalue and subordinate women; social and institutional structures that diminish their instrumentality; double binds that hold mothers responsible for whatever happens with their children and overinvolved if they take that responsibility to heart; social realities that make women vulnerable to sexual abuse and rape while chiding them for being sexually repressed; economic conditions that place them in competitive, adversarial positions with each other in 'spaces' where access to resources is limited – this is the terrain of women's experience that has been hidden from view and thus gone unnoticed in our theories of family functioning. Many of the methods and techniques of family therapy demonstrate a tunnel vision that sees only what is immediately apparent and never explores that which lies below the surface. 'Meaning' is relegated to the margins or confined within the formulae of systems theory.

Therapy, techniques, and women

It has been well established that theories of human development and scales of maturity and individuation have been based on male models. This is also true of theories of human systems. In many ways, these theories have pathologized women, particularly with respect to their roles in family life. In the practice of family therapy the very absence of a consciousness about gender, and the differences in the development of men and women in a patriarchal culture, serve to pathologize women. The following examples, taken at random from family-therapy journals, publications and workshops, illustrate interventions and techniques that, in their very lack of awareness of, and sensitivity to, the meaning they convey to women, reproduce sexist constructs that invalidate women's experience.

We can begin with the familiar pursuer wife and distancer husband, a typology frequently employed in conceptualizing conflict or lack of communication and intimacy between marital partners. While framing the pursuit and distance as a complementary pattern of interaction, maintaining the balance of power between husband and wife, a therapist moves to block the pursuer so the distancer can enter. He suggests that the wife is working too hard; that she should back off, take a rest. (To the degree that *she* works so hard, *he* does not need to work at their relationship. The more *she* pursues, the more *he* will distance. *She* fills their emotional space; if *she* backs off, it will create a vacuum that *he* will fill.)

Such a technique ignores the fact that women are socialized to be the purveyors of relationships, the articulators of feeling, the nurturers of intimacy. In a culture that does *not* put a premium on relationship and intimacy, that comes dangerously close to equating emotionality with irrationality, failure to validate the pursuit of these ends devalues the very behaviours that are socially expected of women. A double bind indeed! Asking a woman to 'back off' from a pursuit of intimacy and relationship will convey the message that *her* pursuit endangers the relational competence of her partner; that her pursuit causes his distance. And what a message for the man – that his capacity for intimacy is contingent on the degree of intensity his wife employs in trying to engage him; that he will withdraw in the face of too much pursuit.

A similar typology is that of the overinvolved mother, peripheral father, and acting-out or problem-bearing child. This time, a therapist uses the father to block the mother's concentration on the child, thus engaging the father in greater involvement with his child while freeing the mother to engage in more complex, adult activities. No matter that the relationships are conceptualized as complementary. The intervention carries the same message as the previous one: mother is overfunctioning, overinvolved, overprotective, and father's peripherality is connected to that. In her socially prescribed role as primary parent, she will be perceived as having failed. His primary socially prescribed role, as family provider, is not at issue; and as a parent, he need only *enter* to set things right. It may balance the system, but what is the effect on the self-esteem of its members? And what of the notion that child rearing is a less than complex or adult activity? This idea delegitimizes the very function that women are expected to perform. (Anyway, maternal functioning is less complex than what – selling used cars?)

Another therapist, faced with a disengaged, distant, often absent father, suggests to the mother that she pretend that she cannot handle the child any more, that she act as if she has run out of alternatives and is giving up. Is this not isomorphic with generations of advice to women to 'act dumb', or 'fake it', so he will feel more competent and take charge? If we ask women to act incompetent on behalf of men, are we not conveying the message that their competence, at least with respect to their relationships with men, puts them at risk?

A therapist working with a couple in conflict because of the husband's infidelity uses a *meta* stance of tongue-in-cheek double-talk, suggesting that the wife might compete with her husband, perhaps 'go into the business' and offer her husband good rates. What is the message? When a woman has an extra-marital affair, it is likened to prostitution. I do not think the therapist thought this; I just think he did not think about the *meaning* his words would convey. A therapist working with a sexually inhibited couple, in the same vein of playful prodding, asks the husband if he would mind if he – the therapist – had a little affair with his wife during the session, noting that she had been making eyes at him, and he would like to 'retaliate'. The message? Men ask each other for permission to 'have fun' with 'their' women; her consent is not even sought! (The word 'retaliate' might have been a 'Freudian slip' – it certainly conveys the message that the women's flirtatiousness is experienced as aggression by a therapist whose experience of his own flirtation is benign.)

A therapist works with a couple which is fighting through their children, a boy and a girl, each of whom is allied with the same-sex parent. The therapist, using metaphor to dramatize the family system, suggests that the boy, who is older, has already removed himself from the parent's bed, only to be replaced by his younger sister. He wonders if the parents will ever let their daughter out, and asks them if she will have to stay home as an old maid for ever to keep her parents apart. After all, the therapist remarks, their daughter is already 13 years old; it will only be three or four years until she has her first affair, or gets married, or has a sex-change operation. (So much for the possibilities for women in this world!) Here the therapist refers to a 13-year-old girl exclusively in terms of her sexuality, thus implicitly reaffirming a limited and stereotyped perspective of women and their psychosocial potential. His view of the daughter is expressed solely in terms of relationships that she might achieve with a man or, failing that, the prospect of becoming one!

A therapist works with a family in which the mother is depressed, the father is alcoholic, and the teenaged son is a high-school dropout. The parents fight a great deal. The mother describes herself as the patient. The father says that he does not like to argue. The therapist, using circular questioning, asks the son what he thinks his mother does to get his father going. The message? Woman as provocateur – not so far removed from questions like, 'How did she get him to hit her?' Later, the mother says her husband drinks and then he gets nasty. The therapist, taking a 'neutral' position, suggests to these battling spouses that their fighting creates emotional intensity. He tells the wife that she was bored with her first husband, that the fighting is a game and she likes it. The message? Women in pursuit of intimacy, of emotionality, bring about their own destruction.

Then there is the therapist who is working with an intact family of four children. The identified patient is an 8-year-old girl who regularly wets her bed, having already ruined five mattresses. The therapist presses for inclusion of the mother's mother in the therapy. He wonders what the mother's life was like when she was her daughter's age. Assuming anger and defiance are connected to the bed wetting, the therapist seeks an answer to the child's anger. Using provocation to increase intensity, the therapist suggests that the child is like her mother, that she has her anger. The therapist comments that perhaps when the mother was pregnant, the daughter was swimming in her anger, in her belly. The message here is twofold. On the one hand, the daughter's bed-wetting symptom is defined and explained as somehow connected to her mother's anger, thus confirming traditional views of maternal destructiveness. This is compounded with ideas of inevitable intergenerational conflict and anger between the women in a family. In this respect, the therapist outdoes Freud by using a *pre-*

natal metaphor.

And then there is the therapist who uses trance with a father who was referred to him for beating his daughter when she returned twenty-five minutes late from a date. The trance is designed to help the father get in touch with the more expressive, trusting, and tender side of himself. The daughter is asked to observe the process quietly. The therapist then points out that the daughter brings her father a sense of trust by being there, quiet and accepting during the session, comparing this to the manner in which a puppy can evoke tenderness by being quiet and still. The message here is only too obvious: the way to a man's heart, the way to avoid being hurt, the way to take care of others, is to be there, quiet and still, much like a puppy. In orchestrating the daughter's quiet acceptance of her father as a remedy for his aggression, the therapist plays on an all-too-familiar refrain.

Of course, these examples are taken out of context – but what context can justify the use of interventions that replicate sexist thinking or that fail to take into account their effect on the sensibility of women in therapy?

The techniques, in and of themselves, are not the problem. It is only when they are put into words and behaviours that they reflect the sex stereotypes and gender biases, the values and belief systems, of the prevailing culture. Only an unused technique can be neutral. As soon as it is put into practice, it will convey meaning and impart significance that will be experienced in particular ways by the members of a family. And such meanings, no matter how much the intention of the therapist is to attach them to the systemic issues of the family, will be determined as well by the gender of the recipient.

Informed intervention therapy

The literature and research that have been generated out of the past two decades of the women's movement has direct bearing on the practice of family therapy. A vast, and certainly rich, vein of writings by, for, and about women has gradually worked its way into the mainstream of research, study, and teaching, as well as into the popular media. Historians have delved into the past for evidence of the way in which women were hidden from view, and to rediscover the contributions of women in every area of human endeavour. Social scientists have studied social systems and institutions, uncovering the patriarchal structures that define the roles and functions of women. Ideologies that devalue women have been analysed. The social, political and economic processes that disadvantage women have been described. Mental-health professionals have explored the psychological development of women and their emotional well-being – or lack of it – as this relates to the issues and conditions of their 'second-sex' status. Women have written about their lives, experiences, and relationships. Essays, letters, biographies, autobiographies, articles, novels, and anthologies of every description have enriched our literature. And people, for the most part, have become more aware of overt sexist language and behaviour and make some efforts to avoid it. Yet family therapy remained, until recently, largely indifferent to the significance that this growing body of knowledge has for our own theory and practice.

As noted earlier, I think the reason for this lies within the limitations of systems theory itself. Systems theorists can become entrenched in the study of systems as if they have no political, social, or economic contexts. Systems practitioners can become so focused on the inner consistency of a given formulation that they lose sight of the larger realities that structure and shape it. And both theorists and practitioners can become so enamoured of the internal logic of a system that they operate and think pragmatically, unaware of the values, subtleties, or meanings in what they do or in how they think. Within systems theory, some practices have evolved that are so focused on 'what works', or on the 'performance' itself of the therapists, that meanings and process are virtually ignored.

Every social, and every human, experience is at once personal and interpersonal; boundaried and continuous; specific and general; felt and understood. That which is internal to any system is also in process, moving within and between context, system, and person. If we continue to understand symptoms primarily in terms of their functions within the family system, then we do not need to understand the immigrant experience, the impact of poverty, the effect of overcrowded living conditions, the punitive classroom situation, the racial slur – or the gender stereotype – as determinants of dysfunctional interpersonal transactions and of familial structure. If we concentrate on hierarchical arrangements within the family, we do not need to worry about power arrangements and inequalities outside of it. If we circle around reciprocal loops between marital partners, we need never concern ourselves with the sexist social conditions that organized and structured that partnership. If we look only at the complementarity in a parental relationship, we do not need to confront a society that assigns the woman the primary responsibility for the children and then blames her for their problems. If we focus on the medium, we do not need to struggle with the message.

Systems theory and systemic practices have, in the past generation, informed and transformed the field of psychotherapy in profound ways. Because of this, because systemic therapy continues to hold such promise for achieving the change human beings desire in their lives, their families, their work, and their relationships, it is important that our theory and our therapy continue to evolve with reference to the new information, meanings, and understandings that have been developed within the women's movement and feminist theory. Here is material that informs us in new ways about the very nature of the family system, and about the experience of women within it.

Most of us, in recent years, have become familiar with the statistics on women in the world of work, as single parents, in marriage and divorce. Most of us are aware that more women seek therapy for themselves and their children than do men; that married men report greater emotional and physical well-being than do married women; that, in fact, married women show poorer mental and emotional health than do either married men or unmarried women; and that for widowers the mortality rate is 61 per cent higher than for married men of the same age. We know that married men experience more dissatisfaction in the marriage if their wives work, and that women who work experience greater satisfaction in their marriage; that 92 per cent of divorced women keep their children; and that single-parent families are really female- or mother-headed households, only one-third of which receive financial support from the father of the children. We are also aware that of violent crimes committed by a relative, 77 per cent of the victims are women; that the divorce rate for women is higher among those with graduate education; that half of all women with children work, but earn 68 per cent of what men earn; that 70 per cent of full-time employed women work in occupations in which over three-quarters of the employees are female; that fewer women than men remarry after divorce – and on, and on.

Such information has a direct bearing on the way we frame a question, deliver an intervention, exercise power, develop a relationship, or offer a direction in the conduct of therapy with families. A brief example should suffice in making my point. In studies conducted in both primary and secondary schools between 1980 and 1986, American University education professors Myra and David Sadker found that boys get far more attention at all grade levels, be it praise or criticism from their teachers, than do girls. Interactions between the teacher and students in the classrooms studied were categorized, in relation to the teacher's response, as criticism, acceptance, remediation, and praise. In every category, the researchers found that boys received more attention from the teacher than girls, and that the domination of boys in the classroom grows as they get older. In films of teacher–student interaction, the observers noted that the boys were asked more challenging questions, were given more praise in response to correct answers, or were coaxed along towards the right answer. Girls were praised more for their neat handwriting and exemplary behaviour than for their academic abilities. In the classroom, boys called out answers to questions without raising their hands eight times more often than girls. In addition, a review of books that have won the Caldecott Medal (the Pulitzer of the kiddie set) showed that for every girl depicted in the books there are ten boys.

What, then, of interrupting women in the therapy? And have we noticed the frequency with which we do this as compared with the frequency with which we interrupt men? Do we listen more to men? Do we block women from talking in order to give men a chance? Do we defer to a man who interrupts but object to a woman doing so? Do we validate a man's efforts in therapy more than a woman's?

Information such as that elicited in the Sadker study can filter into our work, helping us to evolve new techniques and refine old ones. For instance, recognizing that women are not accustomed to having their thoughts pursued, or to receiving as much attention to their thinking as do men, we fashioned an intervention we call interior questioning, a way of referencing an emotional experience to the intellectual process that accompanies it. For example, a woman in therapy might talk about the way her husband's anger makes her feel helpless. She describes upset, distraught, sad, or conflictual feelings. To highlight how she *thinks* about how she *feels*, we might pursue a line of questioning that links these two processes: What do you mean by helpless? How did you arrive at that meaning? What other things make you feel helpless? Why do you think they do? What does being helpless look like? Can you tell when others feel helpless? Or: How do you define anger? How do you know when someone is angry? How do you think anger and helplessness are connected? And so on. Answers can be used to help the client elaborate her meanings and definitions by challenging her to expand, and to own, her thoughts, ideas, and beliefs. The idea – to integrate cognition and experience, understanding and feeling – is, in fact, something of a compensatory intervention. In a world in which women have been trained to enquire of others whether they are cold rather than declare outright that 'it is cold', it is important for therapy to provide them with the opportunity to make declarative statements and to identify their own belief systems. When people understand, they not only feel, but *are*, more in charge. Self-definition is the key to empowerment.

Gender modes and models

As male models of behaviour and male modes of transaction are primary in our society, surely their use in therapy as translated into techniques of intervention needs to be reconsidered. If therapy is to give people a different experience, one that offers alternatives, it would seem important to look at our methodologies for the messages conveyed by the structure and ideology that underlie the methodology itself. For instance, many social analysts have noted that problem-solving modes are more associated with men; that men tend to go after problem resolution whereas women tend to go after the ways a problem is manifested. Men are more likely to be engaged in pursuing ends and women in pursuing means. Of course, these are dichotomized ways of thinking, and both men and women are found along the spectrum between these polarities; but the dichotomy does exist in the way in which modes of expression are perceived and models of behaviour are experienced. Women are caretakers; men are doers. Such are the archetypes, the myths, built on many levels of social text and subtext that are internalized and reproduced by women and men, and by the systems within which they function.

Gender modes and models provide a provocative context within which to consider the choices we make of interventions and techniques between the various methodological frameworks in family therapy. Is problem-solving therapy a male model? Does it affirm or give sufficient expression to female modes of processing experience? Will the therapy of prescription be experienced by women as affirming of relationship or as another expression of the privileged use of authority? Can even a well worded directive fail to objectify women whose experience as objects has been so well documented? Can a functional hierarchy be achieved through behaviours that are at any level disrespectful? Can frames and formulations be used without reference to conditions of sex-role stereotyping? Can we use techniques that exploit the greater access we have to women for creating change? Or, for that matter, can we use techniques that depend on the greater availability of women for compliance?

Again, such questions are not merely rhetorical. They force us to take a critical look at our theory and techniques; to examine the ideology underlying our choice of method. Beginning to make conscious use of female modes of transaction, and models of interaction, will offset the natural tendency to utilize modes and models that are more acceptable in our society because they are associated with authority and power. To help the women in family therapy not only to change, but to be empowered and feel understood, with their self-esteem not only intact but improved, we will need to pay attention to the meta-messages conveyed in the transactional modes we choose, as well as those conveyed in words. Such messages constitute a powerful means of transmitting values, meanings, and attitudes; more powerful perhaps than words because they are hidden, obscured by the structure and content of the technique itself, and so tend to be internalized without the filter of critical thought.

Perhaps the next stage in the evolution of family therapy will be the development of a methodology that is as congruent with the experience of women as of men. This will surely mean a focus on process, the use of relationship and engagement, a comfort with proximity and emotion, and a sensitivity to gendered meanings, differences, behaviours, and beliefs. It will mean not having to sacrifice instrumentality on the altar of power, or relationality on the altar of 'reason'.

Case example

Although this discussion was not intended to be primarily clinical, a case example might be useful in illustrating a feminist rethinking in family therapy. I am reminded of a family I saw recently that was in treatment with a family therapist as part of an ongoing consultation group.

A couple, both in their late 30s, had brought their seven-year-old son for therapy because he had been found repeatedly going through his mother's clothes, touching her undergarments, and occasionally trying on some of her clothing. Although their son had not yet gone outside of the home in his mother's clothing, his parents were terrified that he would. Both parents worked outside of the home. They had been married for twelve years, and had been contemplating having another child before this problem developed. A family genogram revealed intact families of origin, with both sets of grandparents living nearby and visiting the couple frequently. Both grandmothers often provided child care. The father's younger sister lived and worked nearby; the mother was an only child.

The therapist, and the group observing the family, noted poor generational boundaries, an aggressive, sometimes seductive, mother, and a passive father who even described himself as a 'milktoast'. The patient's older brother, age 11, was, in size, behaviour, and choice of heroes, reminiscent of a burgeoning Rambo. The therapist and the group agreed that sex roles were unclear in this family and the parental hierarchy was weak. There was concern about the number of women hovering around the boy, the youngest grandchild in the family. The mother wanted constant reassurance, and even brought in newspaper clippings about cross-dressers who were happily married! Both parents wanted to believe that nothing was wrong with their son, although the father seemed more prepared to intervene forcefully in the child's behaviour if this was recommended. The mother, on the other hand, was protective, fearing that any intervention on their part would make her son feel more vulnerable or hurt his feelings. She did not want him to begin to think that something was wrong with him.

The therapist had four sessions with the family. He suggested that boundaries in the family were unclear, framing this in terms of too many open doors, so that their son was not sure where to enter and where not to enter. He suggested that the mother close the door to the master bedroom and that the father begin to monitor the boy's behaviour, keeping him away from his mother's things. He worked with the father for more engagement with his son, and suggested the mother needed to stop working so hard for the whole family. During the session, the mother's intrusiveness was blocked with instructions that each member of the family was to speak for himself. The therapist suggested that the mother's protectiveness towards her son and the father's distance were interconnected. Both parents were encouraged to strengthen their own familial boundaries, together setting up some rules for interaction with their families of origin. The mother strongly objected to this idea. She saw the families as close, and their interchange as spontaneous. Moreover, their help with the children was indispensable. The father became more active around this question, suggesting ways to structure visits with their respective families.

In the fourth session, it became clear that the mother was not following through on the directive to close her bedroom door and she remained overly close and protective with her son despite her husband's objections. The therapist asked the son what he thought his mother was thinking, why he thought she did not close her bedroom door, why she was not doing what had been asked of her. The mother became quite agitated and the session ended abruptly. The group felt there was a lot of resistance from the mother and that it would be necessary to secure the father's help in disengaging her from the overinvolvement with her son. At this point, I was invited to have a consultation session with the family.

Using a feminist perspective, I framed the family dynamics quite differently. I told the parents that their son loved them both very much indeed, but that his love was more complicated in relation to his mother than his father. I suggested that although their son wanted to be close to his mother because he loved her, he, like many little boys, was always getting conflicting messages. At school, at the cinema, and on television, he heard that boys who were too close to their mothers were sissies or mummy's boys – a fate worse than death! So he did not know what to do with all those good and warm and close feelings he had towards his mother. He certainly did not want to be a sissy. And this made him begin to do some mixed-up things. The mother was right to be concerned and protective because her son really was feeling all mixed up. I suggested that both parents would need to reassure their son that it was good to love and be close to your mother, that it would not make him a sissy. But that mum would then need to help him find ways to be close other than wearing her clothes.

We spent much of the session talking about ways to be close that did not get people into trouble, reaching into the experience and repertoire of both parents for ideas and suggestions. Their thoughts about closeness were translated into behavioural and verbal interventions that they could use when their son got mixed up again and sought closeness by playing with or wearing his mother's clothes. The parents were asked to divide this work in an equitable fashion – that is, one that reflected the expertise and competence of each. I asked them to identify where they felt most competent with their son. Then I worked with them to negotiate where each would engage with their son during the week.

During the session, the mother's interruptions and overtalking diminished somewhat as the father was encouraged to express himself more fully. Feedback centred on their reactivity *vis-à-vis* each other and each was challenged to engage in the session from his or her own perspective rather than in response to the other. Within this framework, I could encourage the mother not to feel she had to fill in the silences left by her husband or the boys. And I suggested to the father that his wife probably often felt lonely, even within the family, and that was why she found it so hard to regulate contact with their parents. I suggested that future sessions might focus on how dad could help mum feel less lonely. During most of the sessions, the boys were excused after being asked if they had any questions or concerns they wanted to express. I thought that in future sessions their son might sometimes be seen with his parents and sometimes alone with the therapist, with the older boy being included on an as-needed basis.

At the end of the session, we talked together about privacy and boundaries versus closeness and spontaneity, and how to keep these from being opposites even though that is how they are so often experienced. I reassured both parents that their son's behaviour was reversible but would continue to need their attention within the range of things we had discussed; some of which would not seem to be directly related to his problem. I congratulated them on being able to maintain close and often mutually satisfying relations with their own parents, even if these might need to become somewhat more structured.

I trust that this case illustrates some of the clinical approaches a feminist perspective will suggest. Each of us will do it differently, but always with a sensibility to the particular experience of women within a culture largely organized by men.

Originally published in Marsh Pravder Mirkin (ed.), *The Social and Political Contexts of Family Therapy*.

Chapter two

Equality, asymmetry, and diversity: on conceptualizations of gender

Rosine Jozef Perelberg

> To have a theory of woman is already to reduce the plurality of woman to the coherent and thus phallocentric representations of theory.
>
> (Gallop 1982: 63)

Introduction[1]

Family therapists' preoccupation with the issue of gender is of recent origin and even today there are relatively few papers on the subject in the literature. When we turn to other disciplines such as social anthropology and psychoanalysis, however, we perceive that the question of gender has, for some time, been taken up by feminist writers who have questioned the assumptions at the very core of these disciplines.

Feminist thinking about the family has made important contributions to the field of sociology, for instance (Thorne and Yalom 1982). First, it has challenged prevailing assumptions about the family, arguing against the ideology of the 'monolithic family' as the only natural and legitimate family form. Second, the family became the subject of social and historical analysis, in which the category of gender played a central role. Third, feminists have pointed out that the various members of a family do not experience that family in the same way. Thus, feminists have challenged the glorification of motherhood and have brought the presence of conflict, violence, and inequality to the forefront of discussions about the family. Fourth, feminist writers have consistently emphasized the connection between the family, the economy, and the State.

In anthropology, feminists have argued that the literature all too often presents a model of society which focuses on male authority roles. Folk models of most societies, in contrast, stress a more complex interaction between male and female roles (MacCormack and

Strathern 1980). In the fields of both sociology and anthropology, feminists have argued that the way gender is perceived raises questions about the assumptions at the heart of those very disciplines. The same process is beginning to take place in family therapy where the few papers which have appeared on the issue of gender fundamentally question the basic assumptions of what is now known as 'systems thinking'. Hare-Mustin's paper is a case in point. She suggests that 'the failure of family therapy theory to deal with gender issues needs to be addressed if a theory that is not just "more of the same" is to be developed' (Hare-Mustin 1987: 15).

This chapter aims to contribute to the conceptualization of gender in family therapy. First, it will review the way in which family therapists have dealt with this issue. It will then briefly look at the contributions made by psychoanalysis and social anthropology. Hare-Mustin suggests that family therapy has not provided a truly new vision of the family: looking at the way other disciplines have approached the subject may enable family therapists to introduce a difference which will make a difference to the conceptualization of gender. I will then present some examples from my own clinical experience, which incorporates contributions derived from the fields of psychoanalysis and anthropology in my practice as a family therapist.

Feminism and family therapy

Family therapy has, for several decades, ignored the issue of gender. This can be confirmed by the following widely accepted definition of the family as 'a self-regulating group system which controls itself according to rules formed over a period of time, through a process of trial and error' (Palazzoli 1978: 3). The emphasis on recursive sequences and circular causality separates the specificity of the family from the historical and social circumstances in which it exists. The family becomes not only asexual but also ahistorical.

The emphasis on circularity has raised particular problems for therapists working with situations where an imbalance and/or an abuse of power exists. Thus, when dealing with child abuse or neglect, family therapists must face the conceptual problem of linking inequality in social relationships with the systemic framework (Carter *et al.* 1986).

As far as gender is concerned, feminist writers have pointed out the contradictions between systemic thinking centred around the notions of circular causality, neutrality, and the existence of a common goal for the whole system, on the one hand, and inherent conflict between the various subsystems within the family, exploitation, and inequality on the other (Libow *et al.* 1982; Pilalis and Anderton

1986). Family therapy utilizes a language that emphasizes interdependence between the various parts of a system, but does not allow for the unequal distribution of power within the family (with the exception of the hierarchical relationship between the generations).

The Women's Project in Family Therapy has played a leading role in the development of feminist family therapy. The issues they raise can perhaps be most readily appreciated from the booklet *Mothers and Daughters* (Carter *et al.* 1982). I remember the exciting impact the authors of the book inspired in the audience of professional women who attended the Women's Project Conference in London in 1982. The weekend conference had a powerful effect on our clinical practice as groups of women started to meet to discuss gender issues in the practice of family therapy.

For me, however, the inspiration they brought to clinical practice contrasted with certain conceptual problems which I indicated in 1987 at the Conference on Gender and Power in Families. Although Walters *et al.* (1988: 12) stress that we should distinguish between the feminist points on which they agree, and the theoretical orientations and methodological approaches on which they diverge, the latter cannot be ignored here since this chapter attempts to clarify some of these conceptual problems.

The two main axes of the publication *Mothers and Daughters* can be identified as

(1) the equation between patriarchy and women's oppression (which, I think, is also present in their latest book (Walters *et al.* 1988));
(2) the discussion of the relationship between mothers and daughters.

The first question, which is found in much of the feminist literature, presents three major problems. First, it is too general, and the term patriarchy remains too vague. It is largely confined to contemporary western society, and is also in some way associated with a specific type of economy. Second, this equation does not take into account the diversity of social organizations to which women belong. Third, relationships between men and women are social and therefore neither fixed nor immutable, as the authors imply.

The explanation of women's oppression as resulting from their economic subordination is derived from the work of Engels (1954). However, Engels is not able to account for the uniqueness of women's position; his scheme does not allow one to distinguish between the position of women and that of other social categories which do not have access to the means of production.

In the late nineteenth century, anthropologists attempted to identify the beginnings of patriarchy, in line with the evolutionist approach of that period. However, Maine and McLennan, founding fathers of social anthropology, argued that any suggestion that a matriarchal order had at any time prevailed was purely speculative and suggested that patriarchy was a universal feature of human society. By confining patriarchy to a specific type of economy, many feminists have failed to understand its universal impact on the structuring of society. Moreover, recent research has demonstrated that relations between men and women are not straightforwardly determined by the economic infrastructure (La Fontaine 1981).

The conceptual problem of *Mothers and Daughters* can also be perceived from its title. The authors discuss the relationship between mothers and daughters almost as if it formed a 'natural unit' which existed in isolation. Any third element is represented as disturbing that unit: 'When they are involved in a triangle, mother and daughter react to each other under the influence of that third person and around issues completely extraneous to their own personal relationship' (Carter 1982: 14). However, it is that very triangle that makes the relationship between mother and daughters possible: there can be no mother and daughter unit without the existence of a father. This point is, I think, acknowledged in their more recent book since a whole section is devoted to fathers and daughters (Walters *et al.* 1988).

The idea that the feminist therapist should concentrate on the mother–daughter relationship is nevertheless still prevalent. Showalter points out that the starting point of the new feminist psychology of women is the analysis of the mother–daughter relationship (1987: 250). Eichenbaum and Orbach (1982: 49) argue that feminist therapy needs to value and meet the unfulfilled longings of the early mother–daughter relationship: 'From our perspective the most critical relationship that is going to come up in the transference is that between mother and daughter.'

Feminist family therapists point out that if the therapist does not recognize the inequality which exists within families, he or she ends up reinforcing stereotyped roles. Hare-Mustin (1978) suggested that Minuchin exemplifies that position by acting as a model for the male executive function, forming alliances most frequently with the father and requiring the father to take control of his family. Her main argument in her latest paper (1987) is that the theory of family therapy rests on normative concepts of the traditional family. The two influential therapeutic models – the psychodynamic and systemic approaches – are both marked by gender bias. Whereas psychodynamic theories exaggerate gender differences (the alpha prejudice), the systemic approach ignores them (the beta prejudice).

What form should a feminist therapeutic strategy take? The feminist approach stresses equality in the relationship between therapist and client (in contrast to the model of therapy in which doctors [usually male] take charge). The family therapist therefore helps the mother to 'develop independence and self esteem'. Osborne (1983) stresses that the feminist therapist must be aware of 'the vulnerability of the women she works with. Whenever possible she shares the process of therapy, explaining to the women what is happening . . . rather than using tricks and deception' (ibid.: 6). According to Osborne, the therapist's aim is to redress the balance in the power relationship between men and women. Pilalis and Anderton (1986) stress that the feminist therapist must assume the role of facilitator and educator (Caust *et al.* 1981; Goldner 1985; Pittman 1985; Taggart 1985).

In short, feminist family therapists note women's asymmetrical position in the family and look to the female therapist to redress the balance, within the framework of a therapeutic system. I would suggest that these statements give rise to five conceptual problems:

(1) Woman is sometimes perceived as a natural, biological category rather than as a gender role, i.e. a cultural construct.
(2) In many feminist writings the very concept of woman becomes problematic because in the final analysis it is perceived as a monolithic entity; the feminist movement of the 1960s and 1970s pointed out that the concept of woman cannot have a fixed meaning (Delmar 1986).
(3) The approach adopts a simplistic dualism which talks of power and lack of power. However, multiple sources of power exist in every society, and these are activated in different contexts. The distinction between power and authority is particularly useful here, and will be discussed later in this chapter.
(4) Women's unequal position is often associated with the development of a specific type of economy. Anthropology and the history of ideas, however, demonstrate the remarkable consistency of the way in which women are culturally perceived, despite differences in the economic structure.
(5) The notion of equality is used to counteract the perception of inequality. The conceptual confusion which exists between the notions of inequality before the law, economic inequality, and differences in status (as an ideological construct) on the one hand, and the right to diversity on the other, will be addressed later in this chapter.

Psychoanalysis and the construction of gender differences

From a very early stage, psychoanalysis maintained that the psychic reality of sex had to be distinguished from the anatomical reality. In his 'Three essays' (1915) Freud suggested that there is no one-to-one correlation between biology and psychology. Men and women are not physically or socially 'made' as male or female but become such. Freud's concept of sexuality does not refer to the biological or interpersonal framework but is linked to his concept of the System Unconscious.

Initially, however, Freud assumed a symmetry in the development of what he called the Oedipus complex. Boys loved their mothers and felt rivalry for their fathers; girls desired their fathers and were jealous of their mothers. Freud was still a 'vulgar empiricist' at that point (Laplanche 1980: 81). In an essay written in 1925, Freud distinguished between the psychosexual history of boys and girls. Until then the boy had been the model for his theory but now Freud recognized the importance of the pre-Oedipal phase in which boys and girls have both feminine and masculine attributes. Both infants in this phase love the mother, and both have to relinquish her in favour of the father. The girl has to move from loving her mother to loving her father, whereas the boy gives up his mother with the understanding that he will later have a woman of his own. In this model, boys identify with their fathers as their masculine identity is established. The little boy learns his role as the heir of his father. The little girl, on the other hand, has to identify with her mother while at the same time abandoning her as a love object and turning to her father instead. For Freud this turning away from the mother is accompanied by hostility.

The importance of the 'pre-Oedipal' relationship with the mother has been more fully discussed since Freud's time (for example, Deutsch 1925, 1930; Brunswick 1940; Chasseguet-Smirgel 1985a, b; McDougall 1985). The powerful character of the primitive maternal imago is experienced by children of both sexes. Both boys and girls desire to be the object of their mother's desire: both would like to give her a baby.

Marie Langer (1989) has suggested that it is at *this* level that one can find an explanation for the stress on matriarchy in early attempts to outline the history of society. Matriarchy thus becomes a myth arising from the personal history of every individual. In the beginning there is an all-powerful mother who nourishes the infant. The father then makes his appearance as the embodiment of the law, interrupting that duality (ibid.: 196).

During this initial stage bisexuality is characteristic of both sexes. What is it, then, that is repressed in the Oedipal phase? In the main body of his work Freud oscillated between two hypotheses. According to the first, the nucleus of the Unconscious in each human being, of what is repressed, is the side that belongs to the opposite sex. According to the second hypothesis, both sexes 'repudiate femininity' (Freud 1919, 1937), a fact which is an essential element of the asymmetry between the sexes. This repudiation, Freud suggests, is the bedrock of psychoanalysis and part of the great riddle of sex (1937: 252).

The distinction between penis and Phallus is fundamental to Freud's differentiation between biological and psychic reality. Penis designates the anatomical and physiological reality (Laplanche 1980: 56). Phallus, on the other hand, exists outside anatomical reality. Lacan suggests that it is the signifier of the mother's desire. The central question of the Oedipus complex thus becomes to be or not to be the Phallus, i.e. to be or not to be the object of mother's desire (D'Or 1985: 102). The role of the father also becomes symbolic – he represents the impossibility of being the object of mother's desire. Freud defined patriarchy, however, as the law of the *dead* father. In *Totem and Taboo* he described the primal patricide committed by the original horde, who killed and devoured their father. This was followed by remorse and guilt (as they both hated and loved their father) and the dead father became more powerful than he had been while alive. This is Freud's myth of the beginnings of society. Gallop has pointed out that if this myth is internalized, then the living male has no better chance of achieving the sovereign position than does the living female (Gallop 1982: 14). However, she also explores the ambiguity of this distinction. Although Lacan's contribution to Freudian analysis was to indicate how the Phallus, unlike the penis, is possessed by nobody (male or female), the confusion between penis and Phallus still supports a structure in which it seems reasonable that men have power and women do not. Gallop points out the biologistic reduction of the Law of the Father to the rule of the actual living male. Most definitions of patriarchy still tend to consider it as the rule of the living male.

Freud suggested that the catastrophe of the Oedipus complex represents the victory of the human order over the individual. His writings are therefore about the creation of this order and how it becomes separate from biology (see also Mitchell 1974, 1984).

Through the Oedipus complex, the individual enters the symbolic order by establishing the differences between the sexes. The opposition between masculinity and femininity is not presented as a *fait accompli* to the child. The individual is not born but constituted through sexual differentiation (Freud 1933).

My work with anorexic patients, both male and female, has provided me with an experience of reconstruction of this process. The notion of reconstruction as used here does not imply that the present is necessarily isomorphic with the past, since over time changes occur in the meanings and functions of conflicts (Sandler 1988). I have found that some forms of anorexia represent an attempt to reject the division of sexes and to recover a time in which there were no such divisions.[2] The problems this poses for therapy are extremely difficult. An example is that of a patient of mine who refused to wear new clothes. She bought them and put them in her wardrobe and did not wear them because they would then become worn and useless. She also obsessively arranged and rearranged the contents of the various cupboards in her home so that there would be no gaps between objects. This can be interpreted as an attempt to create a state of perfection. The paradox was that for her to use me, I would have to be experienced as someone separate from her. Consequently she wanted to preserve me without making use of what I could give her, so maintaining the illusion of not being separate and of preserving me for ever.

For Freud, thus, the formation of the human psyche is linked to the construction of a psychological notion of sexual differences. Gender differences are not pregiven biological facts, but constructions (Mitchell 1984). Psychoanalysis does not exaggerate sexual differences as Hare-Mustin suggests (1987; see also Kaplan and Yasinski 1980), but indicates how the construction of sexual differences is a precondition for the constitution of the symbolic order.

Anthropology and the elementary structures of kinship

Anthropology, especially since the work of Lévi-Strauss, has suggested that the incest taboo separates nature from culture, creating the symbolic order and establishing the distinction between the genders. This contrast between nature and culture must, however, be seen as an artificial creation of culture itself. There is no proof that a society has ever existed in which this taboo has not played a dominant role.

The incest taboo forces one family to give up one of its members to another family, thus producing a system of exchange between families. Lévi-Strauss also pointed out that almost without exception, it has been men who exchange women (1968, 1969). This led him to suggest that the minimal requirements of a kinship system include at least four types of family relations (1968: 46):

(1) a relation of consanguinity between the mother and the mother's brother, who 'exchanged' her;
(2) a relation of affinity (between spouses);

(3) a relation of descent (between parents and children);
(4) the avuncular relationship (between maternal uncle and mother's son). I would suggest, however, that this relationship may also include other members of the mother's family of origin (see also Berenstein 1983).

This fourth pair of terms is a reminder that for a family to be created, the incest taboo requires the existence of another family that has given up one of its women to this family. In western societies this relationship is less important than in many traditional societies because the ideological stress is on the nuclear family. The arbitrary and social characteristics of the kinship system are thus concealed as the nuclear family is regarded as the 'natural' form of family.

Meaning is thus organized around the recognition of difference between nature and culture, relations of consanguinity (blood) and affinity (marriage), the natural and symbolic orders, and women and men.

Gender differences are culturally selected from among biological characteristics and are turned into 'natural differences' between the sexes (La Fontaine 1978, 1981, 1985). What westerners regard as the natural characteristics of men and women are neither universal nor natural (Mead 1935; Rosaldo and Lamphere 1974). The literature abounds with examples which illustrate the variation in these 'natural' characteristics. There are parts of New Guinea, for instance, in which men are prudish and flirtatious, preoccupied with cosmetics and their appearance, while women take the initiative in courtship (Rosaldo 1974).

Lactation and the care of young children have been regarded as major biological determinants of the subordination of women. The human family is, in the final analysis, based on the requirements of human reproduction (La Fontaine 1981). Chodorow (1974, 1978) argued that women's mothering role accounts for their universal subordination. Ortner (1974) suggested that the cultural concepts chosen to characterize women are determined by female physiology. One explanation is that women, when pregnant or caring for young babies, need male protection. The idea of physical strength itself, however, is socially perceived. In societies where the couvade is practised, for instance, women may go to work in the fields almost immediately after delivery, while it is the men that rest.

The anthropological literature provides striking examples of both the diversity of the division of social activities along gender lines and the way in which male activities seem to be more prestigious, even in societies where women have managed to achieve considerable power (Rosaldo and Lamphere 1974).

Writing about the gender role of Vietnamese women, Hoskins (1976) contrasted the formal, respectful language and deferential attitude displayed by Vietnamese wives to their husbands with the role played by many women in running the family business and handling the family income. Both are part of the definition of female gender roles in Vietnam.

The following examples are discussed by Rosaldo (1974). In some parts of New Guinea women grow sweet potatoes and men cultivate yams. While sweet potatoes form the staple diet, yams are a prestige food, the food one distributes at feasts. In the Philippines men used to hunt in groups while women were responsible for tending the gardens. Rice formed the dietary staple but the meat hunted by the men was the most prized food (Rosaldo 1974). Among the Tchambuli of the Pacific the women were traders, in control of the family economy, yet the men were honoured as artists and ritual specialists (Mead 1935).

In order to be a respectable member of the Merina society in Madagascar, one must learn a specific manner of public speech. It is an elaborate form of speech making (*Kabary*) with a fixed formal style which involves quotations and proverbs (Bloch 1975). Men are masters of this formal style in public speech; the women are excluded from *Kabary*. They are percieved as having 'less tact and subtlety than man', and as being unable to help themselves and openly express their feelings (Keenan 1975: 94). These examples seem to be very similar to the much-quoted distinction by Talcott Parsons between men's instrumental role and women's expressive one, which are themselves an ideological statement about role expectations in western culture. Family therapists are familiar with the ways in which wives in the clinic may talk to their husbands in a way that also gives the message 'Don't take me seriously.'

The terms man and woman are therefore social constructs which legitimize patterns of behaviour (La Fontaine 1981). However, most societies – whatever their kinship organization or mode of subsistence – tend to give authority and value to the role and activities of men. The diversity in the relationship between the genders is tempered by a common factor of subordination.

The power of the weak

Does this mean that women never hold power? The distinction between power and authority is both important and illuminating in this context (Bendix 1973). Authority is linked to the idea of legitimization, the right to make particular decisions, and to command obedience. Power, in contrast, 'lies in the possibility of imposing one's will upon the behaviour of other persons' (ibid.: 290). Every society contains multiple sources of both power and authority. The two studies described below have both identified some of the specific sources of power utilized by women who occupy a subordinate position.

Ioan Lewis's study of the contexts in which spirit possession takes place among the Somalis led him to conclude that, far from being arbitrary in its incidence, spirit possession is almost totally restricted to women, specifically women who occupy a peripheral position in society (Lewis 1963, 1971). Spirit possession is perceived by the Somalis as an 'affliction' and, in most cases, rather than exorcising the spirit, a viable accommodation is achieved through women's cults. These can be regarded as disguised protest movements directed against the dominant sex. The spirits which possess women are regarded as amoral, i.e. they lack moral significance. Women who are afflicted by spirit possession cannot help themselves. They are totally blameless; it is the spirits who are responsible for what happens.

The Somalis are a strongly patrilineal Muslim group, where religious life is centred around the cult of Allah. The public cult is almost exclusively dominated by men, who occupy all positions of religious authority and prestige. Women are perceived as weak and submissive and are consequently excluded from the public arena. In this society the prime target of the spirit known as *sar* is women, particularly married women, and more specifically the hard-pressed wife struggling to cope with small children. Through possession, *sar* demands luxurious clothes and perfumes from men. Lewis suggests that this female affliction operates 'as a limited deterrent against the abuses of neglect and injury in a conjugal relationship which is heavily biased in favour of men' (1971: 77). In other words, spirit possession functions as an oblique strategy of attack (Lewis 1963). It is a source of power, although it lacks legitimate authority.

The other research example is derived from my own field-work among the families of mentally ill patients in a London borough (Perelberg 1983a). In one orthodox Jewish family the wife started to behave in a 'strange' way during a period in which she felt heavily pressurized by the numerous tasks which were expected of her during the preparations for a major Jewish holiday. First, she started to reject her feminine role by refusing to do housework, and then she began studying the Kabbala – a mystical subject reserved for men over 40 years old and, even then, under the supervision of someone older and wiser. When the crisis reached a climax with her throwing crockery at her husband, she was admitted to a psychiatric hospital. After this, she was pampered by her husband, who brought her new clothes and even incurred severe debts in order to give her a trip to

Israel, 'the trip of her life'.

The similarity between these two very different examples is striking and both can be perceived as oblique strategies for obtaining benefits in conjugal relationships heavily biased towards men. The concept of the 'power of the weak' is important to an understanding of the ways in which women in different societies may exercise power. This is not to suggest that 'oblique' or 'peripheral' power strategies are equivalent to direct forms of authority. Some of the colleagues to whom I presented this paper expressed their 'discomfort' with the notion of the 'power of the weak'. I think this notion makes the picture more complicated. A model which uses a straightforward dichotomy between power and lack of power could seem more attractive and less ambiguous. It is, however, an oversimplification and does not accurately reflect the complex picture one encounters. Social reality is characterized by discontinuities in which plurality and the coexistence of opposite meanings take place. To reduce those to a two-dimensional picture is to flatten and constrain the field of knowledge. The fact that power can be exercised from a subordinate position is fundamental to both the way in which gender roles are constructed in different societies and the respective positions from which men and women perceive themselves (see also McCormack and Strathern (1980) who have pointed out that most societies tend to present a more complex pattern of interaction between men and women than one would perceive by examining the 'official' system of rights, duties, and authority).[3]

The conceptualization of these multiple hierarchies of power raises important questions for the family therapist: the idea of 'educating' or empowering women which has been proposed by many feminists risks ignoring this complex picture.

Clinical examples

My excursion into the fields of psychoanalysis and anthropology indicated certain points of reference on my 'map' when working with genders. I doubt if these points can be reduced to a consistent order, a united field, without any contradictions. Clinical examples, nevertheless, indicate the way in which these points of reference guide my practice in family therapy:

(1) I include members of the previous generation (especially a representative of the woman's family of origin) in the therapeutic process – either literally or metaphorically.

(2) I bear in mind Lévi-Strauss's minimal unit of a kinship system and explore with families their position in their kinship system

in terms of the various pairs and triads of relationships.

(3) By looking at the different sources of power they utilize, I am able to challenge both men and women.

(4) I am relatively pessimistic about the capacity of therapy to 'eliminate the dominance of male assumptions' (in contrast with the beliefs of Walters *et al.* 1988: 17).

(5) I do not believe that 'education' (of both men and women) is the therapeutic task; rather, therapy should explore the many functions of the patients' conflicts.

'Who needs men!' – the Greensons[4]

The Greensons were referred to the Marlborough Family Service by their General Practitioner (GP) because of the exacerbation in the rows between the 87-year-old mother and the 53-year-old daughter who had lived together for over fifty-two years. The father had died twenty-five years earlier and the two sons had left home. The daughter had been married for a period of six months. She had then left her husband and returned to live with her parents. Since the GP's previous attempts to refer the daughter to individual sessions had failed, he decided to refer both mother and daughter to us. At the first meeting they were seen by my colleague, Dr Varchevker. At the end of the first session he felt that he had been able to identify the function of their fights – that of keeping them bound to each other. Dr Varchevker had tried to intervene in this system by taking mother's side in the battle in order to provoke mother and daughter into responding in a different way. He felt, however, that his interventions had not been taken on board and their response had been 'more of the same'. Dr Varchevker, at that point, felt that there was a risk of him either becoming locked in the role of mother's ally, or in the role of a judge in their battles. He could not join with the daughter, as this would have meant putting pressure on a very old woman, with all the moral, social and emotional implications of such a decision.

He invited me to join him in the second session, behind the one way screen. At the beginning of that session I was able to identify the typical pattern of interaction between the mother and the daughter. In any attempt at conversation between the two, Mary (the daughter) let her mother overpower her and take over, thus allowing herself to be treated as a young girl. She then became more and more frustrated because her voice was not being heard, and either acted out angrily or collapsed. At that point Dr Varchevker maintained his position of supporting the mother, stating that as a parent he could understand the mother's dilemma – that she felt both very worried about Mary, and 'fed up' with her. I noticed that Mary retreated even more at these interventions, as she felt unable to challenge them. I telephoned through into the room and suggested that my colleague ask the mother how she thought Mary would cope when she died. This was an attempt to introduce a different order of reality into the session, readdressing Mary and her mother to the function of their rows. Mary started to cry, and her mother explained that this was because she felt guilty. The ambivalence of their relationship was being expressed in a naked form. I then decided it was important to support Mary from a closer position and raised the question of the protective function of Mary's powerless position for both herself and her mother. I called my colleague out and asked permission to join him in the room. What followed was completely spontaneous; we had not rehearsed what we were going to do, and our debate took on an intensity that reflected the fights between the mother and daughter. A reframe – a retranslation of what their battles meant – was already present then. My main intervention was to confront Mary with the question of why she was behaving towards her mother as if she were hopeless and helpless. Mary started to protest that she was not helpless and I told her that she was *behaving* as if she were so. When the mother started to argue with me, trying to prove that Mary was helpless, I pointed out that she only *believed* Mary was helpless. Dr Varchevker at this point challenged me by saying that as a mother she had to respond to Mary's message to her. The power of this session lay in the re-enactment of the argument between mother and daughter in the debate between myself and my colleague. This debate both included and excluded the mother and the daughter, making them spectators of their own processes and pushing their conflict beyond their usual threshold of tolerance. Mary was encouraged to challenge her mother in a different way. In order to do so she had to give up her omnipotent phantasy that her hostility had the power to damage her mother.

Dr Varchevker and I continued working with this family. At a subsequent session we suggested a role play in which we invited the daughter to role play her father, while Dr Varchevker took the role of the mother. In the dialogue which followed the 'parents' discussed their daughter's situation. We had not indicated what the father's position should be, but were not surprised when Mary played him as supporting her in the discussion with the mother. This role play challenged the conviction that men were useless and it symbolically inaugurated a belief in a strong and helpful father. [5] For the first time since they had come to the Marlborough, the mother was silent, listening to the dialogue. At the end of that session Mary was able to speak with a stronger voice. The role play had actively brought the absent father into the present with the function of supporting the daughter and thus enabling her to separate from her mother.

The Stepford wife: the Masters

The Masters were referred to the Marlborough Family Service by their GP because of Mrs Master's continuing depression, for which she had recently been prescribed antidepressants. The couple had two children in late adolescence and we invited the whole family to come to the session. They were seen by a trainee in our Diploma Course in Family Therapy who was supervised by me from behind the screen using the ear bug. At the first session we were able to identify the main patterns of interaction within the family. In many ways they were typical of so many families in which the woman presents herself as being depressed. Mr Master was prepared to talk about his wife's depression, about when it had started, and the various therapies they had tried. While he related this sequence, Mr Master analysed his wife, criticized and patronized her, always using a very sensible tone of voice. Mrs Master basically smiled and nodded in agreement. The children remained on the periphery of the conversation.

The therapist spent much of the session finding out about the family, their life together and their aspirations for the future. The children were perceived as having let their parents down, having chosen life-styles completely different from their parents. John had recently decided he was homosexual, and Mary was having an affair with a much older, married man. At that moment the channels of communication between these two generations were somehow blocked. Mr Master spoke in a very rational manner about his children being different from them, telling his wife she would have to accept the situation. In that session the therapist pointed out that they were all concerned about hurting each other by expressing their feelings, and that Mrs Master, in particular, felt that she had to shut up for fear of further alienating her children. When the therapist explored the connections with the previous generation, the closeness between Mrs Master and her mother became clear. Whenever she felt she was too depressed, she went to stay with her mother for a few days until she felt better. The distance between the two generations present at the session contrasted with the intense contact between Mrs Master and her mother. Mr Master, on his side, had severed contact with his own parents.

Throughout that session the therapist formulated the problem so that it involved three generations. One of the main interventions, however, addressed the relationship between the husband and the wife. The therapist asked the family if they had seen the film *The*

Stepford Wives. In the film, which is set in a small town in the USA, a group of husbands replace their wives with robots which are in every way like their wives, except that they always look immaculate and do everything the husbands want them to do, but specifically nod at everything they do and say. I had noticed, from behind the screen, the way Mrs Master nodded and smiled at everything her husband said. The couple was then asked when they had decided that that was how they wanted things to be between them.

The whole family had seen the film, and remembered the actors in it. They were intrigued by the comparison with themselves. Mr Master, however, started to say how difficult it was to get Mrs Master to say what she thought. We then suggested that the answer to that problem might lie in the previous generation, and invited them to ask Mrs Master's parents to come to the next session. Mrs Master responded by saying it was the most mind-blowing suggestion she had ever heard!

It is important, I think, to point out that I always treat the grandparental generation as consultants to the therapy. I invite them with the idea that they might have useful thoughts about the problems the younger generation is facing. I think this is extremely important in a setting that has a tradition for blaming the mother (Caplan *et al.* 1985). In my experience, what actually happens in those sessions is not necessarily as important as the very fact that the session takes place.

Mr and Mrs Brown (Mrs Master's parents) came to the next session. The new information that came out of this session was Mrs Master's fear of her father, and Mr Master's fear of both his parents-in-law. Mrs Master talked about how much she had always needed her father's approval and advice. She wanted to please him, as the only way to gain his love, and was afraid to risk his anger. In the session Mrs Master was challenged to tell her father about her ideas. The difficulty throughout was finding somebody who would be able to help her to do so. Mr Master was not able to help her partly because the rules of his own family of origin stated that parents could not be challenged. One had to either conform or leave.

The task was left to Mrs Brown, who then expressed her feeling that throughout her life, she had fulfilled the role of a switchboard in her family. Communication between her husband and her children had always been routed through her. The therapist acknowledged that the family had given Mrs Brown that role, and that she herself had felt she was responsible for working out the relationships in the family. A crucial aspect of this rule for the women, however, was that while daughter and father could not talk directly to each other, mother and daughter were bound together. The paradox was that

Mrs Master, on her side, believed that in the final analysis she had to be there for any conversation to take place between her mother and her father. By helping her daughter to talk to her father, Mrs Brown was challenging this belief at the same time and also making a statement that it was alright for her daughter to leave. She was also telling her daughter that she was not afraid of her husband, and was strong enough to handle him. Mr Brown, in his turn, was being challenged to engage more fully in his relationship with both his daughter and his wife.

Obviously my perception of gender roles and the dominant expectations about them in the wider society was central to these interventions. In the first session I had already suggested that Mrs Master's depression should be reframed as her not being able to speak in a relationship experienced by her as biased towards her husband. They were *both* challenged, however, by my intervention. Once again, the interventions were linked to the idea that the family context must span at least three generations, and include a representative of the mother's family of origin. There is also an assumption about the symbolic function of the third element, here again the father, in the relationship between mother and daughter. The other side of the coin was the way in which both generations of men felt their wives to be inaccessible; they were somehow *frightened* of them. During subsequent sessions it became clear that Mr Master perceived his wife as inaccessible. Mrs Master's 'depression' was thus a 'solution' to a complicated set of issues in that it attempted to 'freeze' the conflicts within relationships in the family.

Some feminist therapists see their roles as specifically and clearly concerned with the education of their clients. In my view this is particularly problematic when one is working with a family whose value system is different from one's own. There is then a risk of wanting to *colonize* the family in terms of his or her own cosmology. The following cases – the Sumas and the Singhs – illustrate this issue clearly.

The family business – the Sumas

The family comprised the mother and father and nine children (five girls and four boys between 16 and 32 years of age). The first contact was with the eldest daughter, 32-year-old Simena, who phoned me saying that her 24-year-old brother Sunjae had become mute and refused to get up in the morning. I invited the entire nuclear family to come to the session.

The Sumas were Kenyan Hindus who had come to England for political reasons, leaving all their property and money behind. They opened a family business but soon after it was established, Mr Suma started to drink heavily and relinquished his position as the family bread-winner. The four eldest sisters looked after the business while the oldest brother attended college and the other children went to school. The relationship between the generations and the genders had become inverted. The women had taken over the task of providing for the family, and the children that of looking after the parents. There had been many conflicts between Mr and Mrs Suma, and they had decided not to speak to each other. They had not talked to each other for some twelve years when they came to the session; any change in that situation would necessarily involve a 'loss of face' for each 'side'. Sunjae, too, had ceased talking to his family. In the two preceding years the three eldest sisters had got married. At that moment in the life cycle of the family, Simena, after her sisters had left home, was at risk of permanently remaining the only one responsible for looking after the family business, her parents, and Sunjae. As her parents were not speaking to each other, she also acted as mediator in their 'conversations'.

The therapy with this family went on for a number of years. Throughout, I was careful to respect the pathways of the family map (Perelberg 1984). Not once, for instance, did I suggest that the mother spoke to the father. As Sunjae's silence had meaning in terms of their religious beliefs, the father was my main co-therapist during that first phase. I did, however, speak about the genders in the family. More specifically, I talked a great deal about Simena's conflicts between, on the one hand, wanting to move on, get married, and have her own family, and on the other, her sense of duty towards the family as the eldest daughter.

After a year of therapy, Simena requested some sessions on her own. I think it would have been extremely difficult for her to have seen a therapist by herself at the outset. In the individual sessions we carried on talking about her conflicts, although I never took a stance or gave an opinion about what she should do. I simply pointed out the various shapes her conflict took. After a while, the mother also asked me for some individual sessions. I then saw her and many of the other members of the family on their own, as well as the mother and her daughters together, and the mother and Simena. Simena wanted her mother's help to negotiate a position in which she could both be a good and dutiful daughter and be able to get married and leave.

An awareness of the family's system of beliefs and the map that guided their behaviour was essential to the therapy. The interventions were syntonic with the principles of the family map.

'You are either in or out' – the Singhs

The Singhs raised important issues about the limit of one's therapeutic powers. A psychiatrist from a psychiatric unit in another borough requested a consultation because Raynu Kahur, a 19-year-old university student, had been admitted to a psychiatric hospital and they found the family very difficult to deal with. Although a social worker had started to work with Raynu, the family opposed this move. I invited the whole family, in addition to the social worker, to attend.

The father, mother, Raynu, and the social worker came to the session. The father was a tall, formidable Sikh, who spoke with a very strong voice. When I asked him at the beginning of the session to tell me about himself he explained that he was a Brahman, from the Punjab. The mother had a deferential attitude towards him and seemed to be in agreement with what he said throughout the session. Raynu had a collapsed appearance, with her head sunk between her shoulders. She looked at the floor during most of the session and it was only towards the end that she felt able to speak.

From the very beginning of the session it was possible to see the way in which the social worker had antagonized the father. She defended what she believed to be Raynu's position, saying that Raynu had been raised in Britain and wanted to be like other people she knew in English society, but that her parents lived in another culture and wanted her to follow in their footsteps. Mr Singh dismissed all this as nonsense, and said Raynu should 'come to her senses'.

During the first session I learned many things about the family. Raynu had started to feel unhappy and to do strange things (by this her parents meant that she had cut her hair and started to go to pubs) a year earlier, at the time her elder sister had left home to get married. Neelo, four years older than Raynu, had married an American and had moved to the USA. The two sisters had always been very close. I expressed to the parents my knowledge that in some Sikh families this would have been a devastating event and the parents both agreed that it was as if they had lost a daughter. As far as they were concerned Neelo had died for them. I asked if they were mourning for her and they agreed with me. I then explored with them what would be worse for them – if Raynu decided to follow in her sister's footsteps, or if she became a chronic psychiatric patient. The parents both agreed that although they would suffer very much if Raynu decided to follow in her sister's footsteps, it would be even worse if she became a chronic psychiatric patient. I told them that I felt it was important for Raynu to know that. I then turned towards Raynu and helped her to tell us how much she missed her sister. When I then asked her if she knew what choices she wanted to make at this point in her life, she started to cry, saying she was not ready for it, that she wanted to be able to go back home to live with her parents and finish university first. The rest of the consultation was spent helping them to negotiate the conditions for Raynu to return home. At the end I pointed out that they could come back to me any time they felt it necessary in the future.

The consultation with this family illustrates the potential pitfalls for the therapist in assuming that his or her life-style is necessarily preferable to that of the family, as the social worker had done. It is often assumed that in the opposition between 'us' and 'them', 'us' is better and that 'their' aim is to become like 'us'.

I think that there are issues that still need to be negotiated in this family. Neelo had had to cross the Atlantic in order to leave her family. Raynu, however, felt it was not yet the time for her to leave home, and she had had a rough time experimenting with leaving. However, the contact she has established with her therapist may enable her to carry on an internal conversation with her in subsequent years.

The importance of these two examples, the Sumas and the Singhs, lies in the way they demonstrate the pitfalls of assuming that the therapist's task is to educate women. The risk is that of attempting to colonize families into one's own belief systems.

Inequality, status, and diversity

Feminists have suggested that they are striving to achieve equality between men and women. The notion of equality made its first appearance in the seventeenth century and reached a peak during the era of enlightenment in the eighteenth century (Mitchell 1976). Under capitalism, the notion of equality referred to equality under the law. After John Stuart Mill,[6] the feminist struggle became an organized political movement for the attainment, among other things, of equal rights. The struggle continues as in no democratic country have women fully attained equal rights with men. For instance, in England it was only the Guardianship Act of 1973 that laid down, for the first time, that the mother has the same rights and authority concerning the custody of a child as the father.

Although husbands and wives in England have equal rights as citizens, many studies have pointed out that government policies tend to embody powerful assumptions about the family and the performance of social roles within it (Nissel 1982). One of these assumptions concerns the social and economic dependence of wives upon their husbands expressed in the Social Security Act of 1948.

Until February 1987, married women could not draw the invalid care allowance for looking after a sick relative since it was assumed that they do not generally work outside the home. These inequalities before the law have wide-ranging implications for the economic position of women (Doyal 1983). Thus, a contradiction exists between the rights of women as full citizens and their legally assumed financial dependence on their husbands.

Equality under the law and economic equality, however, do not necessarily imply equal status. Status is an ideological perception of ranking. We have seen how anthropological studies have demonstrated the low status of women in traditional societies where they participate fully in the productive sphere. In the history of western thought, eighteenth-century ideas of social and political reform did not extend to women who were socially defined as passive, dependent, and politically inferior to men. Jordanova (1980) has shown how well established biomedical traditions have also strengthened the conceptual division between unique feminine and unique masculine attributes. Biological determinism 'explained' women whereas men were defined by their social acts. Women were perceived as closer to nature than men because of their 'physiological' role in sex and motherhood. This explained their exclusion from the political domain and, in more general terms, their overall inferiority to men. Bloch and Bloch (1980) pointed out that even the radical writers of the French Revolution left these ideas untouched. Rousseau, for example, stated that women should remain like children.

Such ideological constructs do not necessarily change as a result of changes in the economic infrastructure, as many studies of both traditional and contemporary societies have shown (Davin 1976). Women can work in the productive system side by side with men and still have unequal status. The struggles for economic and legal equality levels as well as for equal status should, however, be distinguished from the right to diversity. The feminist stress on equality and on 'educating' women paradoxically implies the risk of 'colonizing' women. Femininity, hysteria, and spirit possession are devalued, however, not because of any inferior characteristics inherent in these phenomena, but because of their status in culture.

Conclusion

It may be that the idea that families are systems, which started as a metaphor, gradually became a straightjacket for family therapy. After all, the general notion of systems leaves out certain basic ideas which indicate how families, as cultural systems, are different from other systems. Kinship systems derive meaning from the way in which

they separate themselves from biology, formalizing differences between the sexes and constructing them as genders. In all cultures, however, male and female attributes are valued differently.

'Gender roles' are social, not natural, constructs. Feminist writers have been concerned to show how the differences between the sexes are socially constructed as gender relations. Society attributes distinct ranking to these differences in a hierarchy of status. It is not the differences *per se*, however, that are the sources of inequality; it is their ranking in the hierarchy of status that gives rise to inequality. Rosaldo and Lamphere (1974: 15) have pointed out how Jane Austen, George Eliot, and Virginia Woolf all demonstrated brilliantly that the '"insignificant" details of domestic life can be the stuff of novels'. Feminist sociological writing has highlighted the central significance of the domestic domain; of informal structures as opposed to traditional studies of the formal institutional structures of politics or religion (Raphael 1975; Oakley 1979). The way in which women actually exercise power in these spheres has been demonstrated.

Diversity should be distinguished from economic inequality, inequality before the law, and status in order to avoid a social order dominated by monotony and uniformity. And if we believe what psychoanalysis and anthropology, as our myths of creation, tell us, by not taking on board the constitutive role of 'difference' we would put at risk the very existence of human order.

There is a problem for our model. As family therapists we need to incorporate the concepts of both subordination and diversity into our thinking. This does not necessarily involve linear thought. Perhaps we should think in terms of a structure which includes dominance (Althusser 1967); this would retain the idea of a context that gives meaning to phenomena, while still discriminating between their different values in the system.

Notes

1. This chapter was originally presented as a paper to the plenary of the Second National Conference on Feminism and Family Therapy, held in London in July 1987.
2. I saw these patients in the context of a study of anorexic patients funded by the Medical Research Council and carried out at the Institute of Psychiatry. Dr Christopher Dare provided supervision for the individual psychotherapy we carried out.
3. The literature on women and mental health is highly relevant here (Gurman and Klein 1980). Many important studies have merely tried

to establish correlations between quantifiable variables instead of analysing how specific medical categories – such as depression – are utilized by women (Brown and Harris 1978; Brodsky and Hare-Mustin 1980; Howell and Bayes 1981; Jordanova 1981). Bordsky and Hare-Mustin have suggested that more women are diagnosed as hysterical because hysteria is regarded as a characteristic attribute of women's roles (1980a, b). In my own research in the psychiatric unit of a London hospital, 41 per cent of admissions over a period of a year were of married women, as opposed to 29 per cent of married men. Similarly, almost double the number of women (38 per cent) in contrast to men (20 per cent) named their spouse as the next of kin. Most of the men I saw admitted to the psychiatric wards had been living alone or in hostels and had been brought in by social workers or the police (Perelberg 1983: 142).

4. I am grateful to Dr Varchevker for allowing me to quote from our work together with this family (see Varchevker and Perelberg 1987). All the names and identifying details about this and subsequent families have been changed in order to protect their privacy.
5. It is the symbolic function of the father which is being stressed here. In this case it is, perhaps, more easily perceived as it was not the 'real' father that attended the session. Julia Kristeva (1977) has suggested that language can perform this symbolic function of separating mother and daughter; I think the therapeutic process itself can perform this function.
6. See J.S. Mill (1869) *The Subjection of Women*, London: Everyman (1970).

References

Althusser, L. (1967) *Lire le Capital*, Paris: François-Maspéro.

Barker, D.L. and Allen, S. (eds.) (1976a) *Dependence and Exploitation in Work and Marriage*, London: Longman.

Barker, D.L. and Allen, S. (eds.) (1976b) *Sexual Divisions and Society: Process and Change*, London: Tavistock Publications.

Beauvoir, S. de (1972) *The Second Sex*, Harmondsworth: Penguin.

Bendix, R. (1973) *Max Weber*, London: Methuen.

Berenstein, I. (1983) *Psicoanálisis de la Estrutrura Familiar*, Barcelona: Paidos.

Bloch, M. (1975) Introduction, in *Political Language and Oratory in Traditional Society*, London: Academic Press.

Bloch, M. and Bloch, J.H. (1980) 'Women and the dialectics of nature in eighteenth-century French thought', in C. MacCormack and M. Strathern (eds.) *Nature, Culture and Gender*, Cambridge: Cambridge University Press.

Brodsky, A.M. and Hare-Mustin, R. (eds.) (1980a) *Women and Psychotherapy*, New York: Guilford Press.

Brodsky, A.M. and Hare-Mustin, R.T. (eds.) (1980b) 'Psychotherapy and women: priorities for research', in *Women and Psychotherapy*, New York: Guilford Press.

Brown, G. and Harris, T. (1978) *Social Origins of Depression: A Study of Psychiatric Disorder in Women*, London: Tavistock.
Brunswick, R.M. (1940) 'The pre-Oedipal phase of the libido development', *Psychoanalytic Quarterly* 9.
Caplan, P.J. and Hall-McCorquodale, I. (1985) 'Mother-blaming in major clinical journals', *American Journal of Orthopsychiatry* 55 (3): 345–53.
Carter, B., Papp, P., Silverstein, O., and Walters, M. (1982) *Mothers and Daughters*, Monograph Series Vol. 1, No. 1, The Women's Project in Family Therapy.
Carter, B., Papp, P., Silverstein, O., and Walters, M. (1986) 'The procrustean bed', *Family Process* 25 (2).
Caust, B.L., Barbara, L., Libow, J., and Raskin, P.A. (1981) 'Challenges and promises of training women as family systems therapists', *Family Process* 20 (4).
Chasseguet-Smirgel, J. (1964/1985a) 'Feminine guilt and the Oedipus complex', in J. Chasseguet-Smirgel *Female Sexuality*, London: Maresfield Library.
Chasseguet-Smirgel, J. (1985b) *Creativity and Perversion*, London: Free Association.
Chodorow, N. (1974) 'Family structure and feminine personality', in M.Z. Rosaldo and L. Lamphere (eds.) *Woman, Culture and Society*, Stanford: Stanford University Press.
Chodorow, N. (1978) *The Reproduction of Mothering*, Berkeley: University of California Press.
Davin, D. (1976) 'Women in revolutionary China', in J. Mitchell and A. Oakley (eds.) *The Rights and Wrongs of Women*, Harmondsworth: Penguin.
Delmar, R. (1986) 'What is feminism?', in J. Mitchell and A. Oakley (eds.) *What is Feminism?*, Oxford: Basil Blackwell.
Deutsch, H. (1925) 'The psychology of women in relation to the functions of reproduction', *International Journal of Psycho-Analysis* 6.
Deutsch, H. (1930) 'The significance of masochism in the mental life of women', *International Journal of Psycho-Analysis* 11.
D'Or, J. (1985) *Introduction à la Lecture de Lacan*, Paris: Denöel.
Doyal, L. (1983) *Unhealthy Lives*, London: Women's Studies Unit, The Polytechnic of North London.
Eichenbaum, L. and Orbach, S. (1982) *Outside In, Inside Out*, Harmondsworth: Penguin.
Engels, F. (1954) *The Origins of the Family, Private Property and the State*, Moscow: Foreign Languages Publishing House.
Franchetto, B., Cavalcanti, M.L.V.C., and Heieborn, M.L. (1980) 'Antropologia e feminismo', in B. Franchetto, M.L.V.C. Cavalcanti, and M.L. Heieborn (eds.) *Perspectivas Antropológicas da Mulher*, Rio de Janeiro: Zahar.
Freud, S. (1915/1981) *Standard Edition of the Complete Psychological Works of Sigmund Freud*, Vol. VII, London: Hogarth Press.
Freud, S. (1919/1981) 'A child is being beaten', *Standard Edition*, Vol. XVII, London: Hogarth Press and the Institute of Psychoanalysis,

179–204.
Freud, S. (1923/1981) 'The Ego and the Id', *Standard Edition*, Vol. XIX, London: Hogarth Press.
Freud, S. (1925/1981) 'Some psychical consequences of the anatomical distinction between the sexes', *Standard Edition*, Vol. XIX, London: Hogarth Press.
Freud, S. (1933/1981)'Femininity', *Standard Edition*, Vol. XX, London: Hogarth Press.
Freud, S. (1937/1981) 'Analysis terminable and interminable', *Standard Edition*, Vol. XXIII, London: Hogarth Press and the Institute of Psychoanalysis, 209–53.
Gallop, J. (1982) *Feminism and Psychoanalysis: The Daughter's Seduction*, London: Macmillan.
Goldner, V. (1985) 'Feminism and family therapy', *Family Process* 24: 31–47.
Goodrich, T.J., Rampage, C., Ellman, B., and Halstead, K. (1988) *Feminist Family Therapy: A Casebook*, New York: W.W. Norton.
Gurman, A.S. and Klein, M.H. (1980) 'Marital and family conflicts', in A.M. Brodsky and R.T. Hare-Mustin (eds.) *Women and Psychotherapy: An Assessment of Research and Practice*, New York: Guilford Press.
Hare-Mustin, R.T. (1978) 'A feminist approach to family therapy', *Family Process* 17 (2).
Hare-Mustin, R.T. (1987) 'The problem of gender in family therapy theory', *Family Process* 26: 15–27.
Hoskins, M. (1976) 'Being female', in D. Barker and S. Allen (eds.) *Sexual Divisions and Society*, London: Tavistock Publications.
Howell, E. and Bayes, M. (1981) *Women and Mental Health*, New York: Basic Books.
Jordanova, L.J. (1980) 'Natural facts: a historical perspective on science and sexuality', in C. MacCormack and M. Strathern (eds.) *Nature, Culture and Gender*, Cambridge: Cambridge University Press.
Jordanova, L.J. (1981) 'Mental illness, mental health: changing norms and expectations', in Cambridge Women's Studies Group *Women in Society: Interdisciplinary Essays*, London: Virago.
Kaplan, A.G. and Yasinski, L. (1980) 'Psychodynamic perspectives', in A.M. Brodsky and R. Hare-Mustin, *Women and Psychotherapy*, New York: Guilford Press.
Keenan, E. (1975) 'A sliding sense of obligatoriness: the polystructure of Malagasy oratory', in M. Bloch (ed.) *Political Language and Oratory in Traditional Society*, London: Academic Press.
Kristeva, J. (1977) *About Chinese Women*, London: Calder-Boyars.
La Fontaine, J.S. (1978) 'Introduction', in J.S. La Fontaine (ed.) *Sex and Age as Principles of Social Differentiation*, ASA Monograph No. 17, London: Academic Press.
La Fontaine, J.S. (1981) 'The domestication of the savage male', *Man* 16 (8).
La Fontaine, J.S. (1985) 'Anthropological perspectives on the family and social change', *Quarterly Journal of Social Affairs* 1 (1): 29–56.

Laplanche, J. (1980) *Castration Symbolisations Problématiques II*, Paris: PUF.

Lévi-Strauss, C. (1949/1969) *The Elementary Structures of Kinship*, Boston: Beacon Press.

Lévi-Strauss, C. (1968) *Structural Anthropology*, London: Allen Lane.

Lewis, I.M. (1963) 'Dualism in Somali notions of power', *Journal of the Royal Anthropological Institute* 93(1).

Lewis, I.M. (1971) *Ecstatic Religion*, Harmondsworth: Penguin.

Libow, J.A., Raskin, P.A., and Caust, B.L. (1982) 'Feminism and family systems therapy: are they irreconcilable?', *Journal of Family Therapy* 10: 3–12.

MacCormack, C. and Strathern, M. (eds.) (1980) *Nature, Culture and Gender, Cambridge*: Cambridge University Press.

McDougall, J. (1985) 'Homosexuality in women', in J. Chasseguet-Smirgel (ed.) *Female Sexuality*, London: Karnac.

Mead, M. (1935) *Sex and Temperament in Three Primitive Societies*, London: Routledge & Kegan Paul.

Mitchell, J. (1974) *Psychoanalysis and Feminism*, Harmondsworth: Penguin.

Mitchell, J. (1976) 'Women and equality', in J. Mitchell and A. Oakley (eds.) *The Rights and Wrongs of Women*, Harmondsworth: Penguin.

Mitchell, J. (1984) *Women: The Longest Revolution*, London: Virago.

Nissel, M. (1982) 'Families and social change since the Second World War', in R.N. Rapoport, M.P. Fogaily, R. Rapoport (eds.) *Families in Britain*, London: Routledge & Kegan Paul.

Oakley, A. 'Review essay: Feminism and sociology – some recent perspectives', *American Journal of Sociology* 84(5).

Ortner, S.B. (1974) 'Is female to male as nature is to culture?' in M.Z. Rosaldo and L. Lamphere (eds.) *Woman, Culture and Society*, Stanford: Stanford University Press.

Osborne, K. (1983) 'Women in families: feminist therapy and family systems', *Journal of Family Therapy*, 5(1).

Palazzoli, M.S., Selvini, M., Boscolo, L., Cecchin, G., Prata, G. (1978) *Paradox and Counterparadox*, London: Jason Aronson.

Parker, R. (1982) 'Family and social policy: an overview', in R.N. Rapoport, M.P. Fogaily, R. Rapoport (eds.) *Families in Britain*, London: Routledge & Kegan Paul.

Perelberg, R.J. (1983) 'Family and mental illness in a London borough', unpublished Ph.D. dissertation, University of London.

Perelberg, R.J. (1983a) 'Mental illness, family and networks in a London borough', *Social Science and Medicine* 17 (8): 481–91.

Perelberg, R.J. (1984) 'Familiar and unfamiliar types of family structures', forthcoming in J. Kareem and R. Littlewood (eds.) *Inter-Cultural Therapy: Theory and Techniques*, Oxford: Blackwell.

Pilalis, J. and Anderton, J. (1986) 'Feminism and family therapy – a possible meeting point', *Journal of Family Therapy* 8: 99–114.

Pittman, F. (1985) 'Gender myths: when does gender become pathology?', *Family Therapy Networker* 9 (6): 24–33.

Raphael, D. (1975) (ed.) *Being Female: Reproduction, Power and Change*, Chicago: Aldine Publishing Co.
Rosaldo, M.Z. (1974) 'Woman, culture and society: a theoretical overview', in M.Z. Rosaldo and L. Lamphere (eds.) *Woman, Culture and Society*, Stanford: Stanford University Press.
Rosaldo, M.Z. and Lamphere, L. (eds.) (1974) *Woman, Culture and Society*, Stanford: Stanford University Press.
Sandler, J. (1988) 'Introduction to the first plenary discussion', *Bulletin* 31, EFP, Barcelona.
Showalter, E. (1987) *The Female Malady*, London: Virago.
Taggart, M. (1985) 'The feminist critique in epidemiological perspective: questions of context in family therapy', *Journal of Marital and Family Therapy* 11: 113–26.
Thorne, B. and Yalom, M. (eds.) (1982) *Rethinking the Family: Some Feminist Questions*, New York: Longman.
Varchevker, A. and Perelberg, R.J. (1987) *Who Needs Men? Mother–Daughter, Late Separation*, Edited videotape of family-therapy sessions, with narrative. Marlborough Family Service.
Walters, M., Carter, B., Papp, P., and Silverstein, O. (1988) *The Invisible Web: Gender Patterns in Family Relationships*, New York: Guilford Press.

Part two

Strategies of Intervention

Chapter three

Feminism and family therapy: can mixed marriages work?

Elsa Jones

> When a subject is highly controversial – and any question about sex is that – one cannot hope to tell the truth. One can only show how one came to hold whatever opinion one does hold.
>
> (Virginia Woolf 1929)

Introduction

In this chapter I propose to discuss some aspects of a feminist critique of systemic family therapy, and to consider their compatibilities as well as their (perhaps) irreconcilable differences. I will use some polarized examples, which may well give offence because they illustrate interactions in our practice which are more common than we like to admit. I hope that by leaving some questions unanswered I and other practitioners of family therapy may continue to struggle with the 'unresolved remnant'.

It is a truism that all theory and practice emerge from their multiple contexts – social/political/economic/historical and so on. Thus, the issue for us as family therapists wishing to assess our field from a feminist perspective is *not* to question which approach or school is more or less sexist; we must accept that they all are, since they are rooted in our culture. Rather, the question is: how can we facilitate change in our work with clients?

Family-therapy orientation

This said, it is necessary for me to define where I stand as a family therapist, since the particular freedoms and constraints I perceive will depend in part on my theory and practice model. Thus, as a systemic therapist, influenced particularly by the ideas of the Milan group and the second generation of Ericksonians,[1] I am in some ways less constrained in my work with clients than those workers for whom concepts such as hierarchy and control form an important part of their thinking about families.

I am therefore unlikely to believe in, or to urge families to practise, the exercise of power in intimate relationships which so easily shades over into the abuse of power – by men over women, and by parents over children. However, I am constrained by a belief system (otherwise known as a theory) which urges me to 'be neutral'. The concept of therapist neutrality has caused considerable distress and confusion among systemic family therapists, and I shall not here recapitulate the debate, which is now approaching obsolescence (cf. McNamee [1989] for an excellent discussion of the meaning of 'neutrality' in systemic family therapy and research). I assume in my practice that it is important for therapists to be even handed in their empathy, responsiveness, and attention to all members of the client group.

I assume, since instructive interaction is probably impossible (Hoffman 1985; Cecchin 1987) that therapists must do what they do in such a way as to maximize the likelihood of a sufficient perturbation within the client system to enable the members of that system to reorganize themselves, by drawing on their own resources, in a manner coherent with their own history, beliefs, and adaptive abilities (Tomm 1987).

I assume that it is important to end therapy with an 'unresolved remnant' – i.e. not to strive for complete closure, thus enabling clients to tie up the loose ends and own the changes they have brought about, rather than being left with the belief that the therapist is the source, now and in the future, of solutions. I assume that it is not my business to hold specific goals for client system organization post-therapy nor to urge clients in one particular direction, although the fact that I accept employment as a therapist obviously means that I do have some opinions about the undesirability of suffering, abuse, 'stuckness', and the unhappiness often caused by symptoms.

All this is (fairly) easily said – in practice the thin line between quietism on the one hand, and pushing people around for their own good on the other, requires a constant balancing act.

How does this stand up in the face of a feminist critique, or more ordinarily, in the face of easily observed mundane facts of power differentials between the genders? We are the products of at least 2,000 years of patriarchal[2] culture, which has manifested almost universally across the world regardless of any of the apparent distinctions we are asked to regard as significant: Marxism, capitalism, tribalism, monarchy, democracy – in all these systems men have been the subject and women the other, the object (de Beauvoir 1949; Kappeler 1986). The consequences of this for the way in which men and women construct their gender identity are manifold (Woolf 1929; Spender 1980) and must be our business as therapists.

Truisms

We know (Bateson 1972, 1979) that we cannot not communicate; it follows that we cannot not act. How do we act (perhaps by 'not' acting) when we perceive an imbalance in the way that, for example, a woman and a man in a relationship evaluate their own and their partner's behaviours? She may doubt her worth, diminish herself to boost her male partner's self-esteem, accept responsibility for the relational and emotional well being of the family, remain with a violent partner, lack economic independence, be 'over involved' with her children; he may assume that his emotional distance, difficulties in dealing with or expressing tenderness and intimacy, failure to notice or respond to the feeling states or practical requirements of family members, his resort to verbal or physical domination under pressure, or control of finance, are manifestations of his normative and desirable/superior functioning. If we do not comment on these role values and attributions of meaning, that also constitutes 'action'. When stated thus baldly it is easy to see that all these behaviours and stances are functions of an inequitable relationship in which certain attributes, behaviours, and their educational/cultural/economic consequences are valued while others are not. It is of course also a truism that both men and women function at less than their potential when warped by their adaptation to socially prescribed roles.

We know that in our culture[3] (and more particularly in the subculture of the mental-health profession), male-gendered behaviour is defined as normative and desirable, whereas female-gendered behaviour is defined as proof of mental ill health while also being defined as normative for females (Broverman *et al.* 1970; Shoben 1980).

We know that in our culture, power to act (and to act to the advantage of one's own in-group, whether white, male, middle class, employer – or all of these) is ascribed to and arrogated by certain groups (Kingston 1982) and is expressed in a manner detrimental and oppressive to those groups without equal access to rule making.

We know that, 'firstly, the act of defining a problem and its solution is a social and political act and secondly, over time, in human systems, certain beliefs are accorded more power to influence how situations are defined than other beliefs' (Pilalis 1987: 13).

We know that violence and abuse is more often perpetrated by males towards females and children ('domestic' violence, rape, sexual abuse, pornography, sexual harassment). We know about the differentials between male and female earning power, which start long before job entrance or career training in the pressure of social and educational discriminatory practices. We know about the feminization of poverty, particularly in regard to the post-divorce financial circumstances of men and women (Cross 1985; Goldner 1985b; Myers 1985). We know that these and many other factors form the context from which the family problems with which we work emerge.

We know that as therapists we are more likely to meet the benign end of the spectrum, i.e. those people who show at least some inclination to change, to talk together with outsiders, and to acknowledge shared difficulties.

Problems

Why then have we been so nervous about dealing with these issues in therapy? Why do we flinch when criticized as 'political'? It is interesting that most opinions which run counter to the prevailing ethos are labelled derogatively as 'political', for example the history of the Peace Movement. I grew up in South Africa, and it always puzzled me as an adolescent to observe that teachers and ministers of religion who overtly propounded the prevailing apartheid ideology were regarded as neutral, whereas anyone who spoke out against it, however tentatively, was branded as 'political', reprimanded for inappropriate and unprofessional behaviour, and sometimes lost his or her job.

Example:

> Years and years ago there was a popular type of reframing which went something like this: Mr X repeatedly attacks Mrs X. The therapist is concerned not to fall into the 'more of the same' trap by blaming Mr X for his violence. The therapist punctuates an interactive sequence which demonstrates that Mrs X's passivity, or nagging, or sexual unresponsiveness, or moral superiority, or physical illness, or emotional dependence, or desire to get a job, or close relationship with the children, causes Mr X to feel helpless and frustrated. The therapist describes Mr X as 'one-down' and his violence as his way of responding to his partner's dominance and thus as the interactional equivalent to Mrs X's input. Criticizing this reframing on the grounds that, in the first place, Mr X should nevertheless take responsibility (as should his acculturation) for resorting to violence in the face of helplessness (rather than, for example, crying, development of stomach ulcers, hallucinating, learning to bath the children, and so on) and in the second place, Mrs X was being attacked again by the therapist, led

to the critic being dismissed as a feminist who was incapable of thinking interactionally.

Example:

> In struggling with the problem of interactional equivalence in male–female relationships, one sometimes hears the argument: 'Yes, but women possess and use "down-power", and often benefit considerably from playing the victim.' This is undoubtedly so, but the comment ignores the context in which such apparent choices are made. In the early nineteenth century in South Africa the white Voortrekkers of Dutch and French extraction decided to move away from the Cape and their new British masters into the unexplored (by them) hinterland. Part of their motive was their refusal to comply with the abolition of slavery recently introduced by the British. Many of their black slaves 'chose' to go with them rather than remain in the Cape. Presumably these slaves feared the unpredictable changes of emancipation, and chose the devil they knew. We all know that some prisoners in gaols and concentration camps obtain privileges by acting as trusties; the Page 3 'girls' in certain British newspapers are presumably not tied down before being photographed.

However, these are not free choices or choices free of context. Goldner (1985a: 22) describes 'the complacent brand of moral relativism that allows family therapists . . . to pervert the concept of circularity by confusing an elegant truth, that master and slave are psychologically interdependent, with the morally repugnant and absurd notion that the two are therefore equals'. Like Goldner I do not wish to equate male–female relationships with those of master and slave, or prisoner and keeper, but I agree with her that

> by choosing to highlight the power of weakness instead of the abuse of power, we are utilizing and exploiting our knowledge of the real power differentials between the sexes, while simultaneously keeping this knowledge out of critical awareness and therefore out of our theory.
>
> (Ibid.: 22)

Whilst there exists a considerable body of feminist critique in regard to other psychotherapeutic approaches, in particular psychoanalysis (for example, Mitchell 1971, 1974), it is only recently that family therapists have started addressing these issues in the literature (for example, Goldner 1985a, b; Hare-Mustin 1987), in workshops, and perhaps most difficult of all, in our day-to-day practice.

One of the major reasons for our difficulties in addressing gender discrimination and its consequences is, of course, that we are – perhaps more than in any other situation – part of the system we are attempting to observe. When dealing with alcoholism, school refusal, schizophrenia, and so on, we can, if only temporarily and partially, and with the help of our professional resources such as the use of a team, screen, consultation, and so on, achieve a relative meta-position, stand outside or alongside a system sufficiently to glimpse some patterning and to feel relatively confident about our perceptions, and participate in the system interaction with some hope of introducing difference. However, we are all profoundly determined by our gendered learning; gender is an overarching construct which pervades all our relationships, perceptions, and actions, and is therefore also present, like the air we breathe, in our interactions with clients and colleagues.

Example:

> The clients are a husband and wife, who have been together for about four years and married for about a year. Mr A is a very large man who has been severely violent towards Mrs A and her 7-year-old ESN daughter. Mrs A is a small woman, who suffers from a life-threatening illness and in consequence has had a leg amputated and uses a walking frame. The child is on the at-risk register, and Mrs A and her daughter have spent some time in a women's refuge. The couple want to explore the possibilities of reconciliation, and the therapist has talked with them in detail about the incidents of violence and is now asking whether the violence dates from the beginning of their relationship.

Mr A: No the relationship I would say for the first two years of our relationship, was extraordinary our relationship was. The last two years it has gone downhill fast.

Therapist to Mrs A: Is that how you see it as well?

Mrs A: Mm, Yes.

Therapist: What made the change?

Mr A: Oh I just rebelled; I thought I'm not a woman I'm a man and it's time I stood up and acted like a man instead of being trod on.

Therapist to Mrs A: What do you think he means when he says that – do you understand that?

Mrs A: No.

Therapist to Mr A: Can you explain a bit more?

Mr A: Well she got all the money . . . .
[*later*]
Therapist: So is that part of what you mean when you say you've decided not to be a woman, to be a man.
Mr A: Yeah, I was fed up with being trod on. Absolutely cheesed off with being treated like a woman. She'll go out knowing very well I haven't got a cigarette in the house, and I smoke, she'll go out and take every penny with her, and every half-pack of cigarettes with her and leave me without nothing at all.
Therapist: Explain to me how that has to do with being treated like a woman.
Mr A: Well being left in the house to do the housework . . . .
[*later*]
Mr A: If she's gonna sit there and tell lies, because that's a lie that I've hit her previously [*i.e. before they got married*], that's a lie, I haven't.
Mrs A: No I didn't say that . . . .
Mr A: Yes, you did . . . .
Mrs A: It's the aggression.
Mr A: And the aggression has always been there because of the bloody way you are.
Mrs A: [*inaudible.*]
Mr A: You are a woman not me and it's your place to do a woman's bloody job.
Therapist: I'm sure you've had this conversation many times.
Mr A: Oh yeah, many times!
Therapist: Let's have a different conversation here [*to Mr A*]. What are your views about what a woman's place is and how a woman should be treated? And how a man should be treated?
Mr A: Well I reckon I should be treated the same as her, equal.
Therapist: So explain to me how would that show itself?
Mr A: Well, when I say equal, she'll go out and buy a whole lot of clothes for herself, poor muggins here hasn't got nothing. [*Mr A goes on to give examples of disputes about money.*]
Therapist: OK. So what are the areas in which you think how a woman should be treated and how it should be different for a man.
Mr A: They're supposed to be equal people, men and women, and what they do are supposed to be the same as one another, when they're married anyway. They're supposed to do things together – not in our house. She does exactly what she does and I've got to do what I'm told. I'm told if I don't want to go out I can stay in the house.
Therapist: So do you see her behaving like a woman or like a man when she does that?

Mr A: Well I don't see her behaving as a woman or as a wife neither, 'cause she just does what she wants to do.

Therapist: And is that like a woman or like a man?

Mr A: Like a woman.

Therapist: [*to Mrs A*] What are your views about how a woman should be treated and how a man should be treated?

Mrs A: I don't think there's any distinction.

Therapist: You think they should be treated the same?

Mrs A: Yeah.

Therapist: So in that sense the two of you agree that they should be equal. [*Both nod.*]

Therapist: Do you feel that there's a difference between how the two of you share things out? I mean do you think the two of you share in an equal way or do you agree with your husband it's not equal.

Mrs A: No. Things are not equal.

Therapist: So how . . . .

Mrs A: It's the same like he says about going out. He's right, why should I be a prisoner in four walls? I mean I go to my sister's for a couple of hours or I go round the shops, there's nothing wrong with that. But if he doesn't want to come that's his privilege. If he wants to stay in the house let him stay in the house.

Therapist: How would you like him to behave that also makes him equal with that?

Mrs A: Well, I don't know, you should just be living there, you should be maybe sharing the housework, or whatever's to be done, and go out together, go visit people. But it doesn't work out like that.

Mr A: Because you're all self.

Mrs A: He only comes out when he's in the mood, when he wants to.

Mr A: No. Because you're all self.

Mrs A: But if he's not in the mood or he doesn't want to, tough – and then you just get it in the neck.

Mr and Mrs A, like most of the people we meet in our work, are struggling with the same issues that we struggle with in our relationships with colleagues, and in our personal lives. They share a common ideal of equality, yet find themselves in difficulties regarding their different definitions of what this means: each feels oppressed and sees the other as having greater privileges or power; they are not sure whether equality means sameness and unity, or diversity and independence. As for all of us, the battle is fought out at the mundane level: money, goods, friendship.

Each statement to or about a client therefore also addresses our own history and attempts to define our relationships (current, retrospective, and prospective) with those around us in our working and private lives. This then also makes it harder for us to be sure that we are not simply using the clinical situation to ride our own hobby-horses, work out our own problems, or proselytize our own private beliefs. It is not surprising, though, for anyone observant of the history of feminism that it is by and large the 'sensitive', 'empathic', 'tender minded' and 'self-doubting' revolutionaries amongst us who worry about the validity of our perceptions and the justification for their integration into everyday practice. The upholders of the status quo amongst us are, as ever, calmly certain that their view is objective, rational, scientifically neutral, and uninfluenced by prejudice or self-interest.

Example:

> Two male therapists are consulting behind the screen to a female therapist working with a female client whose difficult struggle with multiple abuses in her intimate relationships elicit considerable concern and empathy in therapist and consultants. The consultants announce that they have arrived at a definitive intervention: they have just invented feminism, and wish to present it to therapist and client as a Good Idea. Humour being a well known aid to creativity and context-transcendence, this suggestion/joke forms a useful part of the consultation. However, the two consultants also expand on the client's attractiveness and particularly her gorgeous legs and suggest (jokingly) that they would be only too willing to help her cheer up. Am I a 'humourless feminist' when I consider such views – even behind the safety of the screen – to constitute a further abuse of an unhappy woman? Is it true that woman therapists are less likely to respond like this to distressed 'one-down' male clients, and if it is true, why is this?

Can mixed marriages work?

My grandmother, whenever she heard about a man and woman having marital difficulties, used to say with a twinkle in her eye, 'Well, everybody knows these mixed marriages don't work.' Are family therapy and feminism compatible? The answer partly depends on what we mean by family therapy and what we mean by feminism. I have already delineated my orientation in family therapy. By feminism[4] I mean particularly a critique of the prevailing patriarchal system within which we live, together with action to change this system to one where men and women can express their similarities and differences in a culture which values diversity without treating difference as the determinant for hierarchical attributions of superiority/inferiority, power/oppression, norm/deviation, or subject/'other'. It may be utopian to hope that such goals can be fully achieved; it seems to me that we should at least strive towards them.

I shall now discuss, briefly, some of the basic assumptions of feminist therapy, and then examine to what extent these assumptions are compatible with, or conflict with, our current systemic therapy.

Feminist therapy

Summarizing the views of many writers, Gilbert (1980) defines feminist therapy as being based on two principles: (1) 'the personal is political' (p. 248); and (2) 'the therapist–client relationship is viewed as egalitarian' (p. 249). Regarding point (1), feminist therapy expects the therapist to enable women clients to distinguish between the social rules they have been taught and the requirements of their personal experience, and to validate their own perceptions; and it expects the therapist also to explore her own gender values and to strive for change rather than adjustment to the status quo. Regarding point (2), clients are encouraged to behave as informed consumers of therapy, which is demystified, to become more autonomous and self-nurturing; and the therapist acts as role model for the client, which may involve appropriate self-disclosure in the form of feedback, confrontation, information about the therapist's own experiences, reading, or the wider social-political context. Gilbert also makes the point that these explorations are likely to lead female clients to experience anger and to disrupt existing relationships: 'This anger, and working through it, are part of the feminist therapy' (ibid.: 249).

Applications to family therapy

Some of the above issues, and in particular those relating to self-disclosure, would have seemed quite incompatible with the practice of family therapy some years ago. However I, like many others, have over the last few years been struggling with my own gendered views and values in therapy. Alongside this, my practice has altered as I have, together with some of my colleagues, incorporated some of the values and techniques of the second generation of Ericksonian therapists (Lankton and Lankton 1983; Schmidt and Trenkle 1985). Milton Erickson was a man of his time, and much of his work with clients seems to me offensively paternalistic and sexist (Haley 1985). However, his belief in the positive resources of each individual, and his ability to activate creativity in others has enriched our practice alongside our increased interest in making therapy a joint exploration towards change and growth, rather than a cure delivered from Olympian heights or a contest between a brilliant and messianic team on the one hand and a fiendishly stubborn (games-playing) family on the other. We now work in a way which we see as 'empowering' clients more than before; we will frequently share our thinking as well as our 'technical' knowledge of systems, and things we have learned from other clients; we will talk about our own family experiences when and as appropriate; tell clients about books or films that bear on their experience; or comment on wider-context issues. It seems to me that this is largely what is meant by the egalitarian principle in feminist theory (Gilbert 1980). We do still work with a screen and a consultant behind the screen, but our willingness to let clients meet consultants if they wish, our clear explanation of why we find it helpful to keep part of the therapy team at a distance, and the nature of the messages coming from behind the screen, allow ourselves and our clients to feel comfortable about this (Killick 1986).

Example:

> Ms B is a 29-year-old woman who was sexually abused over a period of about three years in childhood by her stepfather. She is divorced and has an 18-month-old son. She has been seen together with her mother and younger sister, and also on her own.
>
> The excerpt below is from session 5 (individual session), and demonstrates in particular the following phenomena: the client reports back on new discoveries she has made for herself. She is more assertive, and has used specific issues discussed in therapy to make connections with problems and solutions not yet discussed in therapy, thus transforming changed thinking in one area to changed thought, meaning and action in other areas.
>
> The therapist emphasizes the positive aspects of the client's contribution; explicates, when relevant, systemic connections between thinking and behaviour, and individual change and system change; and gives the credit for change back to the client.

Ms B: I'll tell you what I've been doing, I've been thinking . . . . It's like – um – it's weird – thoughts keep going in my mind, and all of a sudden I start to think, I don't know, I think differently about things, and I'm acting differently.

Therapist: In what sort of way?

Ms B: Well, I don't care any more, and I really don't care – I'm not watching my ps and qs all the time – you know, and I thought so what if they don't like me – I'm not bending over backwards to please all the time. I'm not saying I'm there, you know, but . . . .

Therapist: But you can notice a change.

Ms B: Yeah – and thoughts like, so, just little thoughts like um . . . Why I eat chocolate all the time. I was thinking about it, I thought – I went to buy chocolate, and I thought, I don't need that. I thought, mm you don't need that, I don't need that crutch, that's not getting you over nothing, and I just didn't buy any, and I haven't eaten chocolate for about two weeks now. Now for me, course I used to live on the stuff – forget food. I'm not a big eater in the way of food, but it's nothing for me to eat five bars of chocolate a day, nothing. And then I went on and I thought why are you eating it? Why do you go into that shop, buying chocolate and going home – like a child – and I sat down and thought OK, let me think why I'm doing this now, and I thought it's a comfort, it's like a child again. I can see why, I can see the pattern now. Like – um – I go to a shop and get chocolate – and if something upsets me I eat it – if I feel sad I eat it – or if someone's upset me – I'll eat it.

[*later*]

I even went to a party and put my foot in it – now that's not like me. I mean, usually I'm the sort of person that anyone could say anything to and I'll just go Yeah, Yeah, smile, smile and go into a corner like and ignore it. But somebody upset me and before I knew it I put him in his place and thought God, I've never done that you know. I felt awful and yet I felt good, because they really had a go at me for no good reason, and usually I just think oh what have I done you know, have I put my foot in it? But it was unjust, and I realized it was unjust, and before I knew it I just said . . . I answered him back . . . .

Therapist: And what was the response to you?

Ms B: He was gorgeous to me! It was weird! [*describes detail*] . . . and I couldn't understand it! [*laughing*]

Therapist: That sounds like a very good thing to have learnt.

Ms B: Yes, it's like you are a person 'B', you are a person, and don't forget it.

Therapist: And perhaps that when you stop doing all that, and trying to please everybody . . . .

Ms B: You probably don't please them anyway . . . .

Therapist: Yes, and then they start trying to please you a bit more.

Ms B: That's what happened. Because he's usually never nice to me, never. He just keeps putting me down, putting me down and I usually just keep going oh yeah, that's you. But I just thought, why am I putting up with it? I'm just not having it – if he talks to me like that.

Therapist: But that's great, because it means a lot of those changes, they are beginning to go into things you actually do . . . and I mean that's one of the things that we see here a lot, that when, you know, there's a whole lot of people connected with each other, when one starts changing how they are, then the others start changing too.

Ms B: Yeah, how they expect you. You see my family expects me – [*she describes a pattern where she sits around feeling down and hoping her family will respond positively, whereas they assume (a) that she is a support for them and (b) that she's always 'down' anyway*] and then I sit there feeling useless and then I think, look, I haven't murdered nobody, I haven't robbed a bank, I do nothing disgusting, what have I done that's making me feel so bad?

Therapist: That's also something that you're probably carrying around from when you were little and when you thought, as children do, it's my fault that this sexual thing has happened.

Ms B: Yeah! and that you blamed yourself and were frightened that everyone else would blame you for 'killing' your mother and it's that habit of saying I'm in the wrong, I must try and make it up to everybody, I must lie down and let people stomp all over me . . . It's exciting and it's really nice to start to feel like I don't care, I don't . . . I've wasted all my life caring about everything and everybody and I don't care. I mean I don't go out of my way to hurt anyone, that's just not me – that's not.

Therapist: And you don't have to become that kind of person, but you don't have to let other people hurt you any more.

Ms B: No . . . I'm not gonna let it.

Therapist: And then it's very interesting, if you try it out more [*Ms B giggles*] to see if you get more of what this chap did, which is then . . . .

Ms B: Yeah, it's . . . I just thought, waste your breath boy because I'm not interested. But it would be interesting because people admire you if you've got a bit – you know I've got a lot of strength of character in myself but I don't show it and so – well, people think I'm an easy walk-over.

Therapist: And might like that strong character a lot when they get to see more of her.

Ms B: Yeah – when you think of it – they might respect me more . . . . it's all a new experience innit? And I never even tried not to eat chocolate, that's the amazing thing. Normally on a diet I go out of my way not to eat and all this but I didn't try, it just hit me like, God I haven't eaten it for two weeks . . . .

[*later*]

I feel like I'm coming on now, like I'm getting somewhere. I don't know where I'm getting – different thoughts, different ideas, different feelings . . . I'm still learning that . . . . Whereas before I was so afraid he [*her son*] wouldn't love me too you know I thought this baby isn't going to love me because I was so sure I was unlovable . . . but . . . going through this, and starting on this progress, have taught me that, well, maybe I'm not perfect but I'm certainly not horrible.

Therapist: And so the more sure you are that you're a good enough mother and a lovable mother he will love you the more, you can say . . . .

Ms B: The more confidence I have . . .

Therapist: . . . that's the limit and then you can . . .

Ms B: . . . carry on and instead of being so tense and anxious all the time I just think well – say someone says ooh, you shouldn't have let him do that, I say it's OK. Whereas before I'd say Dafydd! Don't! Now I say, no, let him play, it's his house. Then if I really think something's naughty I'll say no. I warn him and he's starting to listen . . . . Suddenly I'm starting to find my own field with him, not what everybody keeps telling me I should do . . . I mean who the hell are they? He's my baby. See how I'm thinking? It's amazing what the therapy's doing for me, already. [*laughing*]

Therapist: The [*laughing*] let me put that slightly differently because I see lots of people in therapy, and I think, it's amazing what you're doing with the therapy.

Ms B: Oh! (ha ha) Oh dear!

Therapist: It's very important you should also take credit for that.

Ms B: Yeah, it's like I've always wanted to get this off my head you know, all my life, I've never known how to, or . . . I've sat and tried to work out how to . . . . Well I've kept myself sane that's about all that . . . but mm . . . I am the kind of person to think about things and work things out – I'm not sort of irresponsible.

Unresolved difficulties

One might say that it is easy enough to do good feminist therapy with an individual woman. Issues become much more complex when one is also concerned with the interactional systems of men and women, whether because one if working with couples and families, or because of taking a systemic view of working with individuals. It has also struck me, in many discussions about feminist therapy, that there is an assumption that the therapy is for women clients and by women therapists (cf. criteria for feminist theory discussed on p. 72). If the feminist goals of changed relationships and a changed society are to be realized, we also have to address therapy with male clients, therapy with couples and families, and the implications for male as well as female therapists and mixed-gender teams.

(1) If feminism and feminist therapy are women's issues, as is often implied by women who write and talk about it, and by men who ignore it and do not attend relevant conferences, what are the likely consequences of such attitudes?

- Will we help to empower women and oppress men?
- Will male family members and therapy team members feel obliged to skulk around guiltily like woolly-jumpered liberals in a Posy Simmonds cartoon?
- For whom in the family/team would this be most uncomfortable/guilt-inducing/change-inhibiting?
- What form will the backlash take?

(2) Given my orientation, potential system change will obviously not be approached via didactic inputs, statements about family 'pathology' and desirable change, or head-on challenges to existing roles. I assume, however, that every question asked (and not asked) acts as a source of information to the therapist, but more importantly acts as a suggestion/validation/new perspective/perturbation/initiator of a 'search process' for the clients (Tomm 1987).

- If a couple is discussing the feasibility of separation, and I do not ask what the financial implications are for both of them, what are the consequences for their reaching a solution which will be life enhancing for both of them and their children?
- If the presenting complaint includes violence, and I never ask any questions about it during the sessions, how does this influence the meaning clients are helped to attach to the violence?
- If I ask men about their work and women about their children, what are the likely normative conclusions that clients may draw about my views as an 'authority' on 'mental health'?
- If, in my hypotheses and my questions/tasks/statements to clients, I pay attention to the overinvolvement, anxiety, exasperation, neglect, and so on, expressed by mothers to their children, but do not give equal weighting to the 'absence' of fathers, does this sanction the actions of one parent while blaming those of the other?

When I study history, read books, watch the news on television, and so on, I frequently ask myself: 'Where are the women?' When I read the family-therapy literature, watch case presentations, look at current-affairs comments made on the media by family therapists, I find myself asking 'Where (in the understanding of the system) are the (absent) men?' When family therapists act in relation to families as if non-action is not an action, and disengagement is not a definition of relationship, are we being more consistent with our theory or more consistent with our cultural conditioning?

(3) I assume that it is not my business to hold specific goals for client system organization post-therapy. If I were exploring client concerns in regard to stealing, depression, psychosomatic symptoms, disobedience, drug abuse, marital unhappiness, and so on, I would explore exactly how these behaviours show themselves at present, what the influences of wider familial traditions and expectations are on them, and what the consequences for the family system might be were they to change or not to change. If I ask similar questions about gender roles and their relation to satisfaction/dissatisfaction, decision making, finance, role modelling, negotiation, and so on, in the family, am I biasing the course of therapy by introducing gender politics into a non-relevant arena? The newest Hite report (1988) indicates that 98 per cent of the women in her study are dissatisfied with their intimate relationships with men. Is it only by not giving women the opportunity to voice their dissatisfaction that we can hope to save the twentieth-century institution of marriage? If we do not facilitate the expression of such dissatisfaction in relationships, we may be using our influence as therapists to protect men at the expense of women; if we do ask questions to elicit these dissatisfactions, will we be supporting women at the expense of men? Might it be reasonable to assume that men too are disadvantaged by the straightjackets of their gender-role divisions?

- Is it our business to shore up an institution (by keeping silent and helping people to adapt), which is visibly not working well, and which, in the absence of other compensating elements, works less well for women than for men? (Gove 1972)
- Is it our business to explore the flaws in this (crumbling) institution by asking questions about its structure, meaning, and purpose?
- Is it our business to assist in the search for structures of relationship that may enhance the quality of life of all participants therein?
- Can we be 'neutral' when our verbal and non-verbal actions and omissions must inevitably form part of the attribution of meaning that occurs between client and therapist?
- If feminist family therapists persist in their critique of family-therapy beliefs and practice, what form is the response likely to take?

Conclusion

An ecologist is said to be an optimist who works like a pessimist (Schumacher 1987). This is also a good description of my stance in regard to the feminist/family therapy debate.

The feminist critique of family therapy is not something that descended on us from out of the blue. The fact that we suddenly find ourselves in the midst of a proliferation of papers, workshops, discussions, and so on, means that our system has already changed sufficiently to enable a feminist perspective to emerge from within our organization. Therefore as we address these issues they are already in process of shifting. This is a heartening indication of continuous change and adaption within a flexible responsive system. However, in my view there are two risks attached to this responsiveness. The first is that we will feel that any further comment, struggle, critique is now redundant, and that we can relax, having solved the difficulty once and for all. Anyone feeling an attack of complacency coming on should look at the history of the upsurge of feminism and its repeated decline – for example, during the French Revolution, between the two World Wars, and in many other places and eras.

The second danger is spelled out eloquently by Virginia Goldner (1985a) when she discusses her view that feminism has become a fashion in family therapy, thus risking disqualification via cooptation. She suggests that this may most easily come about by

> transforming feminist commentary from a threatening critique into a banal who-could-disagree piece of liberal cant. In the interests of protecting feminists from success on these terms, and in the hopes of reducing our swelling ranks, I would like to present the feminist case in terms that will probably be incompatible with the core beliefs of many committed family therapists. Since I count myself within these ranks, I can only report that subscribing to mutually exclusive visions of truth is a longstanding habit of my mind. It is unnerving, but I want to point out that we often prescribe just such an approach for families stuck in their ways.
>
> (Goldner 1985a: 20)

May we all long continue to follow this prescription! 'The double description (Bateson 1979: 133) that arises from the tension generated . . . is most conducive to the evolution of a more socially just application of systemic thinking' (Pilalis 1987: 5).

Notes

1. I have been particularly influenced, in workshops and conversations, by Marc Lehrer, Phil Booth, and Gunther Schmidt. See references section for relevant publications.
2. Regarding the definition of patriarchy, the Concise Oxford Dictionary defines patriarch as 'Father and ruler of family or tribe', and hence derives patriarchy. Juliet Mitchell (1971), in her discussion of Kate Millet's 'notes toward a theory of patriarchy' in 'Sexual Politics', says that 'Patriarchy is used . . . to mean not the rule of the father but, more generally, the rule of men.' She quotes Millet's definition of patriarchy as a 'universal (geographical and historical) mode of power relationships', and concludes her discussion thus: 'Patriarchy then is the sexual politics whereby men establish their power and maintain control.' Like Virginia Goldner (1985a), I assume it 'is no longer necessary to "prove" the existence of patriarchy'.
3. By 'our culture' I mean specifically the western capitalist post-industrial culture in which I and other British family therapists live. While I assume the phenomena discussed here are widespread, I am confining myself in this section to the culture I know well, and the culture (the USA and the UK) in which Broverman *et al.* (1970) and Shoben (1980) did their research.
4. The Concise Oxford Dictionary defines 'feminism' as 'Advocacy of women's rights on (the) ground of equality of the sexes'.

References

Bateson, G. (1972/1980) *Steps to an Ecology of Mind*, London: Paladin, Granada.

Bateson, G. (1979/1980) *Mind and Nature: A Necessary Unity*, London: Fontana/Collins.

Broverman, I.K., Broverman, D.M., Clarkson, F.E., Rosenkrantz, P.S., and Vogel S.R. (1970) 'Sex-role stereotype and clinical judgments of mental health', *Journal of Consulting and Clinical Psychology* 34(1): 1–7.

Cecchin, G. (1987) 'Hypothesising, circularity and neutrality revisited: an invitation to curiosity', *Family Process* 26(4): 405–13.

Cross, J. (1985) 'Social issues affecting women', *Dulwich Centre Review* 60–3.

de Beauvoir, S. (1949/1969) *The Second Sex*, New English Library.

Gilbert, L.A. (1980) 'Feminist therapy', in A.M. Brodsky and R.T. Hare-Mustin (eds.) *Women and Psychotherapy: An Assessment of Research and Practice*, New York: Guilford Press 245–65.

Goldner, V. (1985a) 'Warning: Family therapy may be hazardous to your health', *The Family Therapy Networker* 9(6): 18–23.

Goldner, V. (1985b) 'Feminism and family therapy', *Family Process* 24: 31–47.

Gove, W.R. (1972) 'The relationship between sex roles, mental illness and marital status', *Social Forces* 5: 34–44.

Haley, J. (ed.) 1985) *Conversations with Milton H. Erickson, M.D.*, 3 vols., New York: Triangle Press.

Hare-Mustin, R.T. (1987) 'The problem of gender in family therapy theory', *Family Process* 26(1): 15–27.

Hite, S. (1988) *Women and Love: A Cultural Revolution in Progress*, London: Viking Press.

Hoffman, L. (1985) 'Beyond power and control: toward a "second order" family systems therapy', *Family Systems Medicine* 3(4): 381–96.

Kappeler, S. (1986) *The Pornography of Representation*, Cambridge: Polity Press.

Killick, S. (1986) 'An investigation into clients' and therapists' account of a Milan-style family therapy session with particular reference to the intervention', unpublished M.Sc. dissertation, University of Warwick.

Kingston, P. (1982) 'Power and influence in the environment of family therapy', *Journal of Family Therapy* 4(3): 211–27.

Lankton, S.R. and Lankton, C.H. (1983) *The Answer Within: A Clinical Framework of Ericksonian Hypnotherapy*, New York: Brunner/Mazel.

McNamee, S. (1989) 'Breaking the patriarchal vision of social science: lessons from a family therapy model', in K. Carter and C. Spitzack (eds.) *Doing Research on Women's Communication: Perspectives on Theory and Method*, Norwood, N.J. Ablex.

Mitchell, J. (1971/1977) *Woman's Estate*, Harmondsworth: Penguin.

Mitchell, J. (1974) *Psychoanalysis and Feminism*, Harmondsworth: Penguin.

Myers, N. (ed.) (1985) *The Gaia Atlas of Planet Management*, London: Pan Books.

Penfold, P.S. and Walker, G.A. (1984) *Women and the Psychiatric Paradox*, Milton Keynes: Open University Press.

Pilalis, J. (1987) 'Consciousness-raising and family therapy', paper presented at the Fifth New Zealand Family Therapy Conference, Hamilton, 14–17 May.

Schmidt, G. and Trenkle, B. (1985) 'An integration of Ericksonian techniques with concepts of family therapy', in J.K. Zeig (ed.) *Ericksonian Psychotherapy*, Vols. 1–3, New York: Brunner/Mazel.

Schumacher, C. (1987) 'Verbal communication', Bristol: Schumacher Lectures.

Shoben, L. (1980) 'The effect of sex-stereotyped conformity and physical attractiveness on clinical judgements about patients', unpublished M.Sc. dissertation, North East London Polytechnic.

Spender, D. (1980/1981) *Man Made Language*, London: Routledge & Kegan Paul.

Tomm, K. (1987) 'Interventive interviewing: Part 2. Reflexive questioning as a means to enable self-healing', *Family Process* 26: 167–83.

Woolf, V. (1929) *A Room of One's Own*, London: Triad, Grafton.

Chapter four

Feminism and strategic therapy: contradiction or complementarity?[1]

Charlotte Burck and Gwyn Daniel

> The oppression of women is like no other form of oppression, because it is entangled through with human love, human need, genuine (core) human satisfactions, identifications, fulfilments. How to separate out the chains from the bonds, the harms from the value, the truth from the lies.
>
> (Olsen 1980)

Hopefully it is not premature to say that family therapists have finally begun to take the criticisms raised by feminists seriously, in particular the almost total lack of attention or mention of gender difference in theory and practice (Hare-Mustin 1978; James and MacIntyre 1983; Goldner 1988). However, the extent to which this will evolve beyond the minimal position, represented by sensitivity to families who are explicitly presenting 'gender issues', remains to be seen. The more demanding task consists in taking on the implications of accepting the way gender and the power invested in gender roles inevitably construct and shape family life. Meeting this challenge involves not only the exhilaration of criticizing conventional practice but also the confusion of 'unlearning' in order to take on board the implications of these new ideas.

For the authors, as therapists, the experience has felt not dissimilar to that of moving from an individual to a systemic perspective. It involves the same need to throw out previously valued ideas and interventions. Looking at our work through the 'lens' of feminism, we are again engaged in the business of questioning every technique and every theoretical formulation. Needless to say, this is a process which is only just beginning.

In this chapter we intend to address the question of family-therapy techniques and approaches which are considered 'unacceptable' from a feminist perspective, and to explore whether and how some of these approaches can be utilized in practice in ways that are sensitive to gender differences, and issues for women in particular. We have chosen to discuss strategic therapies because they have given rise to most criticism from feminists and because they contain most of the features quoted by writers (Libow *et al.* 1982; James and McIntyre 1983; Pilalis and Anderton 1986), who contrast a feminist and a family-systems approach.

We intend, first, to explore briefly the differences and areas of common ground between feminist and family-systems therapy, and then to focus on strategic therapy in particular. We will then look in more depth at the dilemmas faced by women and men who are trying to change with respect to gender roles, and how this affects what the therapist does. We will give examples of strategic techniques which seem useful in addressing gender, and will pay particular attention to the work of Olga Silverstein and Peggy Papp.

Feminist therapy and family therapy

In recent years, a number of papers (Libow *et al.* 1982; James and McIntyre 1983; Pilalis and Anderton 1986) have explored the differences between a feminist and a family-systems approach to therapy. They point to some areas of common ground, the most important of which is the viewing of individual problems as contextual. Both approaches avoid traditional psychiatric labels with their implied blame of the symptomatic person. To this end, both approaches try to relabel or reframe pathology and emphasize positive strengths rather than focusing on failings.

However, these writers also identify various key polarities where the two approaches can be seen to be profoundly different, if not incompatible. The first of these is the way each defines the family. Feminists emphasize the external social context where the woman's experience is formed, whereas family therapists tend to focus more on idiosyncratic family patterns. Feminists are therefore keenly aware of the extent to which unequal power relationships in society are reflected in the family, leading to a conflict of interests. Family therapists, however, tend to see the family as an organic whole, and when they do address issues of power, it is only in terms of generational differences and not the power invested in gender roles (Goldner 1988).

Second, feminist therapists are likely to hold a linear view of causality because they see women's personal difficulties arising from their oppression and marginalization within a patriarchal society. The concept of circular causality, central to family therapy, has led family therapists to look at complementarity in relationships rather than view problems in terms such as an oppressor/victim relationship. However, as Pilalis and Anderton point out, 'feminism provides the supplementary analysis required in family systems theory, and family systems theory provides feminism with a more developed understanding of the processes of problem formation and resolution in the family system' (1986: 105).

Turning to the actual process of therapy, a feminist and a family-systems approach are generally agreed to be at variance in two main areas. (However, there may be an added confusion in that the feminist approach described in the literature has tended to deal with individual women rather than with families.)

The first major difference is that feminist therapists believe in reducing the power differential between therapist and client and aim for a more open and egalitarian relationship. In contrast, the family therapist typically uses 'expert power' (power which is vested in her role as defined by the context) and her interventions are not usually explained to the family. She does not generally, except as a strategy, describe her own personal experiences to the client. Feminist therapists use 'referent' power in which the self 'is utilised as a point of identification in order to aid an individual's self examination and perhaps the reorganization of perceptions of oneself and one's world' (Libow *et al.* 1982: 9). The feminist therapist uses herself as a model of competence and instrumentality, shares her own experiences as a means of universalizing the issues which individual women face, and only uses strategies that are openly shared and accessible. The idea of therapy as partnership is regarded as a particularly important way of emphasizing that, irrespective of differences in wealth, class, or professional status, there is a commonality of women's experience which is a fundamental source of strength.

The second difference which follows from this is that the feminist therapist will place much greater emphasis on the role of understanding as a means of producing change. Family therapists, of course, do not consider insight to be of primary importance, and indeed find that explaining the rationale behind their interventions often makes them less effective. The reason feminist therapists promote insight concerns the issue of power and the belief that understanding the reasons for change is in itself empowering because those changes can then be owned by the woman herself. If change were to occur in a mysterious way, orchestrated by the therapist, the woman may feel further disempowered.

Strategic therapy

Whereas the divergence of attitudes concerning the power relationship between therapist and client and about the role of insight applies to all family-therapy approaches, strategic therapy is most often criticized for putting techniques first and ignoring the implications of these in relation to the wider context. Gurman and Klein argue that strategic therapists

> run the risk of offering couples and families therapeutic directives that, while accurately and perceptively addressing family organizational-transactional dimensions, may fail entirely to grapple explicitly with the substantive details and sources of a woman's suffering and dissatisfaction in her parental and marital role.
> (Gurman and Klein 1980: 173)

The strategic therapist is particularly open to the charge of using techniques in a narrow, symptom-orientated way, and believing that the end of therapy in the form of symptom relief or problem resolution justifies whatever means are used to bring it about. Since strategic therapists are more concerned with problem solving than exploring meaning, they are less likely to question values or assumptions. Values which are unchallenged are likely to reflect the dominant social norms – in other words, white, male, middle-class values.

Strategic therapy has been defined by Haley (1973) as an approach in which the therapist initiates what happens during therapy and designs a particular intervention for each problem. However, within this loose definition, there exist huge differences in approach and it is possible to devise a continuum ranging from a minimalist problem-solving focus at one extreme to a systemic/strategic approach at the other.

The therapy practised at the Mental Research Institute (MRI), Palo Alto (Calif.) lies at the minimalist pole in that its practitioners are only interested in solving the presenting problem and are not concerned with the family structure or belief system, or the wider social context (Watzlawick *et al.* 1974; Weakland *et al.* 1974). They would claim to be working from a value-free perspective on a problem carefully defined and agreed upon with the client. If any attention is paid to the ideas which men and women have about their roles, it is mainly to gain greater leverage in making interventions and getting the client to carry out a directive.

Further along the spectrum, Haley (1976) adopts a broader view which includes family structure, and takes the issue of power in families seriously, albeit solely from a generational standpoint. Consequently he does not address inequalities in the social sphere which can put the woman on a hierarchical level with her children rather than her spouse. Madanes (1981), who uses a similar family model to Haley, describes 'hierarchical incongruity' in couple relationships – by this she means one spouse occupying an inferior position of power in relation to the other spouse. She describes a process whereby the less powerful spouse can gain power through developing a symptom which the more powerful spouse is unable to change. The conflict between the couple is then diverted away from a battle over who is to dominate in the relationship to the issue of whether or not the symptom can be dealt with. If one looks at this struggle bearing in mind existing inequalities of income and status between men and women (women's earnings are, on average, two-thirds those of men – Phillips 1988), it would be highly probable for 'hierarchical incongruities' to tend to cluster in gender patterns, with women being more likely to resort to the power of weakness or symptomatology. Yet in a way that would seem positively disingenuous, if it were not repeated so often in the family-therapy literature, Madanes manages scrupulously to avoid this point, and gives carefully balanced examples where both sexes occupy the position of greater or lesser power.

Clearly there are many aspects of the strategic theoretical framework that can be criticized from a feminist perspective. Most glaring, of course, is the almost total absence of any mention of gender differences. However, an even more problematic area relates to the therapeutic process itself, and the way its practitioners' role is conceptualized and operationalized. If one takes the view that the different socialization experienced by men and women leads them to develop different approaches to problem solving, then the strategic therapies can be seen to accord more with a male than a female perspective. This can be seen in the way that instrumentality, the direct use of therapeutic power, and a narrow problem-solving focus all tend to be paramount. Since the majority of self referrals for family or couple therapy come from women, and the research evidence (Brannen 1982; Willi 1982) suggests that men and women have very different agendas and expectations of therapy, then clearly the way the therapist defines what should be focused upon is highly significant. Women often come to therapy with the idea that they are responsible for the emotional life of the family, and that they must have failed if there is a problem. A straightforward problem-solving approach would do nothing to challenge this view and may accord more with men's expectations of therapy who generally adopt the narrower view that there is simply a problem to be solved (Marianne Walters, verbal communication). It is the authors' experience that many women come into therapy with a wider brief, often wanting a change in relationships in the family, perhaps wanting more emotional involvement from their spouse, and hoping that the therapist will support them in these desires. Men, on the other hand, may either experience the status quo as being to their advantage or be emotionally more distanced from any feelings of dissatisfaction. In this respect too, strategic therapists may indirectly support the man's position.

It is important to emphasize that these are not immutable characteristics of men and women. Rather, they are likely to emerge out of the socialization process and the very different social experience of men and women. In her important book, *In a Different Voice*, Gilligan (1982) describes the way men and women in western society bring very different perspectives to bear on the same moral dilemmas. She points to the way men construct solutions in an abstract rational way, with a clear ordering of priorities while women tend to view the whole context, with an emphasis on the relationship dilemmas arising out of different decisions. Since women appear to attach much more importance and value to the discussion of feelings which are traditionally their 'sphere', the problem-solving approach, which actively discourages emotional exploration, must fail to utilize this area of women's skill and experience. Some interesting research remains to be carried out on the ways men and women view the therapeutic situation, and how this fits with the therapist style, gender, and theoretical orientation. Nevertheless, it does seem that, however neutral and even-handed the therapist tries to be in the choice of intervention or therapeutic alliance, the process in strategic therapy is still likely to accord more closely with men's ways of viewing the world than women's.

It is also interesting to consider the ideas about first- and second-order change, which are central to the strategic approach (Watzlawick *et al.* 1974). Effective change needs to be of second order, in the way the problem is viewed, rather than first order which is at the level of behaviour within the same basic frame of viewing the problem. One can hypothesize that women often come into therapy with a wish, however covert, for second-order change (for example, wanting their male partner to take more responsibility for child care), whereas the man may only see change, if necessary at all, at the behavioural level (for example, helping her a bit more). The therapist's idea of what constitutes second-order change depends upon her value system, which does not necessarily involve challenging or even questioning the family's beliefs about men or women's roles.

Another way in which strategic therapy can be seen to reflect a male value system concerns the conceptualization of the therapist's position as outside the family, acting upon it, rather than as a co-evolving relationship of mutual influence. This mechanistic view is also demonstrated in what Hoffman describes as the strategic therapists' use of the language of power. She comments that many of the articles written by the MRI group in particular are saturated with language which uses 'a vocabulary based on war and adversarial games, with words like "power tactics", "strategy", "one up", "one down" '. She adds 'I am often struck by the resemblance between accounts of therapeutic prowess described within this framework and the sexual performance known as "scoring" ' (Hoffman 1985: 382).

There is the likelihood, therefore, that the problem-solving approach (whatever the sex of the therapist) may, however subtly, disempower women by according more with a view of the world based on men's experience. Marianne Walters emphasizes the need for therapists continually to criticize the process of therapy from a gender-sensitive perspective and to bear in mind that interventions will reverberate differently for men and women (verbal communication 1987). She therefore argues that strategic approaches are generally unacceptable to feminist therapists because they elevate certain more masculine ways of seeing problems at the expense of others. Certainly there are many examples in the strategic literature, from female as well as male therapists, of interventions that are effective in producing change but are at the same time deeply offensive to women. However, does this mean that we should reject all strategic techniques in our repertoire? Or should we assume that an indirect approach always runs contrary to the goal of empowering women?

One of the difficulties in developing a feminist model of family therapy is not only the temptation to focus only on the woman's position, but also the danger of assuming goals with women as to the nature, direction, and pace of change. Alongside this, there seems to be a belief, implicit in much feminist writing on the subject, that insights into the social constraints operating on women, depathologizing individual problems in the light of this understanding, and reframing women's positions in order to focus on strengths, will themselves lead to change. It is the experience of the authors that while most referrals for therapy come from women and they are often the ones most motivated to change, it is also evident that the constraints on women changing do not only come from outside. It is therefore important to find a way of addressing women's as well as men's reluctance to find different solutions to rigid gender stereotypes.

Because women are often the ones most closely connected to and empathetic with other members of the system, whether their parents, their partners, or their children, they may be particularly conscious of the implications for others if they start to change too much. Strategic therapists are often most effective when they pay attention to the constraining patterns which inhibit attempts to change, and when they devize their interventions to take these into account. In reviewing and trying to develop our own clinical practice, it has become increasingly clear that there are valuable strategic interventions which are effective in addressing dilemmas over gender roles and which do not necessarily lead to the problems we have outlined.

We have been strongly influenced in our work by the practice of Peggy Papp and Olga Silverstein who, together with Marianne Walters and Betty Carter, founded the Women's Project in Family Therapy (Simon 1984). Their approach lies at the systemic end of our strategic-therapy continuum, and uses the idea of the 'dilemma of change' which involves laying out for the family the consequences of change, and the consequences of staying the same. Papp and Silverstein do use a number of strategic techniques to highlight the family's dilemma; these techniques are hidden from the client, do not involve the therapist taking a clear personal position, and make ample use of the 'expert' power of the therapist and her team. In our experience, this has been a particularly helpful way of addressing the constraints operating on both men and women, especially those stemming from beliefs about gender roles, which are likely to be those most deeply embedded in the family's fabric of relationships. The therapist can fully address the complexity of issues involved and maintain manoeuvrability without becoming trapped in the position of believing that there is a single right way for the woman to change, or underestimating the strength of the constraints.

The question of power is also more complex than the current debate has indicated. Whereas the strategic therapist uses power in the sense of taking control over the direction of the session and issuing directives, many strategic therapists do work indirectly to reach their goals, often taking a 'one-down' position which means that, far from being seen by the family as too powerful, they are often seen to be quite peripheral to changes that occur. Indeed, some strategic therapists would argue that being dismissed as irrelevant to any changes that take place is the hallmark of successful therapy (Kraemer 1983). This raises interesting issues for the feminist therapist who emphasizes referent power based on sharing experience and providing a strong role model, because this may make the client more likely to attribute change to the therapist's agency. Perhaps as women therapists wanting to empower women it is important for us to feel that our effectiveness in doing this is openly acknowledged and for this reason as well, we are reluctant, paradoxically, to use indirect techniques. Concealing power may come more easily to male therapists who have not had to face this issue in such personal terms.

One advantage of the approach used by the Ackerman therapists,

Papp and Silverstein, is that the therapist can take a position of authority and yet show uncertainty or share a dilemma about the direction of change in a way that addresses complexity. Although she expresses uncertainty, she does so on the basis of discussing the potential losses and gains involved in change rather than adopting a false position of therapeutic impotence.

Beliefs and constraints

In our work in identifying constraints on change we have been particularly interested in the family's belief system, i.e. that aspect of family functioning which includes assumptions, attitudes, myths, and family scripts. Although there are family therapists like Byng Hall (1979) who have paid a great deal of attention to this area, only a few strategic family therapists have been interested in exploring families' beliefs and how these influence and shape the families' interactional patterns (Papp 1983; Keeney and Silverstein 1986). As Papp (1983) has commented, this level is often the most difficult to understand because it is beyond awareness, but can be revealed through the use of language or metaphor. It is often only when the therapist questions or highlights assumptions that the belief system is clarified for the family.

One of the most striking features in the literature is the fact that when therapists do pay attention to the family's belief system they concentrate almost entirely on idiosyncratic beliefs. In this way they have focused entirely on what happens inside the family, as if it were a hermetically sealed system, just as they have done when paying attention to behaviour and interactional patterns as other feminist writers have pointed out (James and McIntyre 1983). It seems extraordinary that no one has taken into account the more widespread beliefs held in our culture.

We have become most interested in examining the influence of beliefs about gender, as most people would agree that they have as much or more impact on interaction and behaviour as actual biological differences. Some beliefs about gender have become more apparent in Britain because women's roles have begun to change, albeit slowly. As women have become bus drivers, fire-fighters, trade-union leaders, and so on, we keep bumping into beliefs about what is 'natural' for men and women. No matter how traditional or from which ethnic group, all families in Britain today will inevitably have come into contact with this process of change in some way. This change is slow, however. Family therapy is a field which, although it defines itself as radical in relation to other therapies, has been shaped mainly by men. Beliefs and premisses have remained unchallenged and therefore largely outside awareness until recently confronted by feminist practitioners.

When can one identify the beliefs about gender which help shape behaviour in families? It has been interesting to examine the stereotypes of men and women which are held in our culture. In a study published in 1970, Broverman asked professionals to identify characteristics of men and women and found that women were seen to be intuitive, nurturing, expressive, and dependent and that men were seen to be assertive, independent, and active. Broverman went on to ask mental-health professionals to identify characteristics of a healthy adult, and found these to be similar to the characteristics identified for men. This study thus demonstrated that men and women are believed to have fairly consistent characteristics allocated in rather stereotypic ways, and that male characteristics are most valued.

Systems thinkers note that personal characteristics are not fixed but are related to context. Many of the stereotypes identified in the Broverman study are interactional – the man does not express feelings, the woman is emotionally expressive and looks after others' feelings, and so on. A study by Manikel in 1978 of perception demonstrated this contextual influence by looking at the differences which emerged when marital partners were tested separately and together. When tested together, women gave up their creativity and their control, and men gave up their emotional responsiveness; both men and women showed more stereotypic characteristics in interaction with each other (Feldman 1982). Sex-role stereotypes are an expression of our society's beliefs about how men and women should be in relation to each other. They have been handed down through the generations and are reinforced in our culture in a multitude of ways. They are also perpetuated through the legal system – for example, the fact that until recently the police did not intervene in domestic violence suggests a belief that men had the right to hit their women partners, and that women deserved it because they were being provocative.

Other beliefs about gender can be identified as operating at a less overt level. These beliefs may never be articulated directly or may not be acknowledged, and yet they seem to organize interactions between men and women profoundly. One such belief, identified in particular by two American writers, Dinnerstein (1976) and Chodorow (1978), is the belief that women's power is dangerous and destructive. Both these writers argue that this belief originates from our early experiences in which the mother is seen to hold the power of life and death and is experienced as all-controlling and all-powerful. They go on to discuss their belief that society is structured so as to ensure that this experience is never repeated, that women should never have power again because it is so overwhelming.

There are many examples of interactional sequences and patterns both in families, and between families and therapists which seem to confirm this belief. In our society, it is women who are most often blamed for the difficulties of their children and, as we have noted, blame themselves when they come into therapy. Family therapists often work to take power away from women, feeling that children need to be separated from mothers who are stifling, over-protective, and damaging, so that they can grow up. Therapists will therefore work to encourage men to take over with the children, relegating women to a back seat – a less powerful and therefore 'less damaging' position.

Powerful women are also seen to be particularly dangerous to men, because another covert belief seems to be that men are fragile and need protecting. This belief seems paradoxical because conventional wisdom has it that men are there to protect women. However, the message conveyed repeatedly through popular culture is that powerful women are castrating, destructive, or mad (see Showalter 1987, or, for example, the film *Fatal Attraction*). This idea leads men to fear women's power, and leads women to constrain themselves from exercising it directly. There are many other such beliefs about gender which powerfully influence interactional patterns in families (Lowenstein 1981; Burck 1986; Daniel and Burck forthcoming) and which have not been taken sufficiently into account in clinical practice.

When an external event perturbs a family system or a family is faced by a life-cycle change, there may be a wish or need for change which may conflict with a premiss or belief about gender which may in turn leave the family stuck or in a bind. Families often develop symptoms at such times of transition when they have been influenced by beliefs which have restricted their ability to adopt new ways of interacting. A crisis will thus produce a rigidification of patterns of interaction which have worked in the past (old ways of behaving), and the family will attempt to respond by changing certain aspects of behaviour to keep things the same, rather than being able to change their premisses and move on to develop more complexity. In these times of high unemployment, for example, families often find themselves bound by their beliefs about how men and women should behave, which limit their options in adapting to unemployment. In one study (Fagin and Little 1984), men were found to become physically ill after a period of some months following unemployment, an example of a first-order change.

There are many dilemmas and paradoxical binds which are encountered in families as women's roles have started to shift (Daniel

1986). As families face change created by outside events or as women themselves actively wish to behave differently, they find themselves confronting internal constraints as much as external ones.

As it is often women who seem more motivated and committed to change, possibly because they are also most unhappy or unsatisfied, we will concentrate for the moment on the restraints and dilemmas faced by women, as these are often unexpected and underrated. As a woman attempts to identify her own needs and find her own voice, she will have to struggle with her socialization in which she had been defined through her relationships with others, and her belief that she cannot act directly, but only through these relationships. She will also be faced with her belief that she is behaving selfishly or bizarrely if she ceases to be primarily concerned for others – her children, her partner – and begins to act on her own behalf. Not long ago this kind of behaviour would have been seen as a sympton meriting hospitalization (Showalter 1987).

As women change their ways of viewing themselves and their positions in the family, issues of loyalty may also arise in relation to their mothers and grandmothers because beliefs about gender are passed from generation to generation. Women who are brought up to value connectedness, and therefore often stay connected to their families of origin, may find that their new perspectives and ways of behaving threaten the old beliefs which shaped their mothers' lifestyles and therefore their whole world view and *raison d'être*. These will be crucial constraints which women will face as they use their strengths in ways not open to previous generations because of the difference in the societal contexts.

Because of the strength and impact of these beliefs about gender, straightforward ways of creating change in therapy seem limited. Some of the feminist family-therapy work described in the American literature seems very straightforward with clear-cut goals of pushing towards change in gender roles and more flexible and evolving interactional patterns for families. No mention is made of the binds produced by the process of change. One interesting example has been the impact of assertiveness training on women and the people around them. Women who have changed their behaviour and attitudes through assertiveness training have sometimes found themselves confronted with increased aggressiveness from their male partners, negative labelling, or difficulty in carrying through the implications of taking more responsibility for their own actions.

Papp and Silverstein

It is particularly because Papp and Silverstein's strategic work addresses itself to the process of change that we have found this approach so interesting and relevant to our work on gender. Their work focuses on identifying the implications of change for everyone in the family, taking into account the family's beliefs as well as its members' behaviour. They highlight both the gains and losses for individual family members and thereby identify the dilemmas which they face in relation to moving on (Papp 1983; Keeney and Ross 1985). Interestingly, this approach also accords more closely with women's ways of conceptualizing difficulties as described by Gilligan (1982).

It is especially the therapist's use of the dilemma around change which characterizes Papp and Silverstein's work. Their clinical work consists of two stages: one in which they investigate with the family the link between their behaviour and their beliefs, and a second stage where they present the family with its own dilemma, reframing the families' view of the problem in relation to the constraints as well as presenting alternatives for change. This model is thus well suited for attending to the constraints around gender beliefs.

In fact although Papp and Silverstein work with beliefs about gender in their clinical work, they do not usually make this overt to the family – that is, they do not say 'we are doing gender work here', or even 'women in our society often experience . . .', and so on. When they give a family an intervention they are often not only reframing the family's view of the situation but are also reframing a societal belief about gender, which they see influencing and constricting the family.

In one example, Silverstein tells the father that his main priority is to provide a perfect mother for his family and that his wife has done and is doing this for him, but unfortunately this requires children, which means that their daughters must stay in the family (Keeney and Ross 1985). She reframes the societal belief that women are to blame, that they are over-protective and do not allow their children to grow up, and makes overt the process by which women adapt themselves to others and therefore allow men to define them. Later she says that she is most worried about what would happen to the father if the daughter were to change as 'he wouldn't know quite how to deal with your mother when she's not a mother'. She also says that she feels that mother 'might be a little tired of being a mother and might not be too worried about giving it up'. Here she has reframed a common societal belief sometimes described as the 'empty-nest syndrome' (Lowenstein 1981), in which women are believed to suffer deeply from the loss of their children, despite findings that women often feel liberated at this time and that difficulties, if any exist, stem from the lack of available alternatives in terms of work, and the renegotiations necessary in the marital relationship (ibid.).

Papp and Silverstein have also described a particularly ingenuous intervention in the form of a debate in which they present the family with the dilemma for change which they have uncovered in the session, by arguing in front of the family about the reasons why things need to move on (Papp 1983). This method of intervening or delivering a message to the family is very powerful, as it often enables the family to hear the intervention without having to defend themselves against it, because someone else is refuting it. Their dilemma is made explicit and is held by the therapy team – one therapist will argue that the family needs to stay the way it is but will reframe the meanings of what is going on, and the other therapist will argue for and present the possibilities of change.

This can also be done by one person holding both positions, a speciality of Olga Silverstein, who shifts from change to no-change in response to the family's moves between stability and change (Keeney and Rose 1985). The therapist can also present a split message on her own by describing a disagreement between the members of the team behind the mirror or between the team and herself.

Feminists among others have expressed concern about the ethical nature of the debate in particular, because of the 'staging' of the disagreement for strategic purposes. They have questioned the performance element and therefore the consequent deception of the family. It seems to us that the positions of the debate can only be delivered if the therapist and her colleagues believe them to fit the family. Within a team, therapists may be drawn to different positions and would therefore present the argument with which they felt most sympathy. We have also been very interested by the meta-message of the debate which conveys that there is no right answer, no 'expert' correct opinion, and can come some way to letting the family witness the team's thinking in the sense of 'referent power'. We are also curious about the impact on a family of a male therapist expressing a dilemma concerning the family's situation, given the identification of this way of conceptualizing problems with women (Gilligan 1982).

Developing clinic practice

We have found that using the split message and the debate are particularly useful techniques in highlighting the crucial importance of gender in the therapeutic context.

First clinical example

In work with a one-parent family, a mother had referred herself and her only son, aged 12, because she was worried she would hurt him.

We had worked a little on issues of non-separation of the parents and the life-cycle issue of this boy's entering adolescence. The therapist then delivered a split message identifying the dilemma around beliefs about motherhood.

Therapist: When I went to talk to my team, there was a disagreement about how they see things, so I'll tell you both sides. Some people think that you are someone who is making great sacrifices as a mother – that you are giving up the next three years to think about James, and look after him, and they feel that's right. Whilst some women are thinking about lots of other things you have decided to put all your energies into being a good mother who sacrifices herself. Now the other people in the team said that wasn't how they saw you at all – they saw you as somebody ready to burst out and get on with things and that you're going to show James, who is at an age when he is becoming more independent, that you too are thinking very hard about how you are going to be in the world.

Mother: I feel on the verge of it.

Therapist: Well that's how they see you. As somebody full of potential to start taking off, both for yourself and as a way of showing James how to become an independent adult.

Mother: As I say, on the verge of it, but I feel he's not ready to be left.

Therapist: That's the other side of it.

Mother: I keep telling myself he should have a Mum and Dad at home and there is only me and I'm going to stick by him until he's ready. And I do have friends who do leave their kids most of the time – are out every evening. Everyone talks about them and I couldn't bear that. I want to bring James up to the best of my ability.

Therapist: Well, that's what the other people feel – that you are providing a good model of mothering that's not around much any more. You're doing everything that you can to do the best for him. I suppose the other group feel that you can get dissatisfied, go a bit sour, and become a stagnant pond and they're asking – are you going to blossom or are you going to be a stagnant pond? The other group are saying – now look, there's a really good model of motherhood.

This intervention was formulated by the team to address what they saw as the 'stuckness' in the family in relation to beliefs about mothering. The presentation of the different views about the current situation – the good model of mothering for the 1980s or the stagnant pond – could be presented in opposition to each other and therefore not disqualified.

Second clinical example

Another family was referred because they were anxious about their young child who was waking with night terrors several times every night. Both parents were very anxious not just about how best to handle this but also about what caused it. The mother in particular felt very responsible and blamed herself. In fact just prior to the appointment with us, the parents had managed to reduce the incidence of the night terrors. We learned that the parents had swopped roles when the baby was 3 months old, as father became unemployed and mother could find work. When their daughter was a year old, the father felt he had to go back to work and chose a child-minder, despite the mother's reservations about this person, to look after the baby. The child-minder subsequently neglected the child, at which point the night terrors started. Prior to the referral the parents had moved home so that the father could get a better job, which left the mother with an unsatisfactory work situation.

With this information the therapist and a colleague from behind the screen presented a debate in front of the family, saying that they had been unable to agree on how they saw the family's situation. The colleague said that she had been very interested and struck to see that it had been Mrs Gordon who had taken on the main burden of feeling responsible for Kate's night terrors, and then started to suggest that it was probably important for her to continue to think about and feel responsible for this even though it was very worrisome for her. If she were to start feeling better about this, her husband might begin to feel more responsible for choosing the child-minder which she probably thought would be very difficult for him. It also seemed that if Mr Gordon did not feel so weighed down by guilt about the night terrors, the issue of her unsatisfactory work might become highlighted and she might not be sure that her husband would be able to handle her disappointment and anger over this situation. In the light of these consequences, the colleague concluded that it was probably important for her to continue to worry about the causes of the night terrors.

The therapist agreed that Mrs Gordon seemed to have taken on responsibility for the causation of the night terrors, but said that she saw the situation very differently. She said she saw a couple who had been very flexible with regard to child-care arrangements in the face of the difficult circumstances of unemployment. They had managed this despite the disapproval from their own families about doing things so differently. She was not so sure that Mrs Gordon could not give up feeling that she needed to protect her husband by taking on all the blame, or that he actually needed the protection she thought he did. Despite the fact that there would be no easy answers about Mrs Gordon's work she was convinced that they would be able to struggle with this, given the way they had managed past difficulties.

This debate reframed the anxiety about the causation of the symptom as something the woman took on to protect the man, making overt a belief concerning the way women deal with and express feelings for their male partners, which would have continued to organize this family. The debate also commented on their successful struggles to change elements of traditional sex roles in the face of external circumstances.

Third clinical example

The Harris family were referred by the mother because of her worries about Danny, aged 11, who seemed perpetually unhappy and was expressing fears about growing up. There were two older brothers and one younger, and the youngest child, a girl, was about to start school. The two female therapists had a tremendous struggle to engage the father, who treated them in an offhand and contemptuous way. Mother talked volubly about her worries about the children and especially Danny. The parents disagreed about how he should develop his male role. The mother, who had been central to the children's lives while her husband maintained a boyish independence on the periphery, was threatened by both Danny's increased distance as he moved into adolescence and the loss of her only female ally as her daughter started school.

As therapy progressed the mother raised more and more complaints about how much of a slave she was to the men in the family. Danny started to refuse to go to school and the therapists worked with the mother to use her strength to get him back to school, as the father did not attend that session. At the following session mother was more angry and assertive about the need to do something for herself and said she wanted to get a job. Her husband said he was happy for her to do this, but his tone conveyed the opposite. The mother immediately began to express doubts about whether the family could manage without her.

At the end of this session the therapists had a debate over the issue of whether Mrs Harris could give up her role of being a martyr to the family. One therapist took the no-change position, saying that Mrs Harris was obviously not yet convinced, and neither was she, that the time was right for her to do more for herself. She was particularly struck by how much Mr Harris seemed to need his wife to be there at home (he would frequently return from work during the day) and this showed how vulnerable he was despite his tough exterior and Mrs

Harris obviously knew this. She recommended that Danny continue his job of providing his mother with worries for the time being. The other therapist argued that Mrs Harris had shown her strength, that she was ready to get a job and that she was sure that Mr Harris would be able to teach the boys how to be more independent.

This debate again presents both the constraints and the wish to move on and challenges both the woman's protectiveness and the man's need for protection.

Conclusion

We have argued that strategic techniques can form part of a feminist approach to therapy. We find Papp and Silverstein's approach invaluable because they have developed a creative range of strategic interventions and in particular emphasize the dilemma of change, which we think accords very closely with women's experience.

Although we have concentrated here on work developed from and influenced by Papp and Silverstein, other strategic approaches can also be adapted to a feminist perspective. As one of the main problems has been the fact that practitioners have tended to be 'gender blind' in their work, practice needs to concentrate on gender as a primary constitutive element of family life.

The MRI approach, for example, places great importance on investigating how people have tried to deal with a problem, on the assumption that these attempted solutions have become the problem, and then directing the client to try something different (Weakland *et al.* 1974). Women who are struggling to change their position in their family, for example, who want more space for themselves but still feel they have to attend to everyone else's needs, may find that their efforts to deal with feelings of guilt lead them to work even harder at attending to everyone's needs, thus perpetuating the problem. An instruction to try doing something different, perhaps by being less predictably competent at home, might produce changes that are surprisingly liberating. This would be particularly so if, as often happens for women, the attempt to deal with the problem through insight and understanding had itself become part of the problem.

The ideas about hierarchical incongruity developed by Cloe Madanes are also extremely useful in addressing gender. Her analysis of the use of the power of weakness or the power of the symptom and some of the very creative therapeutic interventions she has evolved to challenge these patterns have great potential value. What needs to be added is the particular meaning for women of the indirect use of power and an appreciation of the social context in which this takes place.

It is true that many of the strategic approaches have been developed by men (Haley 1973, 1976; Watzlawick *et al.* 1974; Cade 1979; de Shazer 1982) who would claim them to be value free, but as we have argued are actually used in value-laden ways. The clinical literature all too often emphasizes the power and prowess of the therapist and defines the therapeutic context as an adversarial one (Hoffman 1985). However, challenging this macho view of therapy has inevitably led to a polarization which could ultimately reduce the therapeutic options available to feminist therapists.

In our view, the issue of which techniques are acceptable to feminists is less important than the danger of the belief, ever present in strategic therapy, that all problems are technical, and therefore solvable by techniques alone. It seems to us that one of the most valuable contributions that feminism has made is the highlighting of the idea that the family as social institution poses particular dilemmas for women. Family therapists by contrast have tended both to simplify and idealize family life in their attempt to legitimize the systemic approach.

Dilemmas too, are apparent in the interaction between therapist and family, in relation to power and its use in therapy. Whereas feminist therapists working only with women eschew the use of 'expert power' work towards an open egalitarian partnership in therapy, and aim to provide a model of a strong woman, this may translate less effectively into work with families because it may ignore both the constraints from other members of the system and, as we have seen, the internalized societal beliefs about female roles. At times the therapist as role model is too dissimilar from the woman's own experience to be useful. In strategic therapy, there is also a degree of ambiguity about power. The therapist may use expert power in the way she creates the context for therapy and the way she devises and delivers interventions, but she may choose to distance herself from the effects of those interventions and may not be seen by the family or client as particularly powerful or as having been instrumental in promoting change. What effect does this have as a role model?

It is interesting to note, in connection with this, that the word 'manipulative', which is often applied to strategic therapists, is also used in a derogatory way by professionals, particularly about their women clients. Being 'manipulative' (which the Oxford dictionary reminds us also means skilful and dextrous) is often the only way of wielding power open to people who are in a position of little power. Perhaps the association of this word with the implications of having to use power indirectly has led us to discard prematurely techniques which make use of this skill instead of acknowledging its usefulness.

The first stage of the feminist challenge in family therapy has been to make visible that which has been invisible, both in theory and in practice. We believe that this process has inevitably led to some over-simplification of what is meant by a feminist position in therapy. Recognizing the existence of a dual experience in the family based on gender can lead to too much emphasis on 'women's experience' and become polarized and restricted. As we stated earlier, there is always the danger, when emphasizing the need to validate women's experience, of reinforcing stereotypes. Modelling therapy on 'women's ways' and discarding techniques because they reflect male values could lead to failure to use therapeutic opportunities for problem solving, and could idealize women's experience unhelpfully. Some work described by feminist therapists can seem overly straightforward and unidimensional and fails to take into account the constraints and binds that so often characterize women's position in the family or the fact that social change is happening very slowly for women. For us the guiding principles are to take into account the power relations in the family as they relate to men and women's positions in society generally and fully to appreciate the dilemmas involved in any change.

As therapists confronted daily with the painful evidence of women's disempowerment and women's sacrifice of their own selfhood, the challenge to our practice demands both extreme urgency of attention and great delicacy and care in execution.

Note

1. This chapter is a continuation of our attempt to evolve a feminist family-therapy framework and practice. Its theme originally formed the basis of a workshop presented at the Second Annual Conference for Feminism and Family Therapy held in London in 1987, and has evolved and developed from there both in response to feedback from workshop participants and from ongoing discussion and debate about our clinical practice.

References

Avis, J. (1985) 'The politics of functional family therapy: a feminist critique', *Journal of Marital and Family Therapy* 11(2): 127–38.

Brannen, J. (1982) 'Suitable cases for treatment', unpublished paper.

Broverman, I.K. (1970) 'Sex-role stereotypes and clinical judgements of mental health', *Journal of Counselling and Clinical Psychology* 34.

Burck, C. (1986) 'Challenging myths in family therapy: the case of feminism', unpublished dissertation, Advanced Family Therapy Course, Tavistock Clinic, London.

Byng Hall, J. (1979) 'Re-editing family mythology during family therapy', *Journal of Family Therapy* 1: 103–16.

Cade, B. (1979) 'The use of paradox in therapy', in S. Walrond-Skinner (ed.) *Family and Marital Psychotherapy: A Critical Approach*, London: Routledge & Kegan Paul.

Chodorow, N. (1978) *The Reproduction of Mothering. Psychoanalysis and the Sociology of Gender*, Berkeley, Calif.: University of California Press.

Daniel, G. (1986) 'Women in families: dilemmas of change', unpublished dissertation, Advanced Family Therapy Course, Tavistock Clinic, London.

Daniel, G. and Burck, C. (in preparation) 'Patterns and myths – forefronting gender in families and family therapy.

de Shazer, S. (1982) *Patterns of Brief Family Therapy*, London: Norton.

Dinnerstein, D. (1976) *The Rocking of the Cradle and the Ruling of the World*, New York: Harper & Row.

Fagin, L. & Little, M. (1984) *The Foresaken Families*, Harmondsworth: Pelican.

Feldman, L. (1982) 'Sex roles and family dynamics', in F. Walsh (ed.) *Normal Family Processes*, New York: Guilford Press.

Gilligan, C. (1982) *In a Different Voice*, Cambridge, Mass.: Harvard University Press.

Goldner, V. (1988) 'Generation and gender: Normative and covert hierarchies', *Family Process* 27: 17–31.

Gurman, A. and Klein, M. (1980) 'Marital and family conflicts', in A. Brodsky and R. Hare-Mustin (eds.) *Women and Psychotherapy*, New York: Guilford Press.

Haley, J. (1973) *Uncommon Therapy. The Psychiatric Techniques of Milton H. Erickson*, New York: Norton.

Haley, J. (1976) *Problem-solving Therapy*, New York: Harper Colophon.

Hare-Mustin, R. (1978) 'A feminist approach to family therapy', *Family Process* 17: 181–94.

Hoffman, L. (1985) 'Beyond power and control', *Family Systems Medicine* 3(4): 381–96.

James, K. and McIntyre, D. (1983) 'The reproduction of families: the social role of family therapy?', *Journal of Marital and Family Therapy* 9(2): 119–29.

Keeney, R. and Ross, J. (1985) *Mind in Therapy. Constructing Systemic Family Therapies*, New York: Basic Books.

Keeney, B. and Silverstein, O. (1986) *The Therapeutic Voice of Olga Silverstein*. New York and London: Guilford Press.

Kraemer, S. (1983) 'Why I am not a family therapist', *Changes* 2.

Libow, J., Raskin, P., and Caust, B. (1982) 'Feminist and family systems therapy: are they irreconcilable?' *American Journal of Family Therapy* 10(3): 3–12.

Lowenstein, S. (1981) 'A feminist perspective on social work practice. Letter to a son', in D. Waldfogel and A. Rosenblatt (eds.) *Handbook of*

Clinical Social Work, San Francisco: Jossey-Bass.
Madanes, C. (1981) *Strategic Family Therapy*, San Francisco: Jossey-Bass.
Olsen, T. (1980) *Silences*, London: Virago.
Papp, P. (1983) *The Process of Change*, London: Guilford Press.
Phillips, A. (1988) 'Doin' wot comes nat'rally', *New Internationalist*, March: 11–12.
Pilalis, J. and Anderton, J. (1986) 'Feminism and family therapy – a possible meeting point', *Journal of Family Therapy* 8(2): 99–114.
Showalter, E. (1987) *The Female Malady*. London: Virago.
Simon, R. (1984) 'From ideology to practice: the Women's Project in Family Therapy', *Family Therapy Networker* 8(3): 29–40.
Watzlawick, P., Weakland, J. Jr., and Fisch, R. (1974) *Change: Principles of Problem Formation and Problem Resolution*, New York: Norton.
Weakland, J.H., Fisch, R., Watzlawick, P., and Bodin, A.M. (1974) 'Brief therapy: focused problem resolution', *Family Process* 13: 141–168.
Wheeler, D., Avis, J.M., Miller, L.A., and Chaney, S. (1985) 'Rethinking family therapy training and supervision: a feminist model', *Journal of Psychiatry and the Family* 1: 53–71.
Willi, J. (1982) *Couples in Collusion*, New York: Jason Aronson.

Chapter five

The struggle towards a feminist practice in family therapy: premisses

Amy Urry

Since its creation the South West Women's Project[1] has been concerned to bridge the gap between feminist theory and the practice of family therapy. Having developed some basic principles to inform our practice, our aim is to match ideas with action so that these principles become guidelines for behaviour, and not mere academic exercises. In this chapter I shall discuss our framework for therapy and explain how it has come to be constructed. The six basic principles formulated by the project are laid out briefly in Table 5.1.

Before discussing each of these principles in detail, it is worth clarifying what is meant by 'feminism'. The following quotation summarizes our position:

> When we speak of feminism, we speak of the philosophy which recognizes that men and women have different experiences of self, of other, of life, and that men's experience has been widely articulated while women's has been ignored or misrepresented. When we speak of feminism, we speak of the philosophy which recognizes that this society does not permit equality to women; on the contrary, it is structured so as to oppress women and uplift men. This structure is called patriarchy. When we speak of feminism, we speak of a philosophy which recognizes that every aspect of public and private life carries the mark of patriarchal thinking and practice and is therefore a necessary focus for re-vision.
>
> (Goodrich *et al.* 1988: 1–2)

(1) There is a gender system in families. It is based on inequality in the public world which is reflected in the private world. This gender system needs to be recognized, addressed, and challenged.

A family is affected and influenced by the wider society of which it is part; it both reflects the social order of society and helps to maintain this structure. Family members are not free to organize their relationships in a way that they alone negotiate and decide upon. Instead, they are influenced, and therefore limited, by societal expectations and traditions. Among families there is variation in the extent to which each deliberately decides to adhere to tradition or develop new ways of conducting family life. A family therapist can explore with a family the rules, explicit and implicit, that exist to inform members how they should behave.

Given a society which discriminates so clearly between men and women, it follows that many family rules will prescribe differences in male and female behaviour and attitudes. A family therapist can encourage a family to examine how its members came to be the way they are; to look at how they are influenced by both historical and current trends. Perhaps then family members will be in a stronger position to decide how to organize themselves and the extent to which they wish to challenge the patriarchal order that they are maintaining and protecting in their intimate relationships. There may, of course, be disagreement about this among family members.

(2) The structured inequality which exists in families can be examined by identifying the different power bases to which individual members have recourse. These need to be labelled and explored with families.

In any family there are differences between each member's ability to influence what happens within the family. The degree of control an individual has will depend on her or his access to resources (i.e. what she or he can use in order to acquire influence over others) and on how these resources are valued. In many families, for example, a male adult will have greater access to financial resources – for various reasons he will feel obliged to be in paid employment and will be the one designated as the 'bread-winner'. The capacity to earn money is valued highly in our society, and within families it is recognized as necessary for the survival of the family. In the same way a female adult will have greater access to emotional/relational resources as she will be concerned with looking after the emotional well-being of the family members. In our society relational capacity is valued curiously. A woman who is a wife and a mother is not valued highly. Generally there is more prestige attached to, and satisfaction derived from being in, paid employment than being a full-time wife, mother, and home-maker.

The notion of power bases has been developed to describe and explore the differing levels of control (opportunity to influence) that men and women have in their lives. The power bases of money-earning capacity and relational ability are just two examples. There is a wealth of others and families can be admired for their ability to create them, especially in the field of symptoms (Williams and Watson 1988). It is vital to remember that power bases will be valued differently by different

Table 5.1 Therapeutic principles of the South West Women's Project and their implications for practice

Principle	*Implications for practice*
(1) There is a gender system in families. It is based on inequality in the public world which is reflected in the private world. This gender system needs to be recognized, addressed, and challenged.	(a) What are the assumptions about the women and the men in their present and past families? (b) What is the distribution of power? How are decisions made? What happens if one person disagrees? How is language used? This is particularly relevant to expressions of ownership – for example, *your* children but *my* bank account.
(2) The structured inequality which exists in families can be examined by identifying the different power bases to which individual members have recourse. These need to be labelled and explored with families.	(a) What are each person's power bases? The possibilities include finance, children, force, affect, sexuality, fertility, domesticity, relational ability, property, law, language, information. (b) How are these power bases valued? How does this differ in different settings, such as the working world versus the domestic world; working men's club versus a women's group; the family itself versus the therapeutic team? (c) How does access to different power bases vary? (d) Who benefits most from each base and the distribution of bases?
(3) The therapist/therapy team can never be neutral – gender, age, race, profession, and so on will inevitably affect the 'family and therapist system' and therefore the gender and power processes.	(a) What is being communicated to the family by the therapist? Attention must be paid to the significance of the gender of the therapist, the fact that the same message may be received differently by men and women, and the therapists' differential treatment of women and men. (b) To what extent does the therapeutic team agree about feminism and its relationship to therapy? (c) Does the team attend to its own gender processes? (d) Is the team able to make use of its own behaviour to communicate to the family?

Principle	*Implications for practice*
(4) The means are always important in achieving the ends. The therapist must work to understand the values and beliefs that she/he is communicating through her/his own behaviour.	(a) Are the therapist's principles reflected in her/his practice and behaviour? The aim is to avoid feminist ideology and sexist practice. (b) Is the team aware that the use of certain accepted methods and techniques is a betrayal of feminist beliefs and values, albeit that they are being employed towards a sound goal.
(5) Empowering women is an essential part of therapy. It is important to recognize, however, that supporting women therapeutically may not empower but may rather debilitate and promote homeostasis.	Women can be empowered by a therapist in the following ways: (a) validation of a woman's experience and skills; (b) promotion of strength by connecting women positively to their history; (c) challenging assumptions (female and male) by offering alternatives and new choices; (d) calling women by their names and not their roles; (e) avoidance of placing total responsibility for the (dys)functioning of the family upon a woman.
(6) Family interaction is seen in the context of a patriarchal culture. Families cannot be held individually responsible for culturally determined attitudes and interactions. General universal principles can be recognized and shared with families so that consciousness raising becomes part of the therapeutic process.	(a) Therapy should not ignore the outside world and its influences and limitations on the family. (b) Gendered intimacy and familial interaction should be made sense of with the family in terms of the political/social structuring of the outside world. (c) Change within a family and within its gender system must be based on 'the art of the possible' and is not achieved by having unrealistic expectations or by punishing a family for its inheritance from the wider social system.

family members and in different settings. It is also important to realize that when a family comes into therapy it will come into contact with professional people who place a high value on relational ability and emotional well-being. This may be unusual for family members.

A positive outcome can be that the therapy experience is the 'difference that makes the difference' (Bateson 1979): the woman's field of expertise will be given attention and the man will be encouraged to enter this world and concentrate more upon intimate relationships. However, a less positive outcome is that the woman may infer that she has failed: she will have a feeling of responsibility about the relationships in the family and could feel undermined and blamed when professionals tell her that these relationships require attention.

A woman's experience of therapy can be that she is made to feel punished: there are numerous examples in the family-therapy literature of purportedly exemplary sessions which are in fact little more than therapists giving women a hard time, while protecting men in efforts to seduce them into working. We suggest that family therapists need to be sensitive to this and work harder to validate women's experience, avoid punishing them, and push for change.

I ask the reader to read the following example of a family therapy case and to consider the experience of the woman client. I suggest that she is being viewed in a framework of having failed, whilst her husband is presented as the solution of her incompetence. The support she is given by the therapists with their 'paradoxical type of comment' offers some understanding to the woman. However, it falls far short of recognizing her strengths and encouraging her competences. This therapy is exemplary in the way it maintains the myth of male supremacy and reflects a society organized around financial reward.

> The identified patient, Arnold, was an eight-year-old boy who was frequently soiling himself especially when he was at school or away from home. He came at first with only his mother who was encouraged to bring along the step-father and Arnold's two older sisters for the second interview.
>
> Whenever Arnold was soiled and his mother ordered him to the bathroom to wash himself, Arnold had resisted and gone into a temper tantrum. The step-father had not been involved.
>
> A major change in the family functioning was effected by asking the step-father to take a more active part, and by encouraging the mother to allow this to happen. By the time of the third interview soiling was still occurring but the tantrums were no longer taking place. The step-father was directing Arnold to wash whenever he was soiled and this was happening without any fuss.
>
> A few weeks later, at the fourth interview which the step-father was unable to attend because he had a hospital appointment for

himself, a considerable lessening of soiling was reported. However, it was noticed that the mother appeared depressed, and the mother subsystem became the temporary focus for attention by the therapist, but still in the setting of the conjoint interview. A paradoxical type of comment was made by the therapist that with the upheavals of her past life and current worries, it was a wonder that she was not more depressed. All the children were asked to carry out minor domestic chores for their mother, for which they were to be financially rewarded.

(Warner 1980)

In addition, a family therapist needs to be aware that the messages she or he gives to a family may be contradicted by those given by others who belong to the family's network. The extent to which family members will hear and be influenced by the therapist's messages will vary and will be dependent on the family's wider context.

(3) The therapist/therapy team can never be neutral – gender, age, race, profession, and so on, will inevitably affect the 'family and therapist system' and therefore the gender and power processes.

Basic family therapy training tells us that it is not possible to not communicate: all behaviour has a communication value (Watzlawick *et al.* 1967). However, therapists tend to be somewhat irresponsible in recognizing that this rule also applies to themselves. A therapist is part of a team which in turn is part of an agency or a multi-agency structure. Just as a family can be seen to reflect a wider world, so can a therapeutic team. Family members will make assumptions about therapists and therapy based on the beliefs they already hold. It is these beliefs that we often wish to challenge and we are given a golden opportunity to do so by using the behavioural interchanges that occur between therapists and family members; and those that occur between team members.

By assuming or insisting upon therapist neutrality it seems that we are denying ourselves the very factor that makes therapy exciting and possible, i.e. the use of self as another member of the human race. It is fascinating and essential to consider the sense family members are making of a therapist's involvement with them. The intricacies of communication processes are confounding, can lead to much confusion and misunderstanding, and are at the root of all personal contact and relational stability. The more a therapist is in touch with what she is communicating, and with what is being communicated to her by family members' treatment of her, the more empowered she will be.

We believe that it is essential for therapists to recognize that in order to put across a message successfully to a family, they must behave in different ways according to their gender, age, profession, and so on. These factors actually permit differences in behaviour – the same message given by a 60-year-old female consultant psychiatrist might be received differently if it were given by a 30–year-old male trainee social worker.

The fact that a family has been referred or allocated to a psychiatrist rather than a social worker (or vice versa) can operate to give the family information about how the helping professionals are viewing it and its problems. Very possibly this information is ambiguous and can be received in many ways; exact differences in reception are not always easily predicted. However, a therapist may elicit interesting and helpful information by exploring the sense that family members make of their experiences in therapy. For example, with particular reference to gender, a therapist may find it useful to explore or ponder what it means to a family to have a female or a male therapist.

It is always important for members of a team to be aware of what they are trying to communicate through their behaviour. It is not good enough to assume that they are successful in their attempts; the message sent is not always the message received and the same behaviour may be received differently by different members. Exploring these issues with a family provides rich information both about their system, and about the wider social system of which we are all a part.

For a team to function well, there must be some agreement about ideology and a clarification of where the disagreements lie. There must be a clear meeting point between team members about the importance of considering gender processes within the family and within the team.

Finally, it is important to think about what we are in danger of communicating to a family when we rely on one-way screens and supervision from behind these screens. We must be careful that we do not give a message to the family, or indeed believe ourselves, that the more distant and outside a system one is, the more objective and therefore the more one becomes expert. If this really were the case, would we not be endorsing the validity of the traditional male's peripheral role, and disqualifying the real expert, i.e. 'the involved female'?

(4) The means are always important in achieving the ends. The therapist must work to understand the values and beliefs that she/he is communicating through her/his own behaviour.

As feminists, we know that everything we do and say is likely to be received within a sexist structure and will be accommodated so as to maintain this structure. If we give ourselves permission to make interventions which are obviously sexist on the premiss that the final goal is sound, the likelihood is that our only achievement will be to endorse all that we are seeking to challenge. Our aim must be to avoid mixing feminist ideology and sexist practice, by developing feminist practice at all times. I suggest that it is never necessary to use sexist means: there is always another way. To find it does entail working hard to scrutinize methods we have accepted and to devise new ways of working.

There is much debate among family therapists concerning the issue of means and ends. It is recognized that the more inflexible a family is due to a lack of cognitive, behavioural, and practical resources, the more likely it is to encounter difficulties, to throw up symptoms, and become prey to the helping professionals. Family therapy has helped us to understand the powerfulness of homeostatis and the difficulty of change. The positive result of this is that we have more sympathy towards individuals, blame them less for not changing, and see the concept of individual 'resistance' to help and change as naive. A less positive, and possibly dangerous, result is that therapists take on a responsibility for inducing change which gives them an unrealistic and arrogant power and which is fundamentally disrespectful to family members. We can find ourselves in a position where the less resourceful a family is, the more we assume power and control in order to change them for their own good. This can only perpetuate a system of oppression, inequality, and abuse of power.

Family therapy is rich in suggestions as to how we may intervene in people's lives. It is ambitious, optimistic, and above all it offers techniques and a methodology which many of us have embraced as a welcome and necessary relief from too much ideology and conceptualization. The pitfall has been that in our enthusiasm and delight we have not studied the wider effects of our work with our new tools with sufficient rigour.

We must continue to question our assumptions, we must struggle to explore the implicit assumptions we are making when we use tried and tested techniques. For example, is it justifiable to ask families to carry out tasks without explaining why? Is it justifiable to avoid sharing our beliefs and goals with clients; would it not in fact make our jobs more possible if we worked harder to share our frameworks with families?

Some feminist family therapists argue that it is not possible to work in a strategic way with families as this is contrary to a primary feminist principle, i.e. sharing power, not acting in a way that furthers inequality by taking power and control away from those who already experience a degree of resourcelessness.

However, to ban the use of some of the most creative ideas in family therapy seems somewhat harsh. Our task is to be even more creative: for example, a therapist using the concept of the Failed Attempted Solution can work to explore how this solution came to be initially employed; why it is failing now; and can have fun on an ideologically sound basis helping families to devise their own bizarre solutions to free them rather than demanding that they follow the team's prescriptions.

(5) Empowering women is an essential part of therapy. It is important to recognize, however, that supporting women therapeutically may not empower but may rather debilitate and promote homeostasis.

In this section I shall suggest various ways of empowering women in therapy; I shall also examine certain therapeutic behaviours which do not empower women and should be avoided. First, however, it is necessary to pose the question of whether the empowering of women means that men become debilitated. Does this question imply that a man and a woman need compete for a therapist's support in such a way that if one receives it, the other suffers. I believe strongly that an empowered woman does not necessarily lead to an impotent male partner or an unworkable heterosexual partnership. There is, however, a fear, in the therapeutic world at least, of a therapist concentrating too much on giving a woman a stronger and more realistic view of herself. What is at the root of this fear? I shall leave the reader to struggle with this question, only suggesting that all our reactions highlight the essential problem of working in an anti-sexist and therefore anti-societal manner. Therapists may fear that if women become stronger they will no longer protect their male partners and encourage traditional male behaviour. The result will be pressure on both men and women to define themselves differently, to renegotiate their intimacy. Surely, as optimistic feminists point out, this can only lead to both women and men becoming empowered as men will learn to be proud of their emotionality and will be able to develop new relational abilities while being freed from some traditionally male responsibilities. But it is men who are rewarded more for the gender inequality – they have access to more power bases, and male power bases are valued more highly than others. Given our present societal framework, men have more to lose.

Does the empowering of women risk losing men from therapy and from the relationship? If this is a possibility, then we risk being hoisted by our own petard. What would be the consequences? We may feel that a woman would be further empowered by separation from her husband. While we can support this feeling with our knowledge of mental-health statistics for the married and single woman (Sturdivant 1980; Howell and Bayes 1981), we cannot support it through our knowledge of financial and child-care statistics. In short, a divorced woman is likely to be significantly poorer than a divorced man, and she is likely to retain care and custody of any children, but is unlikely to receive a realistic income to support them. At present an alarmingly high proportion of children who are received into care come from single-parent women households.

We argue that we are pushing for change in families and between men and women, which is essential for emotional well-being and mental stability. We also recognize that we are not in step with a large part of society, and any change will not be received easily: hence our fear and precariousness and constant balancing of the cost of staying the same, and the cost of changing. The complexity of this question emphasizes the uncomfortable position we occupy as feminist family therapists. However, those who, like myself, are optimistic about the place of feminist family therapy must turn our minds to ways in which we can work to empower our women clients.

A major guideline is that if a client is not validated about her or his feelings, behaviour, and self, then change will not occur. This truism is often forgotten as therapists rush in with their exciting new ideas gleaned from the latest textbook or workshop. People must feel good about themselves, feel that their way of life, past mistakes, and present dilemmas are at least being approached with sympathy. Our quest for systemic change and solutions must not lead us to forget the real essence of our work, i.e. that we are dealing with the vulnerabilities, fears, strengths, and hopes of individuals. All people, males and females, must feel they are being heard, understood, and respected if therapy is to be successful. In our society, women seldom receive positive messages about themselves in what they do or what they feel. In therapy, it is vital that there is a difference: family therapists must work hard to show they are valuing women's thoughts, feelings, and behaviour (despite their wish to challenge them).

Let us consider a well known family-therapy technique, that of reframing. Minuchin and Fishman help us to understand the need for and skill of reframing:

> Therapy starts . . . with the clash between two framings and reality. The family's framing is relevant for the continuity and maintenance of the organism more or less as it is; the therapeutic framing is related to the goal of moving the family toward a more differentiated and competent dealing with their dysfunctional reality.
>
> (Minuchin and Fishman 1981: 74)

Reframing is a valuable and powerful tool, but without sufficient care its use can lead to problems. If this technique is to be effective, the therapist must have understood and shown that she or he understands already-existing frameworks. If not, the end result of the intervention will be that again a woman will feel that she is being told she has got it wrong. Of course, a man may have a similar experience. However, since women often have more invested in their conceptualization and experience of family life, and since their views and feelings are more often disqualified, there is a heightened need to be aware of women's experiences in family therapy. Reframing can be used effectively with families, but care must be taken not to use them to disqualify and punish.

Let us take an example of a family in which the son is asthmatic. The family's shared reality may well be that his mother has become anxious about, and protective of, her son so that a very close relationship exists between them, and some jealousies have grown in other family members. A therapist may well wish to work to change this; to reconnect the woman with the rest of her family so that she is less isolated, and to challenge the definition of the boy as an invalid, thus freeing him to develop other aspects of himself. It is possible to use some helpful reframes which emphasize both the woman's and boy's competence. It would be unhelpful to tell the family that they need the boy to be asthmatic and therefore dependent on his mother because this protects her from intimacy with her husband and helps her to distance him. This intervention would result in the woman feeling guilty and punished – it would tell her that she has a problem about her marital relationship and she alone is responsible for it. Doubt about her motivation to care for her son would be suggested, along with the implication that she is choosing that he should suffer to help her. Obviously, she would not feel empowered or supported and it is dubious whether any change would follow.

Let us consider the ideas of Minuchin and Fishman regarding the use and importance of increasing intensity in a family. They suggest that for a therapeutic message to be received by a family, it must be *heard* by them:

> Family members have a discriminating sense of hearing with areas of selective deafness that are regulated by their common history . . . . As a result, the therapist's message may never register, or it may be blunted.
>
> The therapist must make the family 'hear' and this requires that his message go above the family threshold of deafness. Family members may listen to the therapist's message, but they may not assimilate it into their cognitive scheme as new information . . . . Families differ in the degree to which they demand loyalty to the family reality, and a therapist's intensity of message will need to vary accordingly to what is being challenged.
>
> (Minuchin and Fishman 1981: 116)

One method of raising intensity is to ask a family to do more of that which they are already doing which we as therapists see as problem inducing. They will begin to suffer more and will then share our idea that change is desirable. There is an obvious need for caution, and recognition that not everyone suffers equally. An example might be the common familial situation where the woman is overburdened by her tasks as child carer and home-maker and the man occupies a peripheral position. If, as experts, we instruct both partners not only to continue to behave in the same way but also to do so more intensely, what messages are we giving to the family about gender roles, and what will the consequences be for the individuals if they follow our directions? The intervention may prove successful and both partners may be pushed into looking at other ways of sharing their lives. However, I suggest that the cost of reaching this point is too high both in terms of individual suffering and in terms of betrayal of feminist beliefs. There are other ways of arriving at the same point, most obviously by exploring with the family members why it is that they are structuring their behaviour in the way they do: in other words, challenging some of their assumptions about family life and male and female behaviour directly, and finding some alternatives.

I must point out here that an equally undesirable intervention in this situation would be that of working to include the man in his family life by instructing the woman to 'take a rest', while he 'takes over'. This disqualifies the woman's expertise, and suggests that anyone is capable of doing her work. Also undesirable is the intervention that focuses upon examining what the woman is doing to 'stop' the man from being part of the family. This gives her inappropriate responsibility, and gives him inappropriate impotence. The result would be extremely punishing towards her and disrespectfully protective towards him.

There are many ways of empowering women, of giving them a sense of their importance, their competences and their possibilities. The remainder of this section focuses upon four important areas where I can suggest specific ways of working to empower women.

(1) *The promotion of women's strength by connecting them positively to their history, on both a societal and a familial level.* The more an individual woman can feel proud to be a woman, and proud of the struggles of all women historically and currently, the more empowered she will feel. When working with families about past generations of women, it often seems difficult to avoid blaming them for what is happening now. Mothers continue to be held responsible for producing the type of people who live in the world today. Again this is giving women inappropriate responsibility and not appreciating their lack of power to alter societal structuring. Clients, and therapists, may not feel pleased about how our mothers and grandmothers behaved towards us, or about what they have handed on to us. We can, however, work to appreciate their experiences and struggles, and to understand the pressures and limitations they faced.

(2) *The challenging of assumptions (female and male) by offering alternatives and new choices.* It would be a mistake to assume that women need always to be empowered by being offered under-

standing and sympathy. A crucial part of feminist therapy is to challenge assumptions – to challenge what is accepted too readily about female and male behaviour – and to press for change in assumptions and therefore behaviour. Often it is unhelpful to challenge an individual's behaviour without understanding it in terms of gender rules and roles. Often it is more creative to challenge these rules and roles, and then behaviour is more likely to change.

(3) *The calling of women by their names and not their roles.* Both in talking to families and in talking about families, therapists can fall into a trap of referring to a woman solely as 'mum' or 'wife'. This can reduce and demean a woman; by using these labels to name women we are not individualizing the women sufficiently. However, we should not forget that we are also working to challenge the low value put on the work of women as wives and mothers so that these roles can attract greater respect and value.

(4) *The avoidance of placing total responsibility for the (dys)functioning of the family upon a woman.* History and current society have given women the idea that they are responsible for the relationships in their family. Therapists can easily collude negatively with this assumption by expecting too much to come from their women clients, both in terms of behavioural change and conceptualization. This may lead to punishment when women do not live up to the expectations of therapists. It may also lead therapists to fail to recognize that men are capable of change, and should not be protected from therapeutic work.

(6) Family interaction is seen in the context of a patriarchal culture. Families cannot be held individually responsible for culturally determined attitudes and interactions. General universal principles can be recognized and shared with families so that consciousness-raising becomes part of the therapeutic process.[2]

Family therapists have been accused (and in my view correctly) of not appreciating fully enough the influences of the political/social world on any one family (Jordan 1981). We have worked hard to understand the effect of transgenerational forces, but have limited our field of vision, and therefore understanding, by paying insufficient attention to community and societal structures. Individuals can only be understood in any depth if we take into account their context – family, community, society, world.

Family therapy has helpfully illustrated the folly of identifying one individual as the patient and working for change with this individual divorced from her or his family context. We are beginning to be aware of a further folly – that of identifying a family as the patient and working for change within it while divorcing it from its wider context.

If we do not appreciate the relationship between the outside world and the family, we risk committing a major error in our work as therapists. We risk giving our clients far too much responsibility about the way they organize their families' lives and thinking. We need to be realistic in our awareness of the choices that people have had, and helpful in our understanding of why they have not realized that there are alternatives. We should guard against unrealistic expectations of what may be possible for them, given societal limitations. The danger is that we can set people up to fail, and to suffer further discomfort by asking them to achieve changes which a large part of society will be working to counteract. Change within a family and within its gender system is best made if based on 'the art of the possible' (Marianne Walters). It is not achieved by making unrealistic assessments of individuals' power, or by punishing individuals and families for their inheritance from the wider social system.

Notes

1. The South West Women's Project in feminism and family therapy was started in 1986 as a forum to discuss and explore feminism and family therapy. Present members are: Rose Caswell, Helen Manning, Cas Schneider, Donna Smith, Amy Urry and Gilli Watson. Acknowledgements to Deb Dobbin, Elsa Jones, Linda Masters, Bebe Speed, and Helen Manning as previous members and to Marianne Walters for help, inspiration and interest.
2. Thanks are due to Marianne Walters for this principle.

References

Bateson, G. (1979) *Mind and Nature: A Necessary Unity*, London: Fontana.

Goodrich, T.J., Rampage, C., Ellman, B., and Halstead, K. (1988) *Feminist Family Therapy. A Casebook*, New York: W.W. Norton.

Howell, E. and Bayes, M. (eds.) (1981) *Women and Mental Health*, New York: Basic Books.

Jordan, W. (1981) 'Family therapy – an outsider's view', *Journal of Family Therapy 13: 269–80.*

Minuchin, S. and Fishman, H.C. (1981) *Family Therapy Techniques*, Cambridge, Mass.: Harvard University Press.

Sturdivant, S. (1980) *Therapy with Women: A Feminist Philosophy of Treatment*, New York: Springer.

Warner, J. (1980) 'Family Therapy: a search for foundations systems and definitions', *Journal of Family Therapy* 2: 267–8.

Watzlawick, P., Beavin, J.H., and Jackson, D.D. (1967) *Pragnatics of Human Communication*, New York: W.W. Norton.

Williams, J. and Watson, G. (1988) 'Sexual inequality, family life and family therapy', in E. Street and W. Dryden (eds.) *Family Therapy in Britain*, Milton Keynes: Open University Press.

Chapter six

The struggle towards a feminist practice in family therapy: practice

Cas Schneider

This chapter presents a single clinical example of feminist-informed family therapy. As such it needs to be read in conjunction with the previous chapter by Amy Urry, which fully describes the conceptual framework.

As a family therapist practising from a feminist perspective, I regard family interaction as occurring in the context of a patriarchal culture. Inequality is recreated in the family structure and transactions within that structure occur in gender-prescribed ways. This, I believe, is constraining for both women and men and leads to much dissatisfaction. When working with families, I challenge gender-related structures and forms of communication, and promote the notions of affiliation and relatedness rather than hierarchy and control.

In my work I attempt to redefine traditionally accepted roles and examine the way in which difficulties often represent a covert attempt to deal with the inequalities and dissatisfaction which result from patriarchal organization. I also focus on redistributing power bases, on transforming covert forms of oppression into overt ones, and on reframing realities so as to offer greater choice. I do this always in full awareness of the limits of change in the therapeutic arena. I also give priority to defining as valid and powerful, ways of being that have been traditionally described as female and hence undervalued. I work towards facilitating the re-evaluation of affiliation, sharing, and emotionality.

A crucial dimension of this approach is the need for gender sensitivity to be applied not only through major interventions during clinical work, but in every interaction with the family. From the first moment at which therapeutic work begins, issues of gender and inequality need to be taken up: this ranges from how and to whom questions are asked, to the labelling and reframing of gender-informed transactions and belief systems. If, for example, in reply to an opening bid, responsibility for the problem is placed on the woman (by how she or someone else responds), a therapeutic moment is created in which gender-informed patterns of interaction can be challenged. Only through this way of working can gender be prevented from being marginalized and become a central and highly effective part of the therapeutic approach.

A clinical example will illustrate these ideas most effectively. The family-therapy team consisted of three people: myself, a colleague who is also a member of the South West Women's Project,[1] and a male colleague. The team had a shared ideology regarding feminist principles and we consciously undertook to address the issues of gender both in our practice with families and amongst ourselves. Although I will not focus on processes within the team, the following gender-related issues arose within the team.

We were confronted with issues of professional hierarchy: the male in our team was a psychiatrist, one of the women was a psychologist, and one a social worker. We had to deal with the conflict that arose between the women in the team and came to understand the extent to which this was enacted in the female dyad as a way of protecting our male colleague from his vulnerabilities. His vulnerability arose from his own personal sense of maleness as a result of his upbringing even though structurally he was in a position of power. Due to our socialization as women we acted in role by 'taking care of him'. We needed to consider the difficulties encountered by both female and male therapists when dealing with families, taking into consideration both issues of gender and our personal histories as they related to gender-determined expectations.

The X family were referred to our team for an assessment of whether or not the two children who had been removed from home should be returned to the family. A care order had been granted on the basis of severe physical abuse and a complex network of professionals was involved with the family. Much of the work with the Brown family focused on the couple relationship.

Patrick and Paula's relationship was extremely entangled. When I was with them, I almost felt as if I were with only one person. They completed each other in the sense that it was very difficult to determine where the 'I' ended and the 'we' began. In conjunction with this behaviour, the couple was very isolated from the outside world and experienced any intervention as highly dangerous and threatening. Due to each individual's lack of self-esteem, a relationship with little individuation developed. The enmeshment led to a precarious relationship as, by definition, neither person felt able to exist without the other.

When Paula and Patrick first entered therapy both partners manifested their fear in a gender-stereotyped way. Paula was upset and tended to withdraw or become paralysed and at times behaved in a 'hysterical' fashion. Patrick denied experiencing anxiety. He explained that Paula was frightened and he was just helping; she agreed with him. Patrick's fearfulness was expressed as rigidity, excessive rationality, great difficulty in allowing access to any feelings, and an abundance of explanations that often prevented me from thinking clearly.

Our basic understanding of the development of Patrick and Paula's relationship was as follows. Paula brought to the relationship many unmet needs for nurturance that she hoped would be met in a non-punishing way by Patrick. However, any demonstration of need in her reminded him of his mother's needs which had been wholly disregarded by his father, for which he therefore felt responsible, as children, from a position of loyalty, often do; he was reminded of this by Paula and so pushed her away. She felt abandoned and crazy as the message she experienced was that he needed nothing and she was 'over-dependent'. Her 'demands' became more extreme as she had fewer legitimate means of expression than her husband, due to her relative lack of power. Patrick felt increasingly burdened, as if he were still a little boy. However, because this was never stated, he tried to control Paula's needs and to make her desires manageable, as his father had done to his mother.

Gender system

Because of their entanglement and internal resourcelessness, Paula and Patrick's roles became caricatures of sexual stereotypes. The following themes emerged:

(1) Patrick occupied a position of superiority in the relationship.
(2) Paula experienced emotionality on behalf of both of them but was then criticized when she expressed that feeling.
(3) Patrick was required to think rationally on behalf of both of them and consequently felt burdened.
(4) Paula protected Patrick from facing his feelings of helplessness and failure because she believed that he was not able to manage and might collapse if she did not protect him.
(5) Paula exerted power through emotional pressures; Patrick did so by rational control.
(6) Patrick's worry was hidden from the outside world and absorbed by Paula who metabolized it (Langs 1979: 98). As a result, she was not free to be strong and active in her own life. This would

have challenged her gender socialization and also make Patrick feel threatened and in a state of neediness – a situation which would terrify both of them. Patrick was prevented from participating fully in his own emotional life.

Rules, roles, and gender-based assumptions

Some of the rules operating in the family were as follows:

(1) They could never disagree.
(2) Paula was held responsible for anything that went wrong.
(3) Men never communicate directly and cannot withstand criticism. The style of communication was one of constant mixed messages which were very difficult to label. For example, one of the shared beliefs was that: Paula is the powerful one, she controls and manipulates, and Patrick falls into line. However, Patrick makes all the decisions and will finally enforce them on behalf of them both.
(4) The idea that women are very dangerous was pervasive. For example Paula cannot help herself because her mother has destroyed her. She is now destroying Patrick, and Patrick's job is to help Paula. This belief undermined women of both generations and continued to cut Paula off from any kind of positive relationship with her mother and from any positive sense of herself as a woman. It also left Patrick feeling disconnected from any true intimacy.
(5) Patrick knew Paula's mind better than she did and hence was allowed no vulnerability of his own. Thus, anything that Patrick did to Paula that she did not like was actually for her own good. (Hence, the relationship can be characterized as being typical of that between an adult and a child rather than between two adults.)

These constructs can be illustrated by a task that Patrick and Paula completed during the therapy. Patrick was asked to write down the kinds of ways in which he viewed Paula and Paula was asked to do the same about Patrick.

Paula (as seen by Patrick)
expects to be told what to do;
never makes decisions;
seeks reassurance;
is tolerated by Patrick in the same way that Paula's mother is tolerated by her father.

Patrick (as seen by Paula)
wants to share responsibility but still retain overall control;
keeps things to himself;
will put up with anything;
is a bad manager;
blames others if something goes wrong.

Power bases

During therapy it is useful to consider the different sources of power to which family members have recourse (Watson and Williams 1988). The value attached to these power bases and the extent to which they have the ability to influence directly, or must be used covertly, should also be assessed (see Table 6.1).

It is interesting to note that the power bases generally more accessible to women (i.e. reproductive and relational power) were not available to Paula. Her reproductive power was eliminated when the children were taken into care and her relational power (earned by being in charge of social networks) was undermined by her estrangement from her family.

Table 6.1 Power bases in the relationship between Paula and Patrick

Power base	*How it is enacted*
PATRICK	
(1) Language and informational power	Use of logic and persuasion.
(2) Relational	Patrick had the support of both his own family and Paula's.
(3) Force	The use and threat of violence.
(4) Ascribed power	This ascribed (rather than earned) power reflects the values of the dominant group. The professional network of social workers, psychiatrists, and probation officers tended to validate Patrick's perception of his wife's instability and his own rationality.
(5) Economic power	Work and income.
(6) Contactual withdrawal	If Patrick were to leave, he would retain the children, both families, and his work. Paula would be left with nothing.
PAULA	
(1) Affective power	Hysteria, emotional battering.
(2) Domestic power	The threat to withdraw domestic services This was a somewhat precarious power base, however, as she had little to back it up with as she had nowhere else to go.

It is important to realize that child-care procedures affect women and men differently due to the different power bases available to them. The statutory agencies often further weaken women who already experience themselves as powerless. They demand that they 'shape up' without taking fully into account the effect of being asked to make major changes when the internal and external sense of being powerless is overwhelming. The felt experience is of unreasonable demands being made without *offers* of help.

One must, however, distinguish between power and influence. For example, hysterical behaviour is temporarily very influential but is not experienced by the user as valid, powerful, or a source of strength or esteem. Nor is it treated with anything other than contempt by others. In comparison, finance, as a power base, has all the opposite attributes.

The structure of this couple system was informed by the historical messages regarding gender that both partners had internalized, in addition to being constantly reinforced by the current attitudes and responses from both families of origin. One of Paula's family scripts was that women's needs are crushing and men are unable to meet these needs. A powerful family script in Patrick's family was that men must be strong and in charge of women who must be kept in check.

The extended family, on both side, felt sorry for Patrick. They saw him as a reasonable man, unlucky to be married to Paula. Paula was seen as manipulative or crazy, and as having no direct form of power. Since she accepted no adult responsibility, she was also seen as having no self. This led to a 'mad-making' belief system whereby Paula 'controlled' everything but actually had no say in anything. Patrick himself felt paralysed and unsure of what exactly Paula expected from him. He felt that he had been put on a pedestal and could not live up to Paula's expectations. Unfortunately, he was not able to say this directly and thus communicated to her that he actually had no needs and could manage perfectly well, if only his wife would stop being so crazy.

The gender-related goals of the therapy were as follows. First, we wished to empower Paula and consequently reduce the amount of overall control exerted by Patrick in the family. By enabling Paula to take responsibility for herself, it was hoped that she would gain a real sense of being able to influence matters. This, in turn, would allow her to give up her emotional centrality. Second, we hoped to help Patrick accept his own feelings, thus enabling him to take the risk of expressing his own needs, thereby enriching his emotional experience. Paula would be freed from the burden of having to express both their needs. Third, we intended to focus on validating Paula's experience as a woman, reframing in a more positive light her relationship

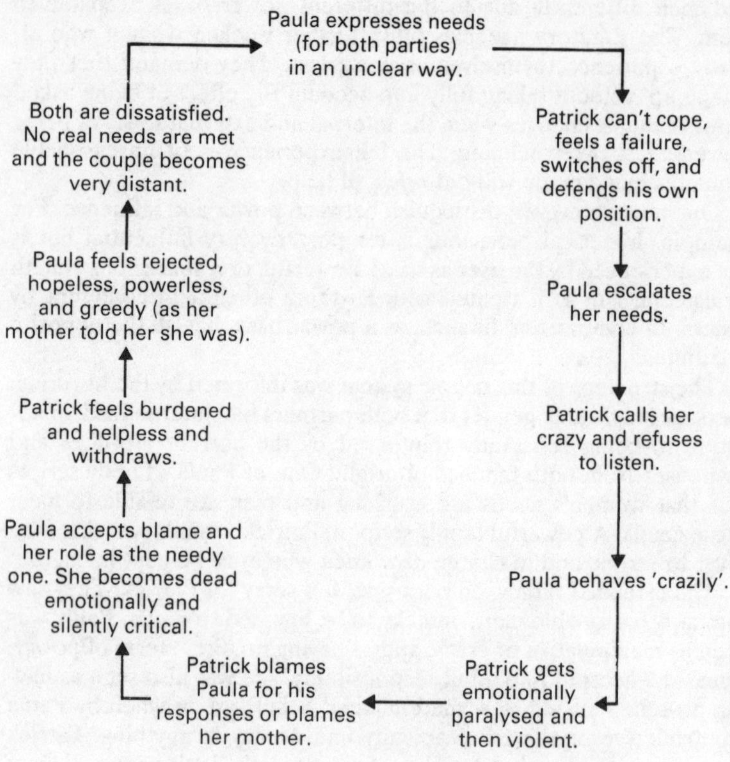

Figure 6.1 The dynamics of the relationship's central contradiction

to significant women in her past. Finally, we hoped to encourage change in their gender-informed relationship, by helping Patrick to move closer to Paula without fear of being 'controlled'. Paula would then be able to challenge Patrick directly and ask for help and support without being labelled as demanding.

The central contradiction was that Paula behaved in a mad fashion so as to make Patrick feel strong. He then acted in an all-knowing manner in order to make her feel 'taken care of'. Figure 6.1 outlines this situation.

The course of therapy

The early stages of therapy concentrated on redefining the couple's shared belief that only Paula had 'problems'. I reframed the perception to include Patrick's difficulty in being 'affected by things', and to cast doubt on the validity of laying all the blame at Paula's door. This reframing used universal principles (see Urry's Chapter 5) behind men and women's socialization to effect change. One example of these principles lies in the way in which men's socialization mitigates against the expression of feeling and women's training leads to the denial of self in the face of the requirement to nurture. Both cultural and personal historical themes were made use of.

The therapy encouraged Paula to discover her own voice. I labelled the communication processes that occurred and showed how Paula came to experience herself as incompetent and nasty. I did this, for example, by pointing out that Paula was blamed for all the difficulties whether or not they concerned her. This process brought about a significant amount of change: Paula became less distrustful of the therapist, much more open to the therapeutic process, and more able to own her own particular difficulties. However, Patrick's inability to take any responsibility for his feelings remained unchanged. Paula actively participated in the process and often continued to protect him, by allowing herself to be the focus of difficulties by deflecting attention and potential criticism away from him.

As the therapy proceeded I became caught up in this web and found myself turning to Paula for change as she appeared to be the one who was responding emotionally, taking responsibility, and actively seeking change. At this point in the therapy, after I had seen the couple for two months, I consulted my colleagues in the Women's Project and realized that the therapeutic emphasis had shifted from empowering Paula to actually adopting the family's belief system. We had come to believe that it was Paula who needed to change and that Patrick was not able to do so. On the one hand I felt unable to challenge Patrick's position out of fear and over-identification with Paula. On the other, I was not able to put myself in Patrick's shoes and understand his position. I was thus replicating the belief that he both could not, and did not want to, relate differently. He did not challenge this attitude because it was both familiar and safe. Thus the cycle continued.

As a result of my new insight, I suggested to Patrick that although Paula had made much progress during the therapeutic contact, he remained remarkably unchanged. We felt that he would not be able to progress until we could find some way of making it easier for Patrick to respond emotionally. When I asked him why he remained so unaffected by things outside himself, he replied: 'Maybe it just seems like that.' Although I agreed with him, I also pointed out that he nevertheless behaved as if he were unaffected.

The following extract demonstrates my attempts to unbalance the system by challenging Patrick directly about his emotional absence and the source of 'power' in the family.

***Extract 1* (30 minutes into the session)**

Therapist: You say that you feel exactly the same. I was saying 'What is it with you that you decide to remain exactly the same despite everything?' Do you remember that?

Patrick: I suppose I don't know what to expect of the way I should be going . . . I don't want it to sound arrogant, or bad towards Paula, but then obviously in some ways I think perhaps Paula . . . the way I see it, we're both dictated by our past upbringing. I think sometimes that what's happened is reflected more directly from Paula's background, although mine is involved. Paula's behaviour is a bit more . . . .

Therapist: Well, I think it's more obvious. It sounds like what you are saying is 'It's more down to her than down to me.'

Patrick: No, I'm not saying that it's more down to her. What I'm saying is that she's always been . . . .

Therapist: Yes. Everyone has always been saying that Paula is the problem. You can see it, that's right, but just because you can see it doesn't mean that your difficulties aren't just as dramatic.

Patrick: No, I didn't say that . . . . You're saying that – that's what I'm trying to avoid saying.

The difficulty Patrick experiences in interacting with me directly about his emotional process is clear, even in this short extract. Having given me the initial responsibility for telling him how to change, he avoids interacting with me directly about himself, by deflecting the attention back to Paula and brings into play the old rule of both blaming her and trying to bring Paula into our transaction.

In this extract I began an antisystemic sequence, both addressing Patrick directly about his difficulties and not allowing him to deflect them on to Paula. This produced anxiety for Patrick and I was also aware of tension in Paula as she watched to see what would happen. It was a new experience for this couple to find a woman asking Patrick to take responsibility for himself and to be pointing out how the usual organization is for Paula to protect Patrick from conflict by saying it was all her fault.

The fact that this challenge was carried out by a female therapist was of particular significance since it models to both partners an alternative reality. Women can challenge and assert with adult compassion. This is an important learning experience for both Paula and Patrick. I began at this stage to challenge this family organization on Paula's behalf as I felt that she required my help before she could begin to undertake this for herself. I was aware that she might experience me as undermining rather than empowering her, but my intention was to begin a process through which she would eventually be able to replace me.

Challenging a man so directly also posed issues for me personally as a female therapist since I had to work against my gender socialization which told me not to appear dominating.

Extract 2

Patrick: I think in some ways I've changed a lot more in the five years since we got married than Paula has because I've had to accommodate . . . when you get married you say right, we go 50 per cent each way and meet in the middle. I've always felt I've gone 95 per cent and Paula's gone 5 per cent.

Therapist: Oh, do you? [*To Paula*] He reckons that he's gone 95 per cent towards you and you've gone 5 per cent. That could make a really interesting argument, couldn't it . . . . Do you agree with this?

Paula: [*In a weak voice*] I don't know really.

Patrick: We had one week, didn't we, well, honeymoon week.

Paula: I know I'm hell to live with.

Patrick: And then within the first two or three days of getting back to work, in the second week of marriage . . . [*To Paula*] . . . I mean, you admitted yourself, didn't you, or you have done before. [*To Therapist*] Paula, because of the way she was treated, overprotected and badly prepared . . . .

Therapist: We are going to get it to be her fault again. I am trying to understand with you how it is. I can hear what you are saying about not knowing what is expected of you, but it sounds like we are getting it to be just Paula and we know that Paula has actually made a lot of strides since all this happened and it feels to us like you haven't actually moved an inch. I mean you said it yourself, you haven't changed at all.

Paula: Maybe he doesn't need to.

Therapist: Well, I'm not so sure. I'm not sure you are either. I feel a part of you knows different, but like many women, you've been taught to take the blame.

As I continued to insist that Patrick should take responsibility and begin to explore with me his part in the difficulties, the tension and anger increased. Patrick used many ways of blaming Paula: he said how accommodating he was and she was not, and he appealed to her to take the blame by invoking a previous time she had done this, referring to her upbringing. The more he felt under pressure the more he appealed to Paula to rescue him. When one tack did not work, he subtly changed his angle of approach.

Predictably Patrick eventually managed to draw Paula in to rescue him. When I directly invited her to express herself she was quite unable to do so even with my support. Instead she provided information to help him and condemn herself, by suggesting that he might not need to change. The oppressive system played itself out. Patrick held his position by blaming Paula. She allows herself to be blamed, on his behalf. The couple system with its gendered consequences is becoming clearer and more intense. The idea that women should take the blame and protect men in the emotional field is a gender-informed transaction. To continue to challenge such deeply held beliefs that have both historical and cultural meaning is a real struggle for the therapist.

Extract 3

Therapist: What I am interested in is how, Patrick, it is possible for you to be so unmoved by things. I mean what do you do that nothing affects you much?

Patrick: How have I been affected? I suppose I still wonder whether the vicious circle is going to be broken.

Therapist: So what would you say the vicious circle was?

Patrick: Well, I mean I think really it started, as I say, more or less the second week we were married, that Paula . . . you know I am not trying to blame anybody, just trying to make a statement. Over the years we have been married Paula always felt that she was thrown in the deep end, that she can't cope and Paula claims that her aggression is a defence mechanism, or survival mechanism. We were married and after about a week she gave up work. Within that first week for some reason, whatever reason, something went wrong.

Therapist: What's your bit of the vicious circle? Forget about her bit. Yes, I want to know about your bit of the vicious circle, because it isn't just down to her.

Patrick: It's the fact that I give in to her I suppose.

Therapist: So, somehow, you always allow yourself to be decided for by things outside yourself. In your own words, 'you give in to her'.

Patrick: We had an example last Saturday. Paula sometimes realizes she's wrong. [*Patrick looks to Paula to rescue him from me. She is able not to respond. Patrick then tells a story about Paula misunderstanding him, constantly pleading with her to back him up.*]

Therapist: [*To Paula*] Right, so he sends out mixed messages.

Paula: Yes. [*In a strong voice*]

Therapist: Because I think one of the things about the vicious circle is it's always Paula's fault. Either she is crazy, or she's got a bad temper or something, and you are always having to accommodate her. What I want to know is what bit of vicious circle you think you are maintaining today?

I continued to unbalance the system by directly challenging Patrick's power and insisting that they develop a new form of organization by not accepting the view of Paula as the sole source of difficulty. Patrick tried to protect his position by continuing to project the difficulties on to Paula to avoid dealing with me.

Patrick referred to an external locus of control; Paula referred to an internal locus of control. For example, Patrick told me that he was waiting for the 'vicious circle' to be broken, probably by me. The responsibility lay outside himself. Paula, however, made statements which related to her own sense of over-responsibility: 'It's probably my fault the circle is still going.'

As the pressure built up, Patrick looked to Paula to back him up. I too felt the pressure to stop and 'take care of him'. Paula resisted and did not respond suggesting to me that change was beginning to take place. Paula was starting to be able to step outside the old system to allow her husband to struggle alone.

When Patrick angrily renewed his criticism of Paula by saying she misunderstood him, I reframed this as Patrick sending out mixed messages. Paula agreed with me. She was beginning to feel empowered and positively engaged in the process of change.

I then overtly labelled the rule as Paula always being blamed as a further step towards empowering Paula and Patrick. This was empowering for both as it freed Paula from feeling she was bad and Patrick from feeling like an outsider who only observed life. It is crucial, in my view, to label overtly insidious rules that have gendered meaning. Their powerful influence lies outside awareness. By clearly talking about the process, its power lessens and choice increases. Suddenly things make sense differently.

Extract 4

Therapist: What I want to know is what bit of the vicious circle you think you are maintaining today?

Patrick: Well I don't know because I would have changed it within the first week of our marriage but if it is still there then obviously something . . . .

Therapist: [*to Paula*] There is something about this first week of your marriage – do you feel so strongly about this point, or is this just Patrick's story?

Paula: Well, I gave up my job didn't I, where I was working, and there was no money then.

Therapist: It does sound like he's angry with you now, doesn't it?

Patrick: I'm not angry with her for giving up the job, I am angry about her giving up the job in that she didn't accept the situation. That's why I get angry. Paula doesn't accept the situation that we together will end up in, that's what annoys me.

Paula: It's always my fault about money. Even though it's five years ago, it's my fault because I gave up my job, although I'm used to it now, he's always telling me.

Therapist: So still it's your fault. He doesn't give up easily. What do you think it is about him? You know last time you came, I said that my experience was that Patrick was pretty unmovable. Now, we know that his dad's a bit like that isn't he, and his dad has been pretty unmovable for all his life, hasn't he? He's just done the same thing for forty years. Now we find that worrying, because we think, I guess, that there are aspects of the vicious circle that . . . .

Paula: [*takes over*]: Okay, Okay. I get the feeling he thinks he's right and I'm wrong. Everything he says and does is right. I think that way of him anyway. [*Patrick interrupts. The therapist stops him and allows Paula to finish.*]

Paula: Because of my upbringing I end up thinking that he must be right. He is all right and I am all wrong. [*Therapist again stops Patrick interrupting.*] It makes me feel I have to go along with him.

Patrick: She thinks I am right. I know I am not bloody well right and she thinks I am. She puts all the pressure on me because of the way her parents are, she thinks I am so different that everything I do must be right, and it's such a . . . .

Therapist: And you don't think you're right?

Patrick: No.

Therapist: Somehow you're not very good at communicating your vulnerability.

Patrick: It gives me a bloody headache trying to . . . .

Therapist: What gives you a headache?

Patrick: Well, trying to convince her that I am not the sort of person she thinks I am. Paula puts me on the pedestal, not me. I can't stand it. I don't know how to be that person.

As I began to sense that Paula was able to continue this challenge directly on her own behalf, I started to talk to her about her feelings about being held responsible for all their problems. Because she was feeling significantly more empowered she was able to comment directly on her experience in relation to Patrick for the first time. In response Patrick became angry and responded in a more emotional way. Paula eventually let me know that she no longer needed me to speak for her (as I had hoped initially), and started to state her own position and her sense of personal meaning.

This change in Paula in turn facilitated a change in Patrick who related his experience of the stress involved in feeling he had to be right all the time. This was the 'flip side' of blaming Paula – but as he had never before been able to own his emotional experience, his feelings were absent until this point. Even though at this stage the change was still of the first order (in that his explanation still blamed Paula), the emotional quality of his expression was entirely different. His emotional responsibility was reclaimed and he began to accept that he could be affected and in turn affect.

As a therapist I experienced a sense of relief that there was a way forward therapeutically. I could now work directly with Patrick's vulnerability which was previously denied and thus gain access to his strength as well as weakness. As Paula had been freed from this oppressive system, I could help her take responsibility for herself and discover her own position.

To use Hoffman's words (1981), a 'step-change' occurred and a therapeutic opening into a new level of work was created.

Many colleagues have, on reading these extracts, felt that Patrick experienced my challenges as a hurtful onslaught. Patrick himself, however, has since said that the session described was the most useful session we had ever had. He subsequently became actively engaged with me and no longer came to the sessions merely because he felt he had to. My interpretation would be that although the original couple system was highly destructive for Paula, it also constrained Patrick emotionally. The fact that I turned to Paula for change (as I had done earlier in therapy) was comfortable for Patrick who felt he could just sit back and wait for things to happen. However, it also told him that I considered him emotionally incompetent, thus leaving him feeling that his emotional life was impoverished. The challenge actually validated his feelings and thus, although experienced at one level as painful and frightening, at another level it was experienced as both liberating and supportive. In addition, the challenge was experienced as helpful because it occurred in the context of a strong relationship between myself and Patrick. I could therefore push for change without endangering the affiliation.

Following the session described I worked intensively with Patrick looking at his family of origin which he had earlier insisted was absolutely perfect. He was able to discover the ways in which he had felt that he had to take care of his mother because of his father's absence, and how alone he felt because of his inability to 'provide'. He described emotionally his asthma attacks as a child and how he felt suffocated and trapped by his mother's need of him and his father's absence.

During this period of work, Patrick was deeply sad and also quite shocked at his new vision. Paula responded to this change with ambivalence but with a wider range of options than previously. On the one hand she felt relieved at not having to take the responsibility and blame for everything, and realized she might be able to accept her own view of things. This was the first time in Paula's life that her own view had been given any legitimacy. However, at another level she became anxious as the change meant that she could no longer hide behind Patrick. There were times when she tried to reactivate the old structure which was at least familiar and predictable. Paula came to see how she blamed Patrick covertly for failing her emotionally, and how she responded to being blamed for everything by communicating indirectly how useless he was. However, on the whole, as the interaction between these two people began to change, Paula was liberated from always being wrong but was also able actually to take responsibility for her own difficulties and begin to request something for herself directly.

Patrick and Paula were trapped by their gender socialization. The role they had each come to play was no accident. As previously mentioned, Patrick had been trained, like most boys, to leave feelings to his female partner and to blame her for family failures. Paula learned that men cannot cope with emotional vulnerability and must be protected even if that involves taking the blame oneself.

The rigidity of these assumptions meant that the cost to both was high. Paula lived in a state of emotional disintegration, feeling she was to blame for almost everything. Patrick lived alone with a headache. By changing Patrick and Paula's gender informed assumptions, therapy was able to give them both greater freedom of choice. Paula could not reclaim herself whilst under threat from the message of blame. Patrick could not find his feelings while on the one hand shielded by Paula, and on the other being given messages of failure. The change for each person began when the original belief was challenged and a new one offered.

As work with Patrick and Paula progressed, both became increasingly individuated. Although there was a seductive inclination to revert to the original rules when under pressure from the family or the wider social network, both Patrick and Paula gradually became able to address their needs both separately and in relation to each other. As one might expect, this put the survival of the couple relationship severely at risk; each began to question whether they would really be able to get what they needed from the other. In my view this was a great step forward.

There are many, many ways of working therapeutically within a feminist framework. The case-study presented here represents one alternative framework offered to two people to facilitate change. However, it must not be assumed that working in this way is easy for therapists. It is difficult at the personal, contextual, and societal levels. It is difficult personally as it requires us to confront our own socialization and ways of relating and being. In exploring alternative realities we have to face both our own and our clients' fearfulness of departing from the established order. Working with a feminist framework challenges our working systems since it is not possible to develop new ways of working with colleagues who hold either hostile or indifferent reactions to radical views without feeling defeated or unsupported. In terms of societal responses, we have to consider the effect of challenging gender construction since change is not easily tolerated.

In conclusion, I would argue that despite the difficulties and the feeling of sailing in uncharted waters, we have no choice but to take up the challenge of feminism in our therapy with families. If we do not, we are deciding to perpetuate oppression. We are deciding to ignore the obviously different effects of family life on men and on women, pretending that the inequality and psychological distress are not related, pretending we know nothing of how gender informs our intimacy even though we will each experience that effect in our own daily lives. In essence, ignoring the issue of feminism would be saying that as family therapists, we will consider context only to the extent that it is comfortable for us as therapists to do so and will ignore anything that is too disturbing.

Note

1. A group of women who meet to discuss the role of feminist thinking within family therapy.

References

Hoffman, L. (1981) *Foundations of Family Therapy*, New York: Basic Books.

Langs, R. (1979) *The Supervisory Experience*, New Jersey: Jason Aronson.

Watson, G. and Williams, J. (1988) 'Sexual inequality, family life and family therapy', in E. Street and W. Dryden (eds.) *Family Therapy in Britain*, Milton Keynes: Open University Press.

Part three

Applications: Specific Clinical Issues

Chapter seven

The mother–daughter relationship and the distortion of reality in childhood sexual abuse

Ann C. Miller

> If we adopt a feminist perspective we will not automatically condemn a mother as 'collusive' if she does not want to believe what has happened, or even if we discover that she did know and did nothing. We will concentrate on giving care and attention to women, recognizing the difficulties of their position, the complexities of their feelings, the meaning for them of what has happened.
>
> (MacLeod and Saraga 1988: 39)

Childhood sexual abuse is now acknowledged as a fact of life. Despite this, ideas about its nature, prevalence, and long-term sequelae are still relatively confused. In a recent study conducted among health visitors, nurses, and medical students in a Secure Unit (Eisenberg and Owens 1987) over half thought the prevalence of incest was one in five hundred or lower.[1] Just over half also thought that some *children* were responsible for the occurrence of the abuse. While high numbers of respondents believed that sexual and relationship problems would be a likely sequela of the abuse, very few thought that anger, aggression, delinquency, prostitution, alcoholism/drug abuse, promiscuity, suicidal behaviour, or mental illness would be connected to it. In contrast, the work of Finkelhor (1984), Briere (1984), and Mullen *et al.* (1988) indicates that many women who were abused as children experience dissociative experiences, feelings of not being real, and out-of-body experiences, and a range of self-destructive behaviours including addictions, self-mutilation, and suicide attempts.

The Eisenberg and Owens findings seem to do no more than reflect the disbelief and denial of what are largely female experiences in British society. The most recent of many, many examples of this attitude in English public life is to be found in Fiona McCarthy's biography of Eric Gill. She reveals that Gill, artist, craftsman, and devout Catholic moralist and paterfamilias, had incestuous relationships with both his younger sisters and two of his adolescent daughters. Two previous biographies (both written by men with full access to Gill's diaries) failed to mention this. On reading the reviews of this book, one is struck by the following statements: 'although, as Fiona McCarthy is careful to state, there is no evidence that the girls suffered any trauma . . . . ' (Clare Tomalin, *Observer*, 22 January 1989); 'Gill felt bothered by it all, of course. "What does God think? Oh dear!" he lamented in his diary. "This must stop!" *But if it had stopped, his art would have stopped as well.*' (John Carey, *Sunday Times*, 22 January 1989, my emphasis).

The aim of this chapter is to explore the way in which the realities of female experience are also denied and distorted *within* the family where abuse occurs. My starting point in thinking about this was four women, seen in my practice as a clinical psychologist, who came to the clinic for different reasons. I will describe each one briefly and then relate some of my experiences when seeing them together with their mothers.

Janine Evans,[2] a working-class woman from a Welsh mining family, was 31 years old, looked young for her age, but had a school-age child.

She lived with their father in a long-term but very unstable relationship. She had been seen at the clinic a year prior to my meeting her when she had been worried about the aggressive behaviour of her son. When I met her she was very distressed about an attack on her a few days earlier by a man in a disco who had followed her to an isolated place and almost succeeded in smothering and raping her. She had survived because she had, over a period of almost ten minutes, fought and screamed and eventually escaped from her attacker. Her mother had accompanied her to the clinic because, since the attack, she was unable to leave the house on her own and had been subject to acute anxiety, fear, and distress. Her assailant had not been found. Although her husband was sympathetic, she felt that he was not good at helping her to talk about it. She also thought he could not understand why she was not 'getting over it'.

When I saw her with her mother, who was clearly concerned about her daughter, I focused on the attack and her feelings in relation to it by getting her mother to find out about it in such a way that Janine was able or willing to tell her. What I then observed was that Mrs Evans, while clearly sympathetic and wanting to be helpful to her daughter, found great difficulty in actually allowing her to speak. Instead she expressed many of her own ideas and thoughts about the situation, and many of her own assumptions about what had happened, which meant that Janine did not in fact have the experience of being heard by her mother. Each time Janine was encouraged by me to tell her exactly what had happened, Mrs Evans found a way to interrupt, change the subject slightly, and talk about her own fear of attack, without ever actually listening to her daughter's experience.

The second woman, Mavis Thompson, was 28, the daughter of a journalist who had abandoned her mother when Mavis was 12. She came to talk about the very difficult time she was having with her boy-friend with whom she shared a very intense and sometimes violent relationship. She was unemployed, despite being a talented journalist, and she was often depressed – staying in her room all day long. After some sessions with her and one session with her brother which focused on their continuing difficulties with their parents, I saw her with her mother. As Mavis started to discuss the decision she had almost arrived at to end her relationship with her boy-friend, her mother, to my surprise, appeared to show disproportionate disappointment. She told Mavis what a nice boy John was and what a shame it was that Mavis wanted to break up with him. Each time Mavis started to explain the way in which she felt exploited in the relationship, and the resolve she was starting to build about the incidents of being beaten, her mother diminished what she said and pointed out another of John's virtues.

The third woman, Julia Panelli, was 40, and worked as a secretary. She had three daughters, the second of whom was congenitally deaf. She was a bright, attractive, and sociable woman but despite this her relationships with both men and women appeared to be rather arid and she was in effect quite isolated. The focus of her concern when she came to see me was her relationship with her mother. She saw her mother frequently, because despite living in different households they had in many respects shared the care of the children. In recent years Julia found that the relationship was becoming increasingly intolerable in so far as every meeting was either full of tension and rather silent, or would erupt to a major row. When I saw her with her mother and daughters, I felt that whatever the conversation between them was apparently about, the real issue at all times was 'Whose version of reality is going to be accepted as true?' It did not seem to matter whether they talked about the children, Julia's social life, her mother's relationship with an aunt, or the reason for coming to therapy. But by far the greatest struggle centred around Julia's father, now dead. Julia had known him only as a very young child (he had left when she was 7) and she had been trying to construct a clearer picture of him by seeking people who knew him and by talking to her mother. Julia's mother's unwillingness to acknowledge that Julia might need some support to build her own picture of her father was profound. Her mother insisted that the only true picture was her own.

Finally, a fourth woman, Marcia Davis, whose situation I shall come back to later, gave the following account of her disclosure to her mother of sexual abuse by her father:

> It was like screaming at someone. You really wanted them to believe you, because you were telling them the truth. She said to me 'Oh my God what will our friends say? What will the neighbours say?' That was all she would say. She did not believe me . . . my greatest fear is of not being believed . . . it's a horrible fear. It is the worst thing about it.

In describing these four women and their mothers, what seems most evident is the way in which the mothers' failure to hear or acknowledge their daughters' experiences amounts to a virtual attack on the daughters' sense of reality. It is as if allowing their daughters to express their point of view, or if once expressed to acknowledge it, would amount to a major threat to the mothers' perception of themselves or of their relationships. This is similar to a pattern of relating which I have observed in interviewing some very young children and their mothers where the little girl is attempting to disclose sexual abuse. The child speaks hesitantly, the mother talks over her, speaking just as she starts, telling her to sit up straight, changes the subject, and so on.

In the literature on child sexual abuse, it has been argued that 'victimology', or the emphasis on studying the *child* in child sexual abuse, simply reflects the prevailing climate in which the role of the male goes largely unchallenged and unexamined. It has also been argued that the woman in the family, the mother, is often viewed in the literature as co-responsible for the abuse in that she colludes with it. Since femininity is, above all, construed as nurturing and protective, the mother who 'fails to protect' the child is seen as pathological. This pathologizing of the woman usually traces a history of pathological relationships with her mother, a history of 'inadequate mothering' or the failure of her mother to protect her against abuse as a child.[3]

However, the analysis that I wish to make in this paper argues that the continuation of male power in the context of child sexual abuse relies on females continuing to distort their own realities such that there is no agreement between the females on the nature of their experience. If the sexual focus of the adult male is the child and not the woman, then adult female sexuality is repudiated. The marital relationship may be one in which the woman is dominated and/or physically abused by her husband, or treated by him as an object. To turn to Eric Gill's biography again:

> Mary Gill meekly accepted her husband's infidelity. She appears in the photographs beaming through spectacles, immersed in her flock of children and grandchildren. When writing about his married life, Gill named his possessions, listing his wife alongside a table, some chairs, knives and forks and a hat. Even in this richly detailed book, Mary Gill remains an incomplete presence.
>
> (Francis Spalding, *The Independent*, 23 January 1989)

One hardly wonders!

An alternative view of marriage is one where the perpetrator is an 'inadequate' man who often attributes this inadequacy to his wife (or his mother).

> In many incestuous fathers there seems to exist a partial suspension of reality. The incestuous father does not realize that the object of his sexual desires is his own daughter (*sic*) and not the juvenile wife or the idealized image of his own mother. This partial lack of reality testing is provided by the possibility of incestuous acting-out, which compensates for the narcissistic pain experienced from rejection by the wife. The rejection itself recalls the deficits in the relationship with his mother.
>
> (Hirsch 1986: 549)

The continuing assault of the father on the child places mother and daughter in positions of mutual betrayal. The daughter betrays her mother by taking her mother's place and becoming 'the other woman'. This confirms the mother's image of herself and her own sexuality as unacceptable, inadequate, or monstrous, and also attacks her capacity to care for and nurture her daughter. The mother betrays the daughter by not responding to her plea for protection. In this situation the daughter implicitly becomes her mother's accuser and joins the father's rageful attack on the adult woman. However, if the father does not cease the abuse by himself, his power can only be reduced and the abuse stopped once the daughter is heard by the mother. Where the mother cannot hear the child or where the child does not find a voice, the outcome for the child can be the adoption of an *illusion* of power by the daughter, as evidenced in the following extract from a session with a woman, who had been abused by her uncle at the age of 7. She had built up a picture of her life and experiences in which the attack was a central organizing feature. She had been referred for severe recurring depression and panic attacks.

> I've kept a guilty secret for twenty-eight years. Everything fits in to why I panic so often. I said to my mum 'my uncle made my bottom

> sore' . . . it must have thrown her at the time. I told her once but never again. I got no response. To me it seems a guilty secret I've always punished myself with. That's why my dad died, I lost the baby, my brother died and that's always been the thing I've never told anybody. I've felt so guilty about it and so ashamed. I wanted to voice it so I could stop punishing myself and that's what I've been doing.

In patiently unravelling her story, it was abundantly clear that *she* took on responsibility for the original event. It was *she* at the age of 7, a curious and excited little girl, who 'should not have looked . . . should have run away . . . should have stopped him . . . should not have been so afraid . . . should have explained myself properly to mummy . . . should not have let him hurt me . . .'.

I wish now to illustrate an approach to women in therapy which not only takes into account the 'difficulties of their position, the complexities of their feelings' but also challenges them to develop ways of redressing the balance of power within the family, while acknowledging that power has been vested in men for a long time within the wider social context. Marcia Davis, who recounted screaming at her mother to try and make her believe her, is a woman of 47 who came to the clinic with her daughter Beryl aged 23. Beryl had become very depressed shortly before she was due to marry, had called off the wedding and had since lived with mother and stepfather. She was now house-bound. Neither Marcia nor Beryl at first really raised their voices much above a low whisper. They had both been abused by the same man, Marcia's father.

Although she had told her mother finally at the age of 14, Beryl had endured the abuse of her grandfather for six years. He had forced her, on her visits to the grandparental home, to engage in oral intercourse with him and she experienced this as both frightening and painful. He always handled her very roughly and threatened to hurt her severely if she told anyone. When Beryl finally told Marcia, she confronted both grandparents, who flatly denied the situation. Marcia remembered her father saying in a tone of shock and reproach 'How could Beryl tell such wicked lies?' He also threatened to accuse Beryl's own father of being the abuser, and this threat apparently had the effect of removing Beryl's father's support for any further confrontation with the grandparents. It also marked the beginning of a rift between Beryl's parents which shortly afterwards ended in separation. Marcia subsequently remarried, but before that she decided to cut off all relations with her own family, so that at the age of 14 Beryl lost her father, her grandparents, her uncles, and her aunts – in effect her whole family.

The following is an excerpt of the session I had with them. They had come without Marcia's husband, or the other member of their family, Beryl's older brother Tony. They had not wanted to push them to come. My co-therapist was Harvey Ratner[4] (HR) who had invited me to join him in his ongoing work with the family. Beryl had been saying that she had felt unafraid only during the year she spent working in Australia; otherwise she was always afraid that 'he is going to get at me . . .'.

ACM: Who is it that's going to get at you?

Beryl: I've always got this fear of my grandfather turning up though he probably never will but . . . I still think he's . . . I feel that he is still after me in some way.

ACM: [*slowly and deliberately*] So, even though your mother makes the best effort she can make by cutting off relationships with him, with her mother, even her sisters, her brother, it hasn't worked . . . it's been a failure in that respect [*pause*] . . . because of the grandfather in your head. [*pause*]

Beryl: [*inaudible*]

HR: [*to mother and daughter*] Something we've talked about is that because of the cut off ten years ago, both of you, but especially Beryl, has been unable to express how she really feels about her grandfather. You [*to mother*] said that you couldn't even bear to go to his house because you'd end up killing him, and you [*to Beryl*] would feel angry with him but the anger has never been directed towards him, to that man who is pursuing you. You've never at any point been able to face him.

Beryl: But this is it, I haven't really got anger. I'm just terrified, I've just got fear there, I don't think I could get angry with him, I don't think I could ever do that . . . sometimes I feel I'd like to say 'Look what you've done to my life', but I couldn't ever actually do that.

ACM: How old is he now? [*Beryl looks at her mother.*]

Mrs Davis: Sixty-five.

ACM: Is he healthy?

Mrs Davis: No in fact . . . .

ACM: [*interrupting, speaking to Beryl*] Is this something you know about or is this information only your mother has? [*Beryl and Mrs Davis speak simultaneously but Mrs Davis dominates.*]

Mrs Davis: I found out recently . . . I phoned my aunt . . . .

ACM: [*to mother*] Let me find out from Beryl [*turning to Beryl*]: what do you think about his health.

Beryl: I think he had a stroke.

Mrs Davis: He had a heart attack recently but he seems to have recovered from it.

Beryl: [*simultaneously*] Something to do with his heart . . . .

ACM: [*to Beryl*] So what do *you* think has happened to him?

Beryl: I don't know. I remember he used to have black hair. Now apparently his hair is white. [*As she talks ACM makes encouraging noises.*]

ACM: So you haven't actually laid eyes on him for ten years?

Beryl: [*shaking her head*] No.

ACM: I see, goodness, no wonder he is so powerful. And is he going to die soon? What is happening? You [*to Beryl*] obviously think he's going to live for ever.

Mrs Davis: I just know that he had a heart attack . . . but he's driving, he can't be that ill . . . it's horrible because when my aunt said he'd had a heart attack, I said what a pity it didn't finish him off . . . I wish him dead and that's a terrible thing to say about anybody.

ACM: [*to Mrs Davis*] I can understand what you're saying [*pause*] but I think for Beryl's sake you can thank your lucky stars that he didn't die. Because it's a bit like . . . you know, some people can't actually ever get over a death unless they have viewed the body, you know?

Mrs Davis: [*nodding her head*] Yes.

ACM: Because Beryl is in the position at the moment that if he dies, before she has had a chance to look at him and even talk to him, she might end up with this grandfather in her head permanently. Or at least I don't know how she's going to exorcise this image, and start to become a grown-up woman and not a little girl who is too frightened to be angry.

Mrs Davis: That's right . . . [*to Beryl*] if he did approach you now you're an adult, you can do something about it . . . .

ACM: That's right, but she doesn't know that, even if you say it to her. Do you know what her vision of her grandfather is?

Mrs Davis: Yes, she has told me how she sees him and the situations he used to grab her in – for example she can't bear the smell of paint or turpentine so I avoid painting the house when she is living with me, because he used to grab her in the workshop. I avoid bringing up things that will remind her of him.

ACM: Well obviously that has been your tack, to try and protect her by taking it all away, putting it away, hiding it. And at great sacrifice.

Mrs Davis: Mmm . . . but obviously not . . . not really . . . to the best end.

ACM: No . . . it hasn't worked . . . it hasn't worked. And that's quite a big realization to take on board when you have made such a sacrifice for ten years.

Mrs Davis: I think if I had had her father's support when I first heard about Beryl I would have gone round there and done something about it. But he backed out because he was threatened by my father. And I didn't feel able to do it on my own. And also my brother and sister were not supporting me at that time.

HR: [*to ACM*] It sounds as though the men in their lives now are continuing the situation in that they're not giving support for this kind of confrontation. Mrs Davis's husband sounds like a kindly person who would not be into confrontation.

Mrs Davis: No, that's right.

A discussion ensued as to whether various men in the family know about the events and whether any of them would support the women in a confrontation with the grandfather. Their opinion was that despite goodwill among those who know, they would not be sufficiently supportive. Mrs Davis was clearly not keen to press them. The conversation then moved to thinking about what it would be like to be in touch again with Mrs Davis's parents. She recalled her own unhappy childhood, particularly her father's violence towards her mother while Beryl listened. I finally brought the conversation back to the question of female resources.

ACM: [*to HR*] The thing I am sitting here wondering about, Harvey, is whether these women can actually solve this problem by facing it, because clearly hiding it has not worked. They've made an extremely good attempt at that, one of the best I've seen, of organizing their lives to hide it and not confront it. But the thing I'm wondering about is whether they see anything they can do, or whether they need their men, and if their men won't help them, then nothing can be done. [*to Beryl*] Where does he live?

Beryl: Parkville.

ACM: You know people in our profession have thought of all sorts of ways to help people try and exorcise ghosts, but it's very much second best. [*long pause*] I don't know whether they have to write off the men in the family as unhelpful or whether they have to look for other women in the family to help them.

At this point HR raised the question of whether in fact Mrs Davis and Beryl do want to make a shift as they are very protective towards one another and he was not sure from previous conversations with them whether they were ready to move out of the safe situation they had created for themselves.

ACM: Well, that's fine as long as Beryl wants to stay with her mother for the next twenty years but I got the impression that she actually had been trying to move out and somehow got stuck.

Mrs Davis: So you think that the thing we really have to do is this confrontation?

ACM: I think Beryl needs to get a look at him . . . [*to mother*] doesn't she?

Beryl: It wouldn't be the same as the picture I've got of him would it? [*She says this to ACM direct, not through mother.*]

ACM: No.

Beryl: That picture you've got in your head isn't there any more, it's not the same.

Later in the session ACM and HR talked at some length with Beryl about how she imagined it would feel like to walk up to her grandparents' house, be in a room in the house, talk to her grandfather, and so on. As we talked about this, mother finally joined in and it became clear that she was preoccupied with the question of whether her mother would continue to disbelieve them both. She again talked about the difficulty she experienced in not being believed by her and thus for this reason wanted to avoid any confrontation with her parents. I raised the possibility that being believed may not necessarily have been the main issue, particularly for Beryl. For her, it may simply be important to raise their voices.

HR: [*to ACM*] I think the problem here is the issue of saying that Mrs Davis has got to find a way out for Beryl when she herself has been subject to the abuse. Then there is also the issue of who can help *her [Mrs Davis*] . . .

ACM: I'm aware of that, I've not forgotten, but we mustn't assume that every woman who's been abused does not grow her strength again. And Mrs Davis has given us a fairly good account of how she has grown strong, and maybe doesn't know her own strength. [*As ACM speaks, Mrs Davis nodded several times and made noises of agreement.*]

ACM: I know she went through a very traumatic experience but I think she has come out the other side.

Mrs Davis: [*very firmly*] Oh I know that I have got the strength, because I've got the anger.

ACM: That's right, that's right, and you need to help Beryl to get rid of this fear.

In this family, several issues could be highlighted – the closeness between mother and daughter, the way in which mother speaks for daughter, their lack of separation, their unwillingness to bring their men to the session. It is also likely that the anger which Beryl has not mobilized must inevitably include much anger against her mother. How could she not know or not guess the truth when she herself had been abused by the same man? There is, though, no hint of this in

Beryl's demeanour. My aim in this session was to support these two women and also to challenge their current arrangements and start to distinguish their separate needs. Beryl's mother has believed her, Marcia's has not. Marcia's intervention as Beryl discusses seeing her grandfather again highlights her own preoccupation with being believed by her mother. This is not Beryl's issue at this point, it is Marcia's and has probably paralysed her throughout. The therapist could have addressed the differences directly by helping them distinguish their separate preoccupations more clearly. However, by simply opening up a new possibility for Beryl, the *idea* of confronting grandfather, and by affirming Mrs Davis's strength as a woman who had recovered from abuse, I hoped to achieve a qualitative change in direction in their relationship. The 'mother who does *not* believe the daughter' was therefore *not* highlighted or amplified (the grandmother–mother diad) whereas the mother who did believe the daughter (mother–daughter diad) was confirmed. The construction of an event, whether in imagination or reality, wherein the females recover their voice with the man who abused them, was framed as one which the two women could achieve alone, with the mother helping her daughter. Further work at a later stage might then address the circumstances that allowed this mother to succeed with her daughter in comparison with the system which had maintained her own mother in silence.

It is tempting, when faced with a woman who appears to be 'failing' in her nurturant role, to focus on her deficiencies and make them a target for change. The mothers of the women I started with, who had such difficulties in acknowledging their daughters, could easily have become a target for blame which therapy may have covertly reinforced.

Work which focuses on the differences and similarities between mother and daughter in being part of a system that include real differences in power between men and women is more likely to seek out the strengths in both mothers and daughters and to help women construct realities in which they can challenge abuses of power. Otherwise therapy runs the risk of reproducing the structures of power that keep women in the position of mutual betrayal.

Notes

1. Prevalence is more likely, according to a variety of studies, to be between one in forty and one in twenty (Markowe 1988; Mullen *et al.* 1988).
2. All names and identifying details have been changed to protect the

confidentiality of the clients.

3. Some of these themes have been very interestingly outlined by McLeod and Saraga (1988) in their recent review of trends in the study of child sexual abuse.
4. Senior Social Worker, Marlborough Family Service.

References

Briere, J. (1984) 'The effects of childhood sexual abuse on later psychological functioning: defining a post-sexual-abuse syndrome', paper presented at the Third National Conference on Sexual Victimization of Children, Washington, DC.

Eisenberg, N. and Owens, R.G. (1987) 'Attitudes of health professionals to child sexual abuse and incest', *Child Abuse and Neglect* 11: 109–16.

Finkelhor, D. (1984) *Child Sexual Abuse: New Theory and Research*, New York: The Free Press.

Hirsch, M. (1986) 'Brief communication: Narcissism and partial lack of reality testing (denial) in incestuous fathers', *Child Abuse and Neglect* 10(4).

McCarthy, F. (1989) *Eric Gill*, London: Faber.

MacLeod, M. and Saraga, E. (1988) 'Challenging the orthodoxy: towards a feminist theory and practice', *Feminist Review* 28 (January).

Markowe, H.L.J. (1988) 'The frequency of childhood sexual abuse in the UK', *Health Trends* 20.

Mullen, P., Romans-Clarkson, S., Walton, V., and Herbison, G. (1988) 'Impact of sexual and physical abuse on women's mental health', *The Lancet* 16 April.

Chapter eight

Intelligence, achievement, and gender: the ramifications of a case-study

Anne Heavey

> The family uses people, *not* for what they are, nor for what they are intended to be, but for what it wants them for – its own uses. It thinks of them not as what God has made them, but as something which it has arranged that they shall be. If it wants someone to sit in the drawing room, *that* someone is supplied by the family, though that member may be destined for science or for education, or for active superintendance by God, i.e. by the gifts within.
>
> This system dooms some minds to incurable infancy, others to silent misery.
>
> (Nightingale 1852; original emphasis)

Awareness would appear to be increasing of the importance of taking on board in family therapy the power dynamics that exist between men and women in the world outside the therapy session (Walters 1988; Goodrich *et al.* 1988). This chapter illustrates an attempt to do so in the case of therapy which the author and a team of colleagues undertook with a family where a young woman was functioning way below her intellectual potential and regarded as mentally handicapped. As a context for the enquiry into explanations for her position, the author reviews the organic, socio-cultural, and emotional factors, and their interplay in the genesis of intellectual impairment, while drawing on psychodynamic and feminist insights into the nature of handicap. The notion of relative mental handicap as a metaphor for the lot of many women in our society is mooted.

In this case it is postulated that, even assuming some subtle organic predisposition to handicap, this woman's condition was ultimately a manifestation of her subordinate role in a family which needed to polarize quite starkly the roles of women and men in the service of the latter's power over the former. The author presents a rationale for using the mother–daughter relationship as the main therapeutic focus and discusses issues arising in therapy around mothering and dependence and separation between mothers and daughters; as well as family beliefs about the vulnerability of women; and the power balance between the marital partners.

Family problems and background

Ruth, aged 28, and her husband David, aged 29, referred themselves for family therapy.[1] Depressed and demoralized, they complained that Ruth's parents, the source of their entire financial support, controlled their lives and interfered in every decision – for example, about spending or David's career. Most recently arguments raged over where they should live, the upbringing of their children, and the amount of grandparental contact. Ruth, who felt no one took what she said seriously, was withdrawing from the close relationship she had with her mother. The latter had stepped up her involvement with the grandchildren, enraging David. Meanwhile, everyone was worrying about Ruth's father, whose heart symptoms had worsened. To begin with, Ruth looked withdrawn and passive, in drab dress and untidy hair. She sat hunched over or sprawled awkwardly, constantly handling her face, her shifting glances alternating with a vacant gaze. Her speech was indistinct and incoherent and she seemed a little deaf. David's appearance, posture, and dress also conveyed his low mood, but his speech, which was articulate, betrayed anger and frustration.

Ruth's mother and father were Roman Catholics and of second-generation Italian and Polish extraction respectively. They met and married when he was a manager in her father's engineering works and spent some years in Canada pursuing his career before Ruth's birth. He returned to take over the family business, developing it into a highly successful concern which was to yield him a large personal fortune. His parents died in their fifties, the father from a heart attack, and the mother from cancer, and he had since lost six of ten siblings through one of the same two conditions. He was now 72, and had thyroid and heart disease. Ruth's mother, at 58, was healthy and energetic. A highly intelligent, articulate woman, who could be taken for a graduate, she actually left school at 14, married at 18, and never developed her education potential formally, or any career outside the home. From an early age the main use of her talents had been to impress men; 'If I had a boy-friend interested in racing cars, I would mug up on racing cars.' She was now a devoted grandmother of seven, but closest of all to Ruth's children, two boys aged 6 and 4 and a girl aged 3.

Ruth's parents shared social and cultural interests but the mother bemoaned her husband's emotional self-control which, she said, deprived her of the arguments she had been used to in her own family and left her carrying worries about his health, which he denied. His preoccupation was with the vulnerability of the women, if he died; he believed that his wife's happiness would depend then on remarriage and that Ruth could not survive without his money (and her husband's protection). Their three sons, whose turbulent teens were a source of poorly resolved conflict, were since married, settled in successful careers, and no longer caused concern.

Ruth, their only daughter and the youngest, had been the centre of their lives since she was born. Pregnancy, her birth, and early infancy had all seemed normal, but compared to her brothers she was slow to walk and talk. 'Attacks', observed by her father from the age of 3 when she would appear to lose contact with her surroundings, was diagnosed and treated as epilepsy until Ruth decided to stop medication just before family therapy began. (Tests, including an electroencephalogram had been equivocal.) The 'attacks', 'tantrums', and her poor academic performance were the subject of further extensive investigation by many experts over the years, revealing, according to her father, a low IQ, although he could not quote the levels.[2] Neither an organic explanation nor confirmation of a language, speech, or hearing problem, suspected by us, had emerged.

She attended several schools including one for the educationally subnormal. She was never to develop any interests or make friends and was said by her parents to be 'incapable' of any independent action (notwithstanding a story of her going on holiday alone in her teens to visit family friends in Italy, where she coped well and enjoyed herself). Like her mother, a career was out of the question for Ruth in contrast to her brothers and father, who were high achievers in the world of work. Likewise, 'it was unthinkable' to her parents that she should ever marry – that is until David was identified as a suitable husband. (His grandmother, who had reared him since his mother died, was known to Ruth's parents.) Although aware of his unstable work record, they felt he could take care of Ruth. Having failed to benefit from his father-in-law's efforts to establish him in a career in publishing, David ran the home and did most of the parenting. Ruth, who he believed did 'not have the wherewithal to cope', let him be the 'top dog'. Neither of them had any friends, and they relied for their social outlets on her socially adept parents.

Theoretical understanding and framework for therapy

The core conceptual framework invoked to address the many complex questions raised by this family's problems, both during therapy and in the subsequent analysis of it, was that which underpins systemic family therapy.[3] Drawing on the Milan school of systemic therapy, strategies were employed to explore and modify the rules and beliefs governing destructive patterns of family behaviour, while taking account of their context (Palazzoli *et al.* 1978; Tomm 1984). We are also indebted to the interpretation of systemic thinking developed by the structural school of family therapy for insights and therapeutic techniques designed to provide family members with direct experience, in the session, of different ways of relating (Minuchin 1974, 1979). Psychoanalytic theory enriched our appreciation of the link between intrapsychic development and the individual's experience of family relationships; and helped to elucidate the many striking defence mechanisms (such as denial, projection, and projective identification) operating in this family (Brown and Pedder 1979). The biomedical model was essential to a full assessment of Ruth's intellectual capacity.

Of particular value in the attempt to draw together this collage of apparently disparate ideas and techniques into an integrative model along the lines explored by others (Rakoff 1984; Kantor and Neal 1985; Will and Wrate 1985) was Kantor and Neal's (1985) idea of disentangling techniques from theoretical schools so that those associated with seemingly incompatible schools could be used together within a framework of shifting stances – that is, different degrees of engagement with or distance from the family. Within this more open framework there was scope for experimenting therapeutically with the therapist's use of her own personality; the pursuit of humour and metaphor (Napier and Whitaker 1978); and attention to gender issues.

Feminist input

From the outset, the problems in this family struck us as particularly interwoven with members' different experiences of their lives as men and women. This understanding evolved in the course of and since therapy in the context of an increasing acquaintance with the contribution to therapy in general (including family therapy) of feminist thinking, to which brief reference is now made. Feminism entails a recognition of gender differences and proposes an analysis of their origins and consequences in terms of the power invested in men over women in our patriarchal society (Goodrich *et al.* 1988).[4] Walrond-Skinner (1987: 74) argues that: 'The splitting, polarising and labelling of characteristics as male or female and all the sex stereotyping that then follows from this process is damaging to men and women, although in different ways, and perhaps too, in different degrees.' She also discusses evidence which suggests 'that women are handicapped both psychologically, developmentally and environmentally in the task of becoming mature and fulfilled human beings' (ibid.: 75).

Concern has been voiced that conventional psychotherapy, particularly psychoanalytically oriented individual psychotherapy, far from acting in the interests of women and challenging patriarchal structures which debilitate them, can re-enact in the psychotherapy relationship the same oppressive dynamics (Smith and David 1975; Penfold and Walker 1984; Walrond-Skinner and Watson 1987). As an alternative, feminism itself has been advanced as therapy for women (Mander and Rush 1974; Ernst and Goodison 1981) and others have struggled to reform existing theory and practice in the creation of a feminist therapy (Eichenbaum and Orbach 1982; Greenspan 1983). Walrond-Skinner (1987), however, questions the efficacy and ethics in some instances of therapy involving only the individual woman, although she sympathizes with feminist therapists' caution in espousing family therapy.

This caution derives partly from the feminist critique of the family as the crucible of patriarchy (Barrett and McIntosh 1982) and partly from the hitherto neglect by family therapists of the crucial variables of gender and power inequalities between men and women – an omission seen as curiously at odds with their putative concern for the context of the individual and the family's problems. Goodrich *et al.* (1988) contend that family therapy 'has dangerously narrowed the notion of system', and 'Since the family is a social unit that expresses society's values, the failure of therapists to address issues of gender role stereotyping and what constitutes a "normal" family perpetuates theory, practice, and training that are oppressive to women.' These writers' own attempts to develop a critique of current family-therapy practice and a cohesive theory of feminist family therapy represent one answer to Walrond-Skinner's (1987) plea for a convergence and cross-fertilization of the two movements, feminism and family therapy, in the interests of women *and* men.

The nature of intelligence and its impairment

Our efforts to understand and work with this family centred primarily on an enquiry into the experiences and roles of Ruth in relation to other members. The nature and extent of her intellectual handicap, and the degree to which her performance was a reflection of this, were considered. Certain historical details suggested she might be mildly mentally handicapped; but she was cared for and behaved as if her capabilities were *less* than those of mild mental handicap; her role functions and associated emotional and social responses were disproportionately poor in relation to the intellectual ability she was supposed to have. Evidence from the family and from our own experience, however, indicated that her intellectual potential might be *greater* than previously suspected – indeed, normal. We wondered how such an apparent discrepancy between her potential and actual functioning as an adult could have arisen, and how she came to be at the centre of an intricate web of protection. Exploration of these considerations is preceded now by a review of the factors that can impair or suppress intellectual functioning.

The origins of mental handicap

The interplay of organic, social, and emotional factors

The origins and nature of intellectual impairment or mental handicap are no less complex than those of intelligence itself[5] – a complexity reflected in the profusion and confusion of the terminology used to address the former.[6] Two main (but overlapping) categories of mental handicap are recognized; pathological or organic, and subcultural. The former arises from brain disease processes originating in genetic or chromosomal abnormalities or from damage before, during, or after birth; often severe, it may be associated with epilepsy and sensory deficits like deafness or poor sight, compounding the handicap; and it spans the social classes but is the mode in the privileged groups, where mild handicap is rare (Penrose 1972). Subcultural or familial/cultural mental handicap (Stein and Susser 1962) refers to the vast bulk of handicap, which is without identifiable organic basis, is usually mild, and clusters in a subgroup of socially disadvantaged families. Its basis is thought to be a combination of polygenic inheritance of low intelligence and severe social and educational deprivation.

Apparent mental handicap may arise independent of social class from physical factors which retard development and learning like unrecognized deafness, poor sight, and the effects of chronic illness and treatment. It may also stem from emotional deprivation, where children lack the security and stimulation to achieve their potential (Bowlby 1965) and from unconscious suppression of a child's achievements by insecure uneducated parents who need to defend a fragile self-esteem (Baroff 1974). However, emotional and social strands in the origin of mental handicap interweave in such a complex way with the organic that objection has been raised to a simplistic disentangling (Sinason 1986), on the basis that, for example, research has shown that learning difficulties are indistinguishable in brain-damaged and non-brain-damaged children. Doll's (1953) distinction between 'true' subnormality attributed to brain damage, and 'pseudo' mental deficiency attributed to the blockage of intelligence by powerful emotional factors, is being replaced by the notions of primary handicap, referring to the original brain damage (if any), and secondary handicap, referring to the result of psychological and social factors contributing to handicap, whether or not there is identifiable brain damage (Sinason 1986).

The handicapping effects of organic defects, of whatever order, may be exaggerated or minimized depending on the response of the environment, including family members and professionals (Symington 1981). This entails a dynamic interaction to which the child is party. Some children with minimal brain damage and subtle language difficulties may incur unavoidable secondary handicap as a result of the reciprocal interactions with carers and peers who are bound to respond differently to their unusual ways of communicating compared with normal children. Hollins (1987) cautions against adopting a blaming attitude in such circumstances. Special schooling with long separation from family following a diagnosis of mental handicap may impede development by depriving the child of the ordinary social and occupational outlets. Further burdens may be conferred by insight into the nature of the handicap, the social stigma of labels like 'handicap', 'backward', and 'epileptic', as well as by an awareness of others' reactions to them, and internalization of these stereotypes (Bicknell 1983).

Psychodynamic understanding

Some defensive uses of secondary handicap have been suggested (Sinason 1986; Stokes 1987), taking account of the observation that all of us can oscillate between handicapped and non-handicapped parts of the personality, entering for a period 'a "stupid" state of mind in order to obliterate aspects of a world that are hated' (Stokes 1987: 4). Sinason (1986) advances the notion of secondary handicap as a protection against the memory of trauma, either of the original organic insult itself or of abuse (physical or sexual). She further distinguishes an opportunistic group in which the original handicap is more extensively exaggerated in order to deal with envy and hostility, and severe personality disturbances (including an attack on intact intelligence) are exhibited; some in this group may have been abused. A 'symptom-trapping effect' has also been described, whereby a defensive acting into the label of mental handicap incurs further disabling labels such as lazy or naughty and psychiatric diagnoses (Bicknell 1983).

Some mentally handicapped children, like those in the opportunistic group above, may have introjected feelings, at first normal for parents of a mentally handicapped child, but later destructive if unresolved: hence the importance for parents to mourn the loss of the ideal child (Bicknell 1983). This is difficult, even in families where organic damage is obvious and powerful projective mechanisms are not so operative; the child can come to represent for them the handicapped and damaged aspects they want to be rid of (Stokes 1987). Resolution entails working through the related death wishes, feelings of hatred, rejection, and guilt; and re-owning the projected handicapped aspects. Only then can the child with his or her handicap, and the parents' depression about it, be properly accepted. Realistic appraisal and encouragement of the child's abilities is thereafter possible.

Failure of this process and denial of feelings, especially guilt, may lead to a compensating protectiveness which inhibits the learning of daily living skills and experience of risks necessary for growth and development. Infantilized and dependent, the child is made to underfunction and its handicap seems worse than it really is. The dread of separation, which is associated with the rejection against which the overcloseness was a defence in the first place (ibid.), may mount to a crisis as parents age and the prospect of parental death raises anxieties about future care of the handicapped person.

Feminist understanding

Psychological separation from their children, whether normal or not, is problematical for many women, particularly in respect of daughters. This is rooted in their strong identification with each other and shared psychosocial experiences (Chodorow 1987). It has been observed that if a mother has been living through her child and has achieved her identity through her mothering role, her sense of who she is may be put in jeopardy and she may feel depressed, empty, and confused when her child separates (Eichenbaum and Orbach 1982). A daughter sensitive to the extreme needs of her mother in this respect may fail to achieve the degree of separation necessary to develop her own potential.

Research points to the influence of the mother–daughter relationship on the daughter's destiny showing 'how the crucial factor generating independence in girls – and thus intellectual achievement – is "freedom to wander and explore", an absence of maternal restrictiveness' (Oakley 1972: 9). But studies of mothers' behaviour towards their daughters engaged in problem solving indicate that while the mother's behaviour may be a response to the child's own difficulties, through her closer identification with a daughter than with a son, the mother may transmit her own fear of failure and lack of self-confidence to her daughter. In becoming women, daughters also learn from their mothers to curb their desires, defer and submit, and acquire a fear of striving for independence or power. Thus, women who do most of the socializing of children, are unwitting agents in the perpetuation of their own oppression down the generations (Eichenbaum and Orbach 1982).

Highly intelligent and achievement-oriented women, it is argued, possess a motive to avoid success and, 'when faced with a conflict between their feminine image and expressing their competencies or developing their abilities or interests, adjust their behaviours to their internalized sex-role stereotypes' (Horner 1987: 183). Concern exists, however, that this focus on women's supposed fear of success may reinforce a popular belief that differences in educational and occupational achievement in men and women arise from innate differences in ability (Paludi 1987), when evidence abounds to show that women's under-achievement, far from reflecting an inferior intellectual capacity in comparison to men, is rather a reflection of the conflicting priorities and restricted opportunities with which they are presented (Curran 1988). Feminist scholarship has revealed how women's intellectual development and success have been suppressed (ibid.; McNeil 1987) and how their knowledge and accomplishments have been devalued or kept 'off the record' in patriarchal society (Spender 1982), depriving women of role models. A study of women's experience of their education found that 'without exception, the most salient feature remembered by all was the sense of activities and aspirations that were forbidden' (ibid.). Oakley (1972) cites a follow-up study of children with IQs of 170 + where no correlation between occupational achievement and measured IQ was found for girls, though there was plenty for boys (two-thirds of the girls had ended up as housewives or office workers).

And why has women's potential been stifled? Educationists from Rousseau in the eighteenth century through to Newsom in the twentieth have held that women were created for the purpose of caring for the family and serving men. Woolf (1928: 37) pointed out that 'Women have served all these centuries as looking-glasses possessing the magic and delicious power of reflecting the figure of man at twice its natural size.' The fulfilment of this patriarchal expectation, that women exist to meet the needs of men, depends on a variety of intrapsychic, interpersonal, and institutional forces interacting to control the lives and minds of women. In the sense that this process thwarts women's intellectual development and achievements in the world, mental handicap can be used as a metaphor for the female condition in general in our society, affecting the mass of women to some degree. For a number, the effects are not just a relative limitation but a stunting so severe, with or without organic influences, that they become clinical cases of mental handicap. This is not to deny that the minds of men cannot also be stunted, only that the social process is different.

The process of family therapy

Explanatory hypotheses

In the context of the ideas and data just presented, the following hypotheses consider how this family's difficulties evolved out of the interaction of socio-cultural influences and previous family events, which in turn shaped the past and current reactions of individuals and patterns of relationships in response to their personal and shared life experiences. Evidence for these statements emerged during therapy sessions.

The case turned on two main beliefs: that Ruth was irreversibly mentally handicapped and that she needed care and protection. These became the focus of a contest between the family and the therapy team.

There was in fact little support for these beliefs. If she were handicapped, it was mild and an organic basis was not in evidence. It could not be attributed here to inheritance of low parental intelligence or social deprivation. The family justified its beliefs and behaviour in relation to Ruth on expert opinion; but, through their interventions, the professionals promoted (unwittingly, perhaps, even allowing for attitudes and practices at the time) an impression of a biological defect and reinforced an image of Ruth as a permanently handicapped epileptic in need of treatment and special care – thus conferring further handicap.

Instead, her greater underlying potential was indicated both by historical accounts (for example, of her travelling abroad separately from her parents) and by our observations in therapy. Moreover, her mother's remark that 'Had she not been in a family of high achievers, she might have been regarded as having nothing the matter with her' supported the view that her intelligence was only low relative to other family members and might have been normal by the standards of the general population. But assuming that her intellectual capacity *was* lower than the rest of the family's and even assuming subtle brain damage (which cannot be conclusively ruled out), Ruth was still functioning well below her capabilities and was disproportionately handicapped in the exercise of her adult role. In accounting for this, her mother's comment indicates that for this family intelligence and achievement had a special significance, partly explicable as the legacy of previous generations of immigrants, reflecting their losses and strivings.

Ruth was also singled out by her gender as the only female child. She was undoubtedly affected by the family's different expectations of male and female members, conditioned by the common social belief that high achievement is predominantly men's destiny; her brothers' abilities were taken for granted as were her father's. But her mother had to mute in herself the intelligence she admired in her husband. Unable to achieve in men's terms, she channelled her talents into the family, her acquiescence in the roles of dutiful wife and mother consistent with the social expectations of women, particularly in the Italian Catholic tradition.

The parents were emotionally poles apart; the mother had subordinated her fiery argumentative temperament to the emotional control of her husband, who thus embodied the social stereotypes of men, in the face of several devastating bereavements and his own brushes with death (through two severe heart attacks). The denied anxieties and vulnerabilities, from which he escaped through driving ambition, were visited again and again upon the women, who were perceived as in need of protection through marriage (and men's money). As in society at large, this was one source of the father's power over his wife and daughter, while they unconsciously carried the burden of his fear of failure and incompetence. Finding it difficult to confront and resolve differences, they avoided conflict and submerged it in their preoccupation with Ruth's welfare. Here they were united in their definition of her as backward and in need of care, and had a common goal in looking after her and her family – a task which, even with its handicapping consequences, had to continue for the sake of marital harmony.

The patriarchal exercise of power through money and the generational hierarchy also extended to David, who personified the family's requirements for a husband for Ruth. He was capable of looking after her, but his failure in a career and alleged fecklessness with money allowed Ruth's parents to maintain control over him and thus over their daughter. Ruth acquiesced in her own oppression in her marriage first because she had internalized the idea of the man as the 'top dog' (her words); second, to protect her husband whose precarious margin of competence she had accurately spotted; and third, as a service to her mother, her model.

The complex interaction between intelligence, achievement, and gender was particularly evident in the mother–daughter relationship. The mother's close involvement with her daughter compensated for the dissatisfactions of the wife's role and the emotional lacks in her marriage. With no alternative in sight it was hard for her to let go of her children through whom her needs had been vicariously met. Her sons were not so readily held or dominated (she could not compete in the male realm they had entered). Ruth, however, as a daughter, the youngest, and appearing to need permanent help was perfectly cast to fulfil her mother's needs to feel competent and fulfilled through caring for others and to experience her own power in relation to them: hence her perpetual mothering of Ruth and her children.

The cost, however, was the sacrifice of Ruth's own autonomy and independent adult life under the guise of a mother protecting her handicapped daughter. But Ruth, in underachieving, was protecting *her*. Aware at some level of the fragility of her mother's emotional position, Ruth was afraid to succeed and expose her mother to the pain of losing her role and perhaps worse, of being surpassed by her daughter. (When asked what might happen if Ruth caught up with her, her mother exclaimed 'I shudder to think!')

Ruth fulfilled the need of family members generally, including her husband, for a receptacle for the disavowed handicapped aspects of themselves. Her containing of the incompetence, vulnerability, and dependency fears of others allowed them to gain unconscious relief and a sense of fulfilment in caring for the person so handicapped. Their need for Ruth in this condition offset the resentment and rejection they would have felt for the container of their negative projections. This was the basis for the difficulty they had in allowing Ruth to separate; it would have entailed their taking back these unwanted areas.

Why now?

The family was immobilized at an earlier developmental stage of its life cycle, preoccupied in caring for Ruth, whose development in many respects had been truncated at a pre-adolescent level. The family as a whole was thus blocked from responding appropriately to other life-cycle issues which time was pressing upon them. First, Ruth's father was ageing, his health was deteriorating, and his death would mean that, symbolically at least, the women would be left in a vulnerable state. What would become of her mother? She was poised either to intensify her involvement with the younger generation, to maintain some role, or she could at last make a life of her own. How would Ruth cope, and could David continue to care for her? But this couple also seemed to be preparing themselves for greater independence, financial and emotional, from the previous generation. Thus, their self-referral at this time could be seen as a bid for freedom in the face of the impending breakdown of the old order.

Practicalities of therapy

The therapist worked with a team who watched from behind a one-way screen and communicated with her through an ear-bug. Team discussions occurred during sessions and always prior to the final message to the family. Study of the therapy was possible between sessions and, since termination, from video-tapes and transcripts of the sessions as well as records of team discussions.

Goals of therapy

The family-therapy team worked with the family towards achieving what the couple wanted – namely, relief from intensely fraught family relationships and the misery and distress (which they shared with other family members) about their feeling that they were totally dominated by Ruth's parents. They also sought greater control over all areas of their lives. In order to accomplish and maintain these results and prevent further disablement, the therapy team explored with the family the need to change the processes which led to the presenting problems, and evolved the following objectives:

(1) to help Ruth and the family to discover and use more fully her intellectual and social capabilities and to support her in developing greater competence and autonomy as she shifted from a child–parent relationship to an adult interaction with her parents;
(2) to enable Ruth's parents to redefine more appropriately their parenting and grandparenting roles, and to encourage them to face avoided conflict-ridden areas such as ageing, concern about the father's health and feared death, and the mother's interest in self-development;
(3) to these ends, to identify and reinforce the strengths and supports both inside and outside the parental relationship, especially for Ruth's mother while she struggled for self-determination as her daughter became more independent of her;
(4) to work similarly with Ruth and David to make their relationship a more balanced one, and support David in responding constructively to his wife's increasing autonomy; and also to increase their self-confidence in their executive functions such as parenting and financial management.

The aim was to match therapeutic interventions to these goals according to the different dimensions of change they entailed – that is, perceptive, behavioural, and affective. Thus the therapy team endeavoured:

(1) to open the family to different and broader perceptions of the roles of men and women in the family and of Ruth's intellectual capacity;
(2) to deal with issues of power, hierarchy, and cross-generational alliances by expanding family members' repertoire of responses through direct experience of alternative interactions – for example, encouraging Ruth to impose limits on her parents' involvement with her children;
(3) to assist the family to explore and resolve conflict and repressed emotions, and support them, especially Ruth's mother, in coping with complex feelings of guilt, inadequacy, and loss, in the face of Ruth's growing competence and independence.

Plan and stages of therapy

Careful thought was given by the team, in discussion with the family, to the structure of therapy over time in terms of which family members attended particular sessions. This process constituted one level of therapeutic intervention since it entailed circumscribing the relationship of the individuals in the subgroups attending a particular session. It was useful in demarcating boundaries, for example in dealing with gender and generational issues.

Eleven sessions occurred at variable intervals over eight months and none was unattended, except the last offered, when it was cancelled by agreement between therapist and family.

Session 1: Ruth and David alone – presenting the main problems.
Session 2: Their nuclear family (a boundary-making composition requested despite their wish to involve Ruth's parents from the beginning) – main emphasis still on delineation of problems.
Sessions 3 and 4: The two couples – intensive work on intergenerational boundaries, issues of hierarchy and power; use of structural techniques, and challenge to the family belief system; mother–daughter relationship identified as a central focus of therapy.
Session 5: Three generations – mother, Ruth, and Ruth's children – to work on the women's common role of mothering and on Ruth's development.
Session 6: Mother and daughter alone – continued intensity and conflict in their relationship addressed; a shift to a mutually supportive adult relationship facilitated; attention drawn to shared experiences as adult women in relation to men in the family; disequilibrium in the family, especially in mother, noted in response to Ruth's increasing independence; mother's supports explored.
Session 7: Ruth's parents alone – strengths and mutual supports

within the relationship reinforced; beliefs about women's vulnerability, potential, and independence addressed; feelings around ageing, illness, and loss explored.

Devoting the *last 4 sessions (8–11)* to Ruth and David's relationship underscored the importance of strengthening its boundary and healthy functioning.

Feminist issues in the therapy process

> The goal of feminist therapy is the attainment of autonomous relating adults, of people being able to be together yet not fearing separateness.
>
> (Osborne 1983)

I now discuss selected aspects of the therapy process which centre mainly on the question of gender. This retrospective analysis draws on video recordings of therapy sessions and notes of team discussions and includes in parentheses statements made in sessions. It constitutes an amalgam of ideas and insights which arose since as well as during therapy.

Our awareness of the inextricable link between gender issues and this family's problems grew gradually, as did attempts to interweave this awareness with the practice of therapy. We were helped by several factors. Workshops and a conference in our work-place addressed the subject of gender and family therapy. In small but significant ways, the effect was to stimulate and legitimize efforts by some therapists to explore and incorporate this thinking in their practice. Also, the fact that four of the five members of our team were women heightened (without necessarily guaranteeing) an increased sensitivity to the power relations of men and women. Although as individuals we differed in stages of feminist awareness, all – including our male colleague – were receptive to discussing the gender issues raised during therapy.

However, we were without the benefit of a coherent framework of feminist family therapy in which to hold our thoughts and feelings about the different plights of the women and men in the family (the therapy predated some of the aforementioned writings on the subject). This and our expounding of the systemic model of family therapy, criticized for its failure to take on board gender issues (Goodrich *et al.* 1988), meant that our work was often not gender sensitive. To the extent that it was, it was related to a growing consciousness of the issues which shaped the attitude of the therapist; this in itself constituted an intervention since attitude communicated itself to the family, often in subtle non-verbal and unconscious ways (some detectable through study of video-tapes of the sessions). At times the therapist also touched more directly on questions of gender stereotyping, trying to link this with the family's problems in a way that might facilitate change.

Having a feminist awareness could be seen to influence the therapist in deciding which of the many themes arising at any one time to pursue; it also put a responsibility on her to avoid sexist practices – difficult within the constraints of the general context of the therapy. However, while remaining sensitive to gender issues, it seemed quite possible to use successfully some of the standard family-therapy principles and techniques, such as the circular questioning of the Milan school or the structural method of alliance building with individuals, to challenge sexist beliefs and behaviour.

Analysis of tapes reveals instances when intervention by the therapist and team were informed by a feminist influence motivated by an intuitive or unconscious appreciation of the issues involved. But equally, while well aware, at times, that power inequalities between men and women in the family had a direct bearing on their painful predicaments, we seemed to be ignoring this link. In these moments we may have been overtaken by feelings of helplessness by reason of our inadequate conceptual and technical framework; or because of identification with (and a transference to us of) the experiences of the women in the family. More open and explicit sharing of team members' responses was one way of ensuring that our sensitivity to the issues was less a handicap and more a source of therapeutic effectiveness.

The mother–daughter relationship

For several reasons, the mother–daughter relationship was chosen as the main focus of therapeutic interventions designed to achieve the goals and objectives outlined. With gender issues so pivotal in this family's problems, this may seem a strange choice, given that these women already carried the burden of responsibility for the family. We may have been influenced by our sense that women are generally more willing to change than men. This may be so because women would appear to have less to lose by changing. It may also explain in part why therapists (especially structural ones) tend to join with men but go to women for change.

But we also felt that this relationship, which carried the greatest emotional intensity, could be most readily escalated towards a crisis, whereupon mother and daughter would have to find new ways of relating; and these effects would ricochet through the whole family system. It was only later that we recognized the moral dilemma

(Walrond-Skinner and Watson 1987). However, given that the women shared handicaps generated by patriarchal society, it made sense to work with them together to foster their competence and independence. Finally, because change in the daughter was likely to threaten and isolate her mother more than any other family member, work with both enabled the therapist to be in touch with and support the mother in her struggle to adapt.

In order for Ruth to 'grow up', her mother had to change her perception of her. This was very stressful since it forced her (like other family members) to re-open the feelings of inadequacy and failure which had been incorporated by Ruth. She also had to deal with the loss of aspects of her role as protector of Ruth and the grandchildren. It was important that the separation should not be seen as a wrenching apart of the women but rather as a redefining and restructuring of their roles and interactions so that their continuing bond would be mutually empowering. The challenge was to find ways of building Ruth's confidence without knocking her mother down. The task was made more difficult by the fury aroused in team members by the mother's interaction with her daughter and the temptation to blame her (notwithstanding systemic wisdom); the therapist felt less strongly in these respects, probably because, through her much closer contact, she sensed the mother's vulnerability behind the frantic domination of her daughter.

The therapist began working directly with the women in response to the mother's incessant thwarting of her daughter's every effort to communicate while at the same time insisting that they had 'no conflict' in their relationship. This was an opportunity to try to make the denied conflicts explicit and to facilitate some degree of resolution through direct experience in the session. The therapist allied herself with Ruth, supporting her in expressing herself and in challenging her mother. This early work was coloured by the presence of the men. Afterwards the therapist was self-critical of allowing them to witness this disempowering of the mother, since she realized that patriarchal culture feeds on men's encouragement and exploitation of rivalry and competition between women and also on blaming mothers. However, the issue arose while the men happened to be present, and thereafter the therapist made a point of seeing the women together without them. Bearing in mind the overall goal of developing a co-operative, supportive relationship between the women, there may have been some advantage in the men's presence at the outset; it enabled them to raise their consciousness of the women's situation and alerted them to the implications for them of change in the women, and the need to think about ways of coping. Meanwhile, they were not allowed to interrupt; this was a counter to the usual male domination of verbal interactions (Spender 1980), and gave the women maximum space in the context of their presence.

The next session centred on the theme of mothering (especially of daughters); Ruth and her mother were seen together with Ruth's children who provided an intergenerational backdrop for addressing the reality that, despite being a mother herself, Ruth remained in a child-like role *vis-à-vis* her own mother. Their presence also lent an immediacy to the exploration of Ruth's developmental process and the mother's related guilt and anxieties, reflected in her criticisms of Ruth's handling of her children, especially the little girl, and her need to usurp Ruth's mothering role; it also provided an entrée into addressing the mother's own vicariously fulfilled needs for care and feelings of competence.

Mindful of the painful path which the mother had to tread as her daughter was 'going through the developmental stage she should have done years ago' (the mother's words), the therapist strove to be supportive of her as well as maintaining her alliance with Ruth and challenging the mother's beliefs about her daughter's capabilities. This approach was complemented by positive reframing and affirmation both of Ruth's mothering and of her mother's ability to be a good grandmother. Ruth was struggling to articulate her need for autonomy, and her wish for her father to believe that she was capable of speaking her own mind. Her mother's critical competitiveness was softened as her fragility began to show in the face of Ruth's new assertiveness. She was startled by Ruth's statement that she 'just woke up'. Ruth joined the therapist in developing the notion of 'waking up' as a metaphor for her emergence from her long suppression. It seemed that the metaphor was equally apt for the mother's process and indeed for that of the members of the therapy team themselves as they tried to grapple with the gender issues.

Women together

Session 6 was set up for mother and daughter alone, to continue the focus on their relationship as adult women. Several reported examples of Ruth's emerging independence and the associated emotional disequilibrium of her mother were addressed, using the strengths, warmth, and humour in their relationship. Ruth smartly reframed her mother's pejorative reference to her 'rebelling' by stating quite firmly and simply 'I want to be an individual.' At the moment when the mother said despairingly that Ruth's behaviour was 'eccentric' and an 'overkill', and 'upsets me so much I can't hold together on it', the therapist earnestly asked Ruth: 'Who could support your mother while she's having to live with your standing up to her in this way . . .

so strongly and independently?' Ruth sat upright and, with more expression in her face and voice than heretofore, revealed her mature concern for her mother. She assessed perceptively the merits of the various figures in her mother's life – her father ('probably not'); several of her mother's friends (definitely, except one having trouble with her husband); and 'even my brothers'.

The mother's distress and need for comfort was acknowledged, while Ruth's strivings for autonomy were encouraged. The content of the question and the manner of the questioner presupposed that Ruth possessed the wisdom and judgement to see to her mother's needs in a responsible adult way and this may have allowed the women to experience a reversal of their usual entrenched roles in respect of caring. This process was reinforced by the therapist's consulting of Ruth who, thus invited into a co-therapy role, could identify with the therapist as a model of competent womanhood. For her part, Ruth taught us a lot; the importance of not assuming that marriage could or should be expected to meet the needs of mothers' disengaging from their children, and the value of a network of women friends as sources of emotional support to women (Osborne 1983).

Then the mood lightened temporarily as the women shared a joke about the mother's youth, mythically misspent courting boys from a tender age and 'mugging up' on their interests. But since her marriage in her late teens, the mother found the productive business relationship between her husband and her father had been 'terrible for the family'. When the therapist asked who it affected most, she replied plaintively, 'Me, a bit . . . I was the wife of one and daughter of the other . . . Even to this day, it is not easy to be a sister, daughter, wife. If you're pleasing one, you're upsetting the other.' The therapist went on to point out the similarities in the positions the women both held in relation to the older generation and their husbands. This therapeutic line was motivated by the aim of increasing their understanding of their common lot as women, defining themselves in relational terms and bearing the brunt of power struggles between men in the family. The fact that the therapist was a woman, though not addressed directly as an issue with the family, was significant in so far as her presence and willingness to address gender issues reinforced their solidarity as women together.

Meanings of loss

In the meeting that followed with Ruth's parents alone, enquiry into their experiences of having a handicapped daughter revealed their different perspectives. Ruth's mother spoke wistfully of the loss of the 'daughter she [Ruth] could have been as an educated, intelligent woman', whereas her husband said firmly that he 'had come to terms with the fact that she's not about to look after herself if she didn't have money or didn't have [David]'. When his wife questioned this he conceded that she had now 'improved a great deal', but his wife retorted that it was not so much that Ruth had improved but that 'our observation of her has improved . . . I'm talking of what was there and we're recognizing'.

Later when the therapist steered the discussion away from Ruth to the couple's thoughts for the future, her father was found to be preoccupied with his wife's vulnerability were he to die, and his wish that she would remarry, dismissing fears about his own ill-health. The therapist chose to track this theme with the aim of emphasizing his wife's resilience rather than the fears that lay behind his defensive façade. To a question about whether she 'could have a life by herself', Ruth's mother responded 'I'm trying to find out. . . . I'm testing my ability to be an individual'. This echoed her daughter's similar wish for individuation, and suggests that patriarchal structures are, at least in part, at the root of the more problematical mother–daughter struggles with separateness, identification, and closeness (Eichenbaum and Orbach 1982; Chodorow 1987). The therapist indicated in various verbal and non-verbal ways her support for the self-development course she had already embarked upon; this was seen as crucial in enabling her to get in touch with and use her own internal resources, so that she could be more accepting of the changes in her daughter.

It seemed that the therapy so far was effecting constructive practical change in the women's lives. There was also evidence of the couple's enhanced ability to express and tolerate differences of opinion. Behind their reserve one had the sense that there was adequate mutual affection and probably sufficient strength in their relationship to help them withstand the unearthing of buried conflicts as Ruth was drawing away. While acknowledging and reinforcing this strength from time to time, the therapist could then use opportunities to unveil the influences of gender stereotypes on the family's fortunes, working to free individuals from the constraints of rigid beliefs.

The way ahead

By now intergenerational conflicts were easing but, not unexpectedly, Ruth's new-found assertiveness was making its presence felt in her marriage, whose hitherto unruffled state had existed at the cost of her autonomy. In recognition of this, the last four sessions were devoted to the couple to explore, stimulate, and support their ability to adjust. The level of resilience and affection evident in their relationship and good therapeutic rapport permitted considerable immediate challenge to the status quo. David, clinging to the belief that his wife's 'limitations [were] set' such that she could not exhibit any 'initiative', was pursued on what might be the implications for him should this change.

Turning to Ruth, the therapist addressed her participation in her own subjugation; she vigorously questioned her on how long it would be before she would demonstrate to others her ability to think, decide, and act for herself – that is, take the initiative; and on the pros and cons of so doing. One is open to the ethical charge that as the woman, in an already down position, she was being put under undue pressure in the service of therapeutic expediency. The contrary view is that this approach was efficient in empowering her and conveyed the message that she was strong enough to take it, especially as her husband too was made to work hard. The enquiry also laid bare Ruth's consciousness of her subordinate role in her marriage, modelled on her mother and other women around her, and she justified its retention to protect her husband who she saw as suffering the effects of an 'unhappy childhood'.

The next session revealed that as Ruth's development continued, further signs of marital strain emerged. The therapist tried to be supportive of David (who was visibly under threat) by addressing his vulnerability in the context of an exploration of his family background. Later the focus for rebalancing their relationship was shifted to the less threatening theme of parenting and their need for greater confidence and a 'united front' in the face of grandparental interference. Meanwhile, split messages from the therapy team acknowledged their progress as well as their fears of the consequences of change in the power dynamics of their relationship, counselling caution in the hope of encouraging them steadily to embrace their new roles and achieve personal growth.

Some effects of therapy

By the following meeting several significant changes were manifesting at different levels; the couple was visibly happier, Ruth in particular looking smart and lively; they reported that the presenting problems had largely resolved; and in addition, shifts in several family relationships were apparent. Ruth was said, for the first time, to have been negotiating forcefully with her father for greater control over her financial affairs. She was clear, in response to the therapist's probe, that she alone should have this control and not her husband, who, it was postulated, might also want it. She was now expressing ambitions to develop new interests and friends and to go out to work, in spite of David's discomfort. He remarked that both her parents (perhaps her mother more so) were taking her more seriously. The latter was said to be content with the new grandparenting arrangements and her relations all round with the couple were much easier. David was feeling a greater sense of his own competence in relation to his father-in-law, who told him that he had come to realize 'that we [Ruth and David] are much older people than we were before'. In the last session attended, Ruth demonstrated her ability to offer comfort and support to her husband, whose grandmother was dying. A phone call before another meeting (offered because of this stress) revealed that she had died; but by mutual agreement the session was cancelled because they seemed to be coping satisfactorily.

Follow-up

Eighteen months later family relationships were amicable; Ruth was attending Italian classes and had developed her first ever friendship; David had found a job; Ruth's father no longer needed his heart tablets; and her mother was enjoying life anew and was generous and philosophical in her appraisal of the effects of therapy.

Conclusion

When asked in the last session how, as a family, they had accomplished all of this, David reckoned that something must have happened between Ruth's parents to create 'a turning point'. Ruth fancied that the breakthrough had been her father's being able, at last, to express uncharacteristic but healthy rudeness and anger towards his wife. Their insights suggest that the crucial step in therapy was a shake-up in the parental marriage, whereby the rigid demarcation of the partners' gender roles and behaviours, which had stifled their own lives and those of the subsequent generations, was giving way to greater flexibility in their expressions of attributes and feelings. They could then *all* look forward to a greater share in the richness of human experience. These intuitions are interesting, for they can be interpreted in terms of a coming together of systemic and feminist models of change in families.

It is interesting to speculate on the degree to which the outcome of therapy with this family was influenced by the feminist perspective introduced, however sporadically in this case. Much work is required on how best to integrate feminist thinking into our work as therapists. Only through proper attention to gender issues (as well as to the wider sociocultural context) can we co-create truly liberating therapeutic experiences for those who consult us. Continued sharing of our separate explorations in this area should speed us in this enlightened direction.

Notes

1. In order to protect the identity of family members, recognizable features such as names, addresses, occupations, and so on, and other factual details have been altered. The author is indebted to them and wishes to acknowledge their inspiring courage. The collaboration of the therapy team in the work forming the basis of this chapter is especially acknowledged.
2. Reports of a low IQ would not conclusively indicate an organic basis or discount improvement in IQ level. Though of interest, the figures were not pursued to avoid focusing on what might have run counter to the therapeutic aim of developing Ruth's intellectual potential, whatever the measures stated.
3. Systemic family therapy, which has its origins in the scientific model of General Systems Theory (Bertalanffy 1962), is based on a notion of the family as a system, defined in terms of individuals who have evolved patterns of relationships over time. Their behaviours, including symptoms, are said to serve different functions for the system as a whole, and have reciprocal effects on individuals and relationships (Grinker 1975; Marmor 1983; Gorell Barnes 1985). Family therapy is concerned with how stress and symptoms in the individual may be relieved by altering dysfunctional patterns of relationships in the family.
4. A general distinction is made between *sex*, which has a biological basis, referring to maleness and femaleness, and *gender*, which is regarded as mainly a social construct. Thus, a certain group of psychological attributes, behaviours, and social roles is stereotypically assigned to one sex, and a different group to the other (Hilgard *et al.* 1979; Goodrich *et al.* 1988). A gender dualism results in which the attributes of masculinity are deemed more worthy than those of femininity, and confer on men privileges and power over women. These power dynamics have been institutionalized in our society, creating what is known as patriarchy.
5. Intelligence comprises different mental capacities which interrelate to such a degree that they suggest the existence of a general intelligence factor (Hilgard *et al.* 1979). This can be viewed as a global capacity for comprehension, reasoning, and purposeful action, which enables the individual to deal effectively with the environment. Tests of different abilities, such as those related to language and visuo-motor skills, may be sampling a fundamental faculty like judgement or good practical sense and initiative. Both general and specific measures of intelligence correlate well with academic achievement in school, but to a lesser

extent with intellectual and creative achievement in later life and with problem-solving ability in everyday living. In these latter respects other less readily measurable aspects of personality, which bear on the person's emotional life and social relationships, are relevant.

6. The discussion of the nature of intellectual impairment is bedevilled by the use of terms which are often confusingly interchanged, despite having specific meanings (Heron and Myers 1983). Intellectual impairment denotes a loss or abnormality of psychological function and structure, including that which is physiologically or anatomically based. Mental disability refers to the restriction or lack of ability to perform activities within a normal range as a result of this impairment. Mental handicap means the social, educational, and emotional effects of impairment and disability that limit normal fulfilment of roles. The term mental subnormality refers to scores on intelligent tests which fall below the normal range for the general population; the concept of mental retardation covers the notion of developmental delay. 'Backward', a lay term, can mean any of the above.

References

Baroff, G.S. (1974) *Mental Retardation: Nature, Cause and Management*, New York: John Wiley.

Barrett, M. and McIntosh, M. (1982) *The Anti-Social Family*, London: Verso.

Bicknell, J. (1983) 'The psychopathology of handicap', *British Journal of Medical Psychology* 56: 167–78.

Birch, H.G., Richardson, S.A., Baird, D., Horobin, G., and Illsley, R.L. *Mental Subnormality in the Community*, Baltimore: Williams & Wilkins.

Bowlby, J. (1965) *Child Care and the Growth of Love*, Harmondsworth: Penguin Books.

Brown, D. and Pedder, J. (1979) *Introduction to Psychotherapy*, London: Tavistock Publications.

Chodorow, N. (1987) 'Feminism and difference: gender, relation, and difference in psychoanalytic perspective', in M.R. Walsh (ed.) *The Psychology of Women: Ongoing Debates*, London: Yale University Press, 249–640.

Craft, M., Bicknell, J., and Hollins, S. (eds.) (1985) *Mental Handicap. A Multi-disciplinary Approach*, London: Bailliere Tindall.

Curran, L. (1980) 'Science education: did she drop out or was she pushed?', in L. Birke, W. Faulkner, S. Best, D.K. Janson-Smith, K. Overfield (eds.) *Alice Through the Microscope: The Power of Science over Women's Lives*, London: Virago, 22–41.

Doll, E.A. (1953) 'Counselling parents of severely mentally retarded children', in C. Stacey and M. Demartino (eds.) *Counselling and Psychotherapy with the Mentally Retarded*, New York: The Free Press.

Eichenbaum, L. and Orbach, S. (1982) *Outside In . . . Inside Out . . . Women's Psychology – A Feminist Psychoanalytic Approach*, Harmondsworth: Penguin.

Eichenbaum, L. and Orbach, S. (1983) *Understanding Women*, Harmondsworth: Penguin.
Ernst, S. and Goodison, L. (1981) *In Our Own Hands: A Book of Self-Help Therapy*, London: The Women's Press.
Forrest, A., Ritson, E., and Zealley, A. (1978) 'Mental handicap', in A. Forrest *et al.* (eds.) *Companion to Psychiatric Studies*, Edinburgh: Churchill Livingstone, 306–24..
Goodrich, T., Rampage, C., Ellman, B., and Halstead, K. (1988) *Feminist Family Therapy: A Casebook*, London: Norton.
Gorell Barnes, G. (1985) 'Systems theory and family theory', in M. Rutter and L. Hersov (eds.) *Child Psychiatry: Modern Approaches*, Oxford: Blackwell Scientific, 216–29.
Greenspan, M. (1983) *A New Approach to Women and Therapy*, New York: McGraw-Hill.
Grinker, R. (1975) 'The relevance of general systems theory to psychiatry', in L. Arieti (ed.) *American Handbook of Psychiatry, 6*, New York: Basic Books, 252–72.
Heber, R. and Garber, H. (1971) 'An experiment in the prevention of cultural–familial mental retardation', in D. Primrose (ed.) *Proceedings of the 2nd Congress of the International Association of Scientific Study of Mental Deficiency*, Amsterdam: Swets & Zeitlinger, 31–5.
Heron, A. and Myers, M. (1983) *Intellectual Impairment. The Battle against Handicap*, London: Academic Press.
Hilgard, E., Hilgard, R., and Atkinson, R. (1979) *Introduction to Psychology*, 7th edn, New York: Harcourt Brace Jovanovitch.
Hollins, S. (1987) Personal communication.
Horner, M.S. (1987) 'Towards an understanding of achievement-related conflicts in women', in M.R. Walsh (ed.) *The Psychology of Women: Ongoing Debates*, London: Yale University Press, 169–84.
Kantor, D. and Neal, J.H. (1985) 'Integrative shifts for the theory and practice of family systems therapy', *Family Process* 24: 13–30.
McNeil, M. (1987) 'Introduction', in M. McNeil (ed.) *Gender and Expertise*, London: Free Association Books, 1–10.
Mander, A.V. and Rush, A.K. (1974) *Feminism as Therapy*, New York: Random House.
Marmor, J. (1983) 'Systems thinking in psychiatry: some theoretical and clinical implications', *American Journal of Psychiatry* 140 (7): 833–8.
Minuchin, S. (1974) *Families and Family Therapy*, London: Tavistock.
Minuchin, S. (1979) 'Constructing a therapeutic reality', in E. Kaufman and P.N. Kaufman (eds.) *Family Therapy of Drug and Alcohol Abuse*, London: Tavistock, 5–18.
Napier, A.Y. with Whitaker, C.A. (1978) *The Family Crucible*, New York: Bantam.
Nightingale, F. (1852/1978) 'Cassandra', in R. Strachey (ed.) *The Cause*, London: Virago.
Oakley, A. (1972) *Sex, Gender and Society*, London: Temple Smith.
Osborne, K. (1983) 'Women in families: feminist therapy and family systems', *Journal of Family Therapy* 5: 1–10.

Palazzoli, M.S., Boscolo, L., Cecchin, G., and Prata, G. (1978) *Paradox and Counter-Paradox*, New York: Aronson.

Paludi, M.A. (1987) 'Psychometric properties and underlying assumptions of four objective measures of fear of success', in M.R. Walsh (ed.) *The Psychology of Women: Ongoing Debates*, London: Yale University Press, 105–202.

Penfold, S. and Walker, G. (1984) *Women and the Psychiatric Paradox*, Milton Keynes: Open University Press.

Penrose, L. (1972) *The Biology of Mental Defect*, London: Sidgwick & Jackson.

Rakoff, V. (1984) 'The necessity for multiple models in family therapy', *Journal of Family Therapy* 6: 199–210.

Sinason, V. (1986) 'Secondary mental handicap and its relationship to trauma', *Psychoanalytic Psychotherapy* 2 (2): 131–54.

Smith, D. and David, S. (eds.) (1975) *Women Look at Psychiatry*, Vancouver: Press Gang Publishers.

Spender, D. (1980) *Man-Made Language*, London: Routledge & Kegan Paul.

Spender, D. (1982) *Invisible Women*, London: Writers & Readers.

Stein, Z. and Susser, M. (1962) 'Families of dull children', *Journal of Mental Science* 66: 1296–310.

Stokes, J. (1987) 'Insights from psychotherapy', paper presented at International Symposium on Mental Health, 25 February.

Symington, N. (1981) 'The psychotherapy of the subnormal patient', *British Journal of Medical Psychology* 54: 187–99.

Tomm, K. (1984) 'One perspective on the Milan system approach', *Journal of Marital and Family Therapy* 10: 113–25, 253–71.

von Bertalanffy, L. (1962) 'General systems theory: a critical review', in *Yearbook Soc. Gen. Sys. Theory* 7: 1–21.

Walrond-Skinner, S. (1987) 'Feminist therapy and family therapy: the limits of the association', in S. Walrond-Skinner and D. Watson (eds.) *Ethical Issues in Family Therapy*, London: Routledge & Kegan Paul.

Walters, M. (1988) *The Invisible Web: Gender Patterns in Family Relationships*, New York: Guilford Press.

Warner, J. (1981) 'Family therapy: a search for foundations: II, Communications, boundaries and control', *Journal of Family Therapy* 3: 201–9.

Will, D. and Wrate, R.M. (1985) *Integrated Family Therapy*, London: Tavistock.

Woolf, V. (1928) *A Room of One's Own*, London: Hogarth Press.

Chapter nine

Working with women in families

Jane Conn and Annie Turner

This chapter examines issues of power and control between men and women both in society and in the agency/therapist/family relationships.

Introduction

> There was once upon a time a little country girl, born in a village, the prettiest little creature that ever was seen. Her mother was beyond reason excessively fond of her, and her grandmother yet much more. This good woman made a little red riding hood for her; which made her look so very pretty, that everybody called her Little Red Riding Hood.
>
> (Perrault 1695: 122)

In Perrault's version of this tale, mother sends Red Riding Hood on an errand for her ailing grandmother; a helpful act ending in tragedy as both grandmother and Red Riding Hood are devoured by the big bad wolf. While the importance of the meaning children (of all ages) may find in fairy tales has been fully explored elsewhere (Bettelheim 1976), this tale offers further meanings. Mother, in trying to help sick grandmother, sends a good, polite, pretty, girl child to care for her. Courtesy leads the child to reveal her destination, so that both her grandmother and herself are devoured by the male wolf. The wolf is, of course, 'bad' – but should her mother have let her go? Can the mother be blamed for allowing her to go? Is Little Red Riding Hood also to blame – should she have told a stranger where she was going?

These issues could, of course, be explored fully, but here serve to highlight some of the dilemmas inherent in the societal and familial context in which many women in this country live. This chapter considers these issues in relation to a particular group of women – those whose children have been in, or may be received into, the care of the local authority. Substitute care implies that the parental care is not good enough.[1] As child care and child rearing are traditionally associated with mothering, parental care becomes more particularly identified with maternal care. There are, of course, exceptions, as with any generalization, but as women are still seen primarily as the nurturers of homes and family, it is their position on which we will focus.

In doing so we wish to bring together feminist thinking and family-therapy practice. This chapter will examine the difference between the two with regard to the family and its connection with the wider context. We will consider how this integration may offer a more helpful framework in working with families when the quality of parental care is being questioned. A feminist analysis offers a perspective on the basic inequality of a woman's position, in both an intra- and extra-familial context. The introduction of a therapeutic agent to work with the family can, in trying to be helpful, reinforce the assumed failure of the mother, and therefore increase a sense of hopelessness and impossibility of change. Feminist thinking offers a theory of society; family therapy offers a theory of change.

> Men come into therapy asking, 'What went wrong?'; women come in asking, 'What did I do wrong?'.
>
> (Walters 1987)

This chapter will illustrate this idea by case examples. The 'therapeutic agent'[2] is a social worker using family-therapy techniques, thereby combining the power of the 'therapeutic agent' and that of the local authority, with its statutory responsibilities and powers in relation to child care. She[3] may be directly working with the family herself, or acting as consultant to the family social worker.

Differences between feminist and family-systems approaches

There has been much discussion in recent years about the feasibility of incorporating feminist and family-systems thinking into clinical practice. For example, does the concept of neutrality eschew the therapist's own value system, and does the notion of non-alliance with any family member preclude usefully addressing the inequity of power within the family? Does the notion of hierarchy always reinforce male superiority? Is it imperative to accept the circularity of Madanes's view (1984) that the powerful are always dependent on the powerless, thereby giving the latter power over the former?

Neither of these schools incorporate as a central theme the concept of gender differentiation as a universal principle of social and political life, underpinning the social fact of male domination in material and political societal structures. Family-therapy theory has been traditionally a 'men's study' (Spender 1981) constructed mainly from a male view of the world and family. In a patriarchal society, as Rich (1976) commented, 'objectivity is the name we give to male subjectivity'. Patriarchy, sexism, and oppression are terms which do not appear often in family-therapy literature, even in writing by women – in itself an indication of the pervasiveness of the patriarchal belief system. Patriarchy has been defined by James (1984) as the social arrangement of male dominance alongside a belief system and symbolic means by which every person becomes a gendered being. In examining this belief system, Baker Miller (1976) concludes that hiding the existence of the unequal power relationship between men and women is an essential mechanism for perpetuating male dominance.[4]

Towards integration

To incorporate feminist thinking into a theory of family work requires a shift in the application of key concepts, given that these have developed with little consideration of gender differentiation. For example, a modification of the concept of neutrality would mean exploring with the less powerful the possibilities of increasing their power, while maintaining a view of the impact of this on the more powerful, in order to avoid a return to the status quo. Drawing hierarchically appropriate boundaries between subsystems must include an analysis of the power relationship between men and women, in order to avoid the trap that they have equal status. The neatly circular notion of the weak ultimately being as powerful as the strong seems to serve the interests of some more than others, and like the Confucian ideology of feudal China (Goldner 1985b), or the Thatcherite ideology of contemporary Britain, it rewards the powerful and silences the weak.

Agency/therapist/family relationship: issues of power and control

Before considering examples of family work to illustrate and locate these issues in practice, it seems important to consider the relationship between the agency, therapist, and family in a more general sense. The use of power in the relationship between the therapist and family has been the subject of some debate within different schools of family therapy. Structural, strategic and Milan systematic therapies each use a model of expert power. Structuralists use this notion quite directly with the family; therapists who also incorporate feminist thinking into their work would argue that this overt use of expertise is particularly helpful in working with women in families as it offers a model of woman working actively and instrumentally (Caust *et al.* 1981).

The Haley model of strategic therapy pays considerable attention to power issues between the therapist and the family but, without a feminist analysis, strongly reinforces the masculine value system, as Hoffman (1985) has argued. It could be argued that Papp and Silverstein (1983) have addressed these issues differently through the notion of the three-way debate, when the covert rules preventing change are made explicit to the family. Given a different meaning by the subtleties of the debate, it gives the family a message that there is no 'correct' solution other than the one they find for themselves by observing their dilemma differently.

The Milan systemic school, with its understanding of relationships as reciprocal, subsumes the concept of power within this notion. It therefore does not address the context of patriarchy, and the social system to which women (and men) belong. Differences in thinking based on sex, culture, and race influence both family and therapist. A possible way forward in addressing this issue could be to acknowledge that both men and women influence family rules, without losing sight of the wider context which determines who has most influence, based on economic and social constraints (Bennett 1983).

Feminist family therapy offers a framework for the use of authority and expertise without working oppressively. Families, and the women within them, have a right to expect a service from the therapist, and owning a level of authority and power which the positions then affords is an important part of modelling a position for women which can empower them in relation to other family members and ultimately in relation to society.[5]

From the time of referral there is a further level of interaction between the agency, therapist, and family. In this instance the agency is a Social Services department, although the families discussed in the following section have necessarily also had contact with other agencies such as the education and health authorities. A family therapist makes some assessment of the interaction between the family and network of agencies, and incorporates this thinking into the work. A feminist family therapist also considers the organization of these other agencies and their expectations of parents. The mother would be the parent who would normally have to negotiate these contacts; therefore feminist thinking would particularly address these interactions in the context of the position of women in families, and in the wider society. If a woman is 'one down' to begin with, and seen to be 'failing' as a parent by school or general practitioner, she will be 'two down' by the time she gets to the Social Services. Thus, in trying to be helpful it is all too easy for the Social Services further to undermine her strengths.

It is also important to consider the position of the social worker. She is working within a male-dominated, hierarchically organized structure. (Some 91 per cent of Social Services personnel at directorate level are male and 9 per cent are female, according to Brock and Davis 1985.) Her position in the structure therefore reflects the position of many of her women clients, at least partially.

However powerless the social worker may consider herself to be within a Social Services structure, to the family she is the 'face' of the organization, and therefore appears to wield its legal and organizational powers. It is extremely important that the worker finds a way to maintain boundaries for herself, both in terms of the appropriate use of personal and professional authority and the appropriate use of the organization.

It is useful for the social worker using family-therapy techniques also to consider the professional system of family therapy, and the extent to which it is governed by hierarchically ordered assumptions. Goldner (1985b) suggests that status within the therapeutic system, as within the family system, is derived from externally structured social hierarchies.

Having drawn attention to the particular position of the female social worker, and the differences between this and that of the recipient of the service, it is also important to consider the commonality of experience. Feminist thinking would especially locate this around the issue of dependency, i.e. that a woman's potential is inhibited by her own experiences of dependency. Women are raised to provide nurturance, care, and attention, and to have others depend on them emotionally (Eichenbaum and Orbach 1983). Again trying to be helpful, women working with families in a Social Services setting will not only experience these issues themselves but may replicate them with their clients, providing for them so well that their own power and potential are not energized.

The other important commonality in the context of this chapter is that of conflict resolution. What the rules are and who makes them, and therefore who demonstrably holds the balance of power, are a frequent source of family conflict (Hare Mustin 1978). Gilligan (1982) draws a distinction between a male approach to conflict resolution, which she views as hierarchically ordered, and a female approach. This, she explains, is an assessment of the network of relationships surrounding the problem. Baker Miller (1976) explores the similar notions of connection (female) as opposed to the 'aggression' of hierarchy. She considers this concept to have important potential for a more co-operative way of living together, thus benefitting both men and women.

The context of practice

The context of the following two case examples is a centre, funded by Social Services, which acts as a specialist secondary resource, to which social workers refer when they feel 'stuck' in their work with a family. Referrals can only be made when there is a child in the family who may be, or has been, received into care.

The following case example illustrates the use of a feminist approach to working with a professional and family system, addressing issues of power between men and women. An approach to conflict resolution which makes an assessment of the network of relationships surrounding the problem is used.

Case 1

The W family (Figure 9.1) was referred to the centre by an area-team social worker. Norah W is the mother of five children, aged 6, 7, 9, 15,

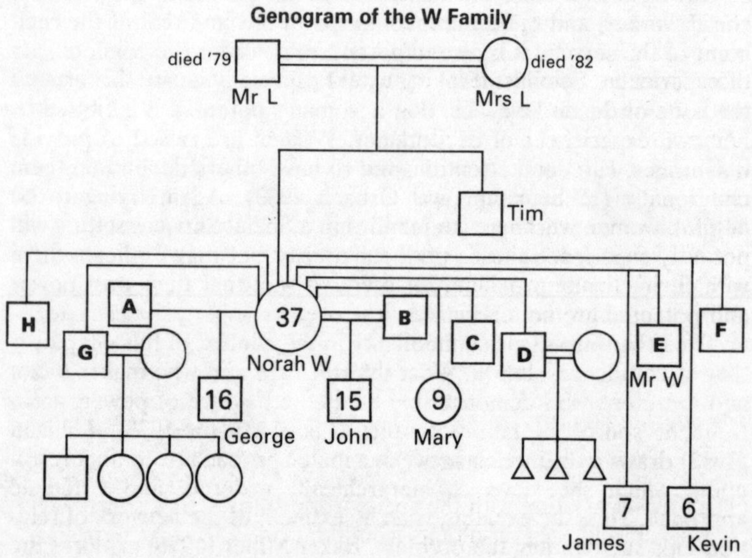

Figure 9.1 Genogram of the W family

and 16 years. The 9 year old is a girl, the rest are boys. Each child has a different father, and each of these five relationships ended while Norah was pregnant. Norah W has had eight cohabiting partnerships (A–H). At the time of referral all the children were the subjects of Interim Care Orders; the eldest had been placed in a residential establishment away from the borough, and the youngest were in a foster home. This situation had been preceded by several years during which the children had been received into care on Place of Safety Orders, returning home after several weeks.

The area team was requesting that full Care Orders be made in respect of the children; child-care planning within the agency indicated placement away from home, but also required some work with Norah W and the children about their removal from home, and plans for the future.

The social worker had known the family for a long time, and felt very unclear about how to undertake this work.

Family history

Norah W had been sexually abused by her father and her brother (she had no other siblings), and had left home at 17 years of age, never having talked about this either within or outside her family. Her brother was later convicted and imprisoned for child molestation. Norah W maintained frequent contact with her mother after leaving home. She had quite an unsettled life, with different partners, but there was no involvement of external agencies until after her mother's death in 1980.

Norah W had no more children after this date, but formed two relationships with men, one of whom sexually abused three of the children. One of these men was also physically violent to Norah and all the children, who were frequently left alone overnight, or for short periods of time during this period. The children came in and out of care during this time; when Norah W was alone she demonstrated an ability to care for them. This was destroyed as soon as she became re-involved with one of these men.

The consultation

This took place in three stages:

(1) an initial meeting with the social worker, the senior social worker, and the consultants from the centre, to consider the agency/family relationship;

(2) a meeting with the social worker, the family, and the centre consultants;
(3) a final meeting with the social worker, her senior, and the centre consultants to discuss the family meeting.

The initial meeting clarified that the social worker's closeness to the family was immobilizing her. The senior social worker was trying to make appropriate decisions by maintaining a distance from the work; this created further anxiety in the social worker who responded by trying to draw him closer to the work; his response was to become more distant. In order to intervene in this cycle it was felt important to concentrate on the issue of control in the agency/family relationship.

The social worker had known the family for five years, and had tried to be a supportive partner for Norah W. However, according to Norah W's 'map of the world' (Elkhaim 1986), partners were dangerous and not to be trusted. An adequate care of the children was further questioned by the Social Services and other agencies, so was the social worker's attempted support of Norah W. As another woman she felt sympathy for Norah W. However, the demands of the agency and her own position as a statutory worker were such that she felt she had to take an authoritarian stand, which for her mitigated against offering support. Her confusion confirmed Norah W's view that partners could not be trusted.

The social worker's close association with the family and her observation of the abuse and neglect of the children was making it even more difficult for her to negotiate a clear contract and relationship with Norah W. Her (male) senior social worker had, in order to be helpful, tried to preserve the boundaries of his own role by maintaining a distance from the problem. This, however, had left the onus for change with the social worker, confirming Baker Miller's view (1976) that women carry the responsibility for change.

In order to help the social worker establish a clearer position in relation to the W family it seemed important to discuss the back-up she needed from her own professional support system. This included listening carefully and examining with her why she felt unable to move forward with the work, and helping her to make an assessment of the messages she thought she was receiving from Norah W about the care of the children. It was recognized that both she and her senior were trying to be helpful but the unequal distribution of power between them (in terms of both gender and hierarchical position) was preventing them from moving forward. Linking these issues to the relationship between the agency and Norah W, and to Norah W's own experiences, made it possible for the senior social worker to take responsibility for making several suggestions for change – for example, himself observing the family session from behind the one-way screen,[6] (with Norah W's permission), and offering several supervision sessions specifically to discuss this work.

The family meeting

The initial hypothesis was that Norah W's relationships had to end before her children were born because male partners were dangerous to their own children. Her mother, from a distance, helped her maintain sufficient distance from men to preserve her children's safety. Her mother understood from her own marriage that she had not felt powerful enough alone to make changes. After her mother died, the Social Services tried to step in at times of crisis, in order to help Norah W to resist the abusive power of men. The agency context, however, also communicated a condemnation of Norah W as a parent by removing her children from her several times. Her mirroring confusion (Reder 1983) about whether the Social Services were there to help or condemn meant that no one was sure how to proceed.

A constant thread in the family meeting was to bring out Norah W's strengths and to reinforce these, while acknowledging that male power was sometimes too strong to be withstood on one's own, even as an adult.

Norah W became clearer that she was not sure she felt strong enough to care for all her children on her own, that everybody needed adult company. The view was changed by introducing the notion that it was very hard for her as a woman alone to be powerful enough to change things if a man was abusing his power, particularly if certain things had happened to her as a child, when she would have felt less powerful.

The view changed from 'As a mother I should be able to protect my children by myself at all times' to 'Because of abuses of power which are not my responsibility, I may not be able to carry out my responsibilities as I would wish.'

Continued work around this theme enabled Norah W to clarify what she wanted for her children, and allowed them to hear her reasons for this. This included thinking that her younger children should be together in a long-term foster home, as long as she was able to retain some contact with them.

The final consultation

A child-care review had been arranged for each child, and the senior social worker had arranged for an independent chairperson to be present so that he or she could offer active support in discussing the complexities of the work during the reviews, and participate in planning the work around each child's future.

As consultants, we said that it would be hard for Norah W not to continually blame herself, as a mother, for the way the children were treated, and that the more she blamed herself the more she would have to fight to get them back, and fail, distressing both herself and them. It seemed important, therefore, to continue working with her in the context of her own past experiences, so that she might feel the need to blame herself less. Her eldest son had elected to live with her, and together they had negotiated this with Social Services, in conjunction with a request also to do some work together on his past experiences to enable him, as a young man, to try and relate to people close to him in a different way.

The further impact of feminism on clinical practice

Feminist thinking made a valuable contribution to this work. It offered an understanding of the context of the Social Services as a hierarchically ordered and male-dominated institution which therefore influenced employees to seek solutions from this perspective. This gave an important clue to the 'stuckness' of the relationship between the social worker and her senior social worker. Using a hierarchically ordered problem-solving approach meant that the senior social worker maintained his distance at a point when the social worker needed more support in order to disentangle herself from the impact of the work with Norah W on her professional identity.

The latter's experience of dependency as a woman meant that she was drawn to a nurturing approach in her work with Norah W, but became confused about whether this was appropriate given the statutory nature of her role, and her position within a system which validated hierarchically ordered solutions. She was therefore unsure about how to proceed.

Redefining the senior social worker's use of his position meant that he could create a supportive network around the work. He maintained his own position by using someone senior to himself appropriately, thus not going directly against the ordering of the organization, while still examining the network available to himself differently. This offered a model of taking control of the use of support systems, which freed the social worker to use both him and herself differently in relation to Norah W. She encouraged the latter to look more closely at support systems which were available to her, instead of encouraging her to try to provide this support entirely herself, and in so doing unwittingly undermining Norah W's competence.

Norah W found her solution in a church based network, which gave her a greater sense of self esteem, by providing her with a context in which to help others.

Case 2: Family work in a Social Services department

The following example illustrates how, without meaning to, helping agencies and helpful family members can reinforce a view of a woman as depressed and not coping rather than experiencing the positive process of grieving.

Family background

Roberto and Angela T met and married in England. Both their immediate families live here, quite close to each other; the further extended families live in Italy. Both their families wanted to have consistent contact with them, and although they were also important to Roberto and Angela T, they did not want to be quite as closely involved as their families wished. Roberto T was described as drinking heavily, sometimes physically abusive and violent, and a womanizer,

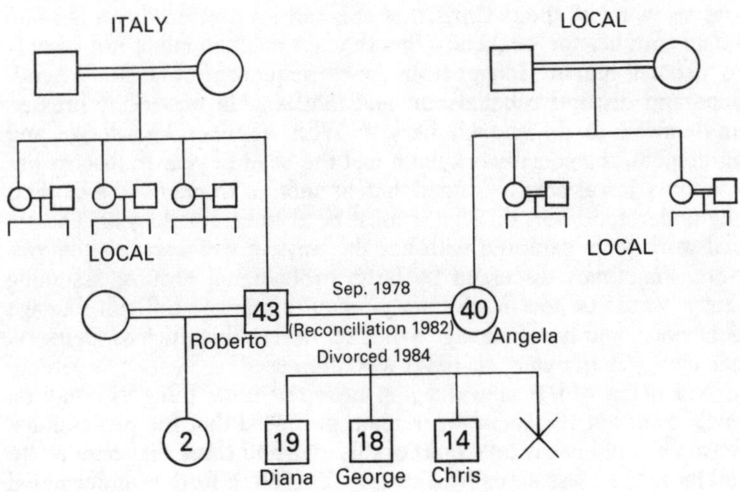

Figure 9.2 The T family

often staying away from home for a few days.

He finally left the family home, but visited regularly. There was a reconciliation several years later; he was again violent, and he started to drink heavily once more. This time Angela said 'enough was enough' and filed for divorce. After Roberto left, she discovered she was pregnant and had a termination. The extended family on both sides maintained close contact.

All three children have had some school attendance problems. The two eldest are now both working and 'doing well'. Diana is engaged and George has a regular girl-friend. Chris is seen as the difficult son; George takes on the role of trying to discipline him, and occasionally one of Angela's brothers does the same.

Angela was described as being depressed. She has had Valium prescribed by her doctor. She also has some gynaecological problems which have caused her discomfort. The professional network and family have the idea that Angela is not well enough to control Chris. In particular, his school wanted the department to consider care and, with the family's agreement, referred them to the centre in order to discuss this further.

The school

Prior to meeting the family, there was a discussion about how the area team could deal with the school's concern. The head of the year was so worried about Chris that she had even offered to take him home with her for weekends. She thought that she might not be able to 'protect' him any longer from the consequences of his non-attendance and disruptive behaviour, and that Angela was too depressed and unwell to do enough herself. With Angela's knowledge and agreement, the social-work team met the head of year to discuss her concerns. It was acknowledged that, as another woman and a mother, she understood how difficult it must be at times for Angela. The social-work team explored with her the ways in which such situations were sometimes discussed by large professional groups, assuming that it would be too much for a woman to manage difficult teenage behaviour, and how language which reinforces this, such as 'being on her own' (Chapman *et al.* 1984) was often used.

Not living with a man did not mean the same thing as being on one's own, but the social-work team proposed that the professional network could easily take hold of this idea and think they needed 'to do' more than was actually necessary. This often further undermined a mother's position. The head of year said that she had not seen the situation in this way before, and thought the planned family meeting would be very useful. She decided to try to be helpful in a different way, by reinforcing the strengths of Chris's home life in meetings at the school.

Family meetings

The initial working hypothesis was that Diana and George were now spending a great deal of time outside the home, and might soon be physically leaving. The family's view of Angela was as the deserted wife, depressed and unable to control her youngest son. The family therefore might not be able to help her get strong enough to withstand further loss. Chris's behaviour, escalating at this point, was bringing in people outside the family in an attempt to get help of a different kind. In trying to be so helpful, no one was actually paying attention to Angela and talking to her about what she wanted.

Angela, Diana, George, and Chris were invited to the first family meeting. Only Diana and Chris came. Chris thought that he was the problem of the family. Diana thought that no one could do more to help them. They were both very worried about their mother. The following excerpt is taken from a letter sent to Angela following the meeting:

> We have been wondering what your view is about the kind of contact we have offered. Perhaps you feel there is nothing much that we can do to help, or that what we might be offering is unlikely to help you with the problems you are having at present? On the other hand, maybe you have some ideas about the kind of people you would find useful and would be prepared to share your thoughts about this with us?

Angela, Diana, George, and Chris attended the next meeting. It became clear, through circular questioning (Campbell *et al.* 1983) that Diana, George, and other family members did not think that Roberto had fulfilled his family responsibilities as a husband and family man, and were trying to make up for this themselves. In so doing Angela's own competence had been undermined, so much so that she had begun to believe in her own frailty, and her slumped posture indicated this. When this belief was strongest, Diana and George acted intuitively, and started to give Chris orders. They did not necessarily give the same orders, or indeed the orders his mother would have given. He did not obey their orders, but occasionally his mother gave him orders, which he obeyed.

The termination and the divorce had distressed Angela. It became clear that other members of the family had forgotten that she needed to grieve. Grieving as she was, and not in the best of health, Angela had managed to limit contact from other members of the family when it seemed to undermine her, and to organize her own family group so that there would be a clear sharing of domestic tasks.

The workers itemized Angela's achievements one by one, and described her feeling 'low' as a grieving process, both for past losses, and in preparation for Diana and George's leaving home (which was due to happen during the next six months). Chris's rebelliousness was described similarly. As they did this, Angela's posture became straighter. She said that she had thought that she had 'the last word about the rules in the house', but now realized that this was not how her family saw things. She would make sure that it was she in the future who told Chris what to do, and not someone else in the family.

The helpful substitute mothering from the school had mirrored the helpful substitute mothering in the family. The centre's systemic approach had enabled the area-team social worker to resist a similar mirroring, and gain a perspective which she could then maintain at the education panel's final meeting. This also proved useful to reinforcing the message to the head of the year.

Angela was presented as a woman on her own who was depressed and not coping. A feminist analysis explored dependency issues for women, i.e. providing care for others at the expense of their own needs. A particular aspect of this approach was the use by the workers of the 'language of action' (Marianne Walters, personal communication, 1987) in this piece of work, i.e. using 'doing' words rather than 'being' words in order to move from a position of hopelessness to possible resolution.

Conclusion

It is a comment on power relations within society that it is the post-war regrouping of the white, middle-class, nuclear family of the 1950s (Parsons and Bales 1955) which has influenced the field of family therapy. In Goldner's (1985) opinion, this narrow and exclusive section of the population has been used as the example of normal family life for all. In her view this has contributed to the minimal impact of family therapy on the wider society.

Feminism offers women the possibility of change that does not simply occur within the current sex-role stereotyping which for women, at best, means more of the same, and at worst, an even greater burden. Working to validate and empower families as part of a process of change is not alien to family therapy; recognizing that men and women do not have equal power, whatever their circumstances, is a novel concept. Therefore the implications of a feminist perspective for practice in family therapy lie in maximizing and using every observable shred of power when working with women in families, and bringing this analysis into the therapy in whatever way seems appropriate. In this context, the notion of power is to be responsible and active oneself, not to have power over others (Burck 1986). The latter simply replicates the abuse of power which at worst shows itself in cases of sexual abuse and violence.

It is not surprising that many articles on possible meeting points for feminism and family therapy end with the words 'and this is only a beginning'. Some beginnings take longer than others.

Notes

1. We are not concerned here with care placements when parental care is not available, i.e. through sickness or death.
2. We will use the term 'therapist' until the discussion includes the Social Services department, when we will use the term 'social worker' to refer to someone working within a Social Services department using family-systems and family-therapy techniques.
3. We will use 'she', as the therapist/social worker is female in both instances. In this chapter, we do not need therefore to address the relationship between the female client and male therapist, or indeed relationships within and without male/female therapy teams.
4. The importance of finding a way to maintain an appropriate position has been extensively explored elsewhere in various ways. These include the use of teams, the concept of 'mirroring' family issues, network meetings, and working with 'underorganized families'. Useful references include Carpenter *et al.* (1983), Dimmock and Dungworth (1983), Jones (1983), and Reder (1983).
5. Details have been altered sufficiently to preserve anonymity.
6. The centre has a one-way screen, and family/agency systems work as a team, with one person conducting the interview and the other behind the screen.

References

Baker Miller, J. (1976) *Towards a New Psychology of Women*, Harmondsworth: Penguin.

Bennett, F. (1983) 'The State, welfare and women's dependence', in L. Segal (ed.) *What is to be done about the Family?*, Harmondsworth: Penguin.

Bettelheim, B. (1976) *The Uses of Enchantment*, Harmondsworth: Penguin.

Brook, E. and Davis, A. (1985) 'Women and social work', in E. Brook and A. Davis (eds.) *Women, the Family and Social Work*, London:Tavistock

Library of Social Work Practice.
Burck, C. (1986) 'Challenging myths in family therapy: the case of feminism', unpublished dissertation, Advanced Training in Family Therapy, Tavistock Clinic, London.
Campbell, D., Draper, R., Pollard, D., and Reder, P. (1983) 'Working with the Milan method, twenty questions', *London, Institute of Family Therapy, Occasional Paper 1*.
Carpenter, J., Treacher, A., Jenkins, H., and O'Reilly, P. (1983) 'Oh no, not the Smiths again', *Journal of Family Therapy* 5(1): 81–96.
Caust, B., Libow, J., and Raskin, P. (1981) 'Challenges and promises of training women as family systems therapists', *Family Process* 20(4): 437–47.
Chapman, J., Martin, C., Park, S., Potts, J., and Schiccitano, M. (1984) 'Proposed guidelines for non-sexist language policy', *Australian Journal of Family Therapy* 5(4): 237–44.
Dimmock, B. and Dungworth, D. (1983) 'Creating manoeuvrability for family therapy in Social Services departments', *Journal of Family Therapy* 5(1): 53–69.
Duncan, R. (1986) *History and Herstory*, London: Robson Books.
Eichenbaum, L. and Orbach, S. (1983) *What Do Women Want?*, Glasgow: Fontana.
Elkhaim, M. (1986) 'A systems approach to couple therapy', *Family Process* 25: 35–42.
Freidan, B. (1981) *The Second Stage*, New York: Summit.
Gilligan, C. (1982) *In a Different Voice*, Cambridge, Mass.: Harvard University Press.
Goldner, V. (1985a) 'Feminism and family therapy', *Family Process* 24: 31–45.
Goldner, V. (1985b) 'Family therapy may be hazardous to your health', *Family Therapy Networker* November: 19–23.
Gorell Barnes, G. (1987) Draft paper for the Association of Family Therapy Conference.
Hare Mustin, R. (1978) 'A feminist approach to family therapy', *Family Process* 7: 181–92.
Hoffman, L. (1985) 'Beyond power and control: toward a 'second order' family systems therapy', *Family Systems Medicine* 3(4): 381–96.
James, K. (1984) 'Breaking the chains of gender: family therapy's position', *Australian Journal of Family Therapy* 5(4): 241–48.
Jones, E. (1983) 'Leaving the motherless family – the problem of termination for the family therapist', *Journal of Family Therapy* 5(1): 11–22.
Papp, P. and Silverstein, O. (1983) *The Process of Change*, New York: Guilford Press.
Parsons, T. and Bales, R.F. (1955) *The Family, Socialisation and the Interaction Process*, New York: Free Press.
Perrault, C. (1695/1974) 'Little Red Riding Hood', in I. and P. Opie (eds.) *The Classic Fairy Tales*.
Pilalis, J. and Anderton, J. (1986) 'Feminism and family therapy', *Journal*

of Family Therapy 9(2): 99–113.

Radcliffe-Richards, J. (1980) *The Sceptical Feminist*, London: Routledge & Kegan Paul.

Reder, P. (1983) 'Disorganised families and the helping professionals: "Who's in charge of what?" ', *Journal of Family Therapy* 5(1): 23–36.

Rich, M. (1976) *Of Woman Born*, London: Virago.

Rutter, M., Dardney, L., Skuse, D., Quinton, D., and Mrazek, D. (1984) 'The nature and qualities of parenting provided by women raised in institutions', *Journal of Child Psychology & Psychiatry* 26(4): 599–625.

Spender, D. (1981) *Men's Studies Modified: The Impact of Feminism on the Academic Disciplines*, Oxford: Pergamon Press.

Walters, M. (1987) 'Personal Communication', Bristol Conference.

Wheeler, D. (1985) 'The fear of feminism in family therapy', *Family Therapy Networker* November: 53–5.

Part four

What About Men?

Chapter ten

The place of men in a gender-sensitive therapy

Margaret O'Brien

Until recently gender-sensitive therapy has been women centred. Writers and clinicians concerned to highlight the gender dimension of psychological distress and its treatment have focused on the specific nature of female experience.

Accordingly, as this book indicates, there have been significant advances in our understanding of women's psychology, theoretical developments about the mother–daughter relationship and female sexuality being important examples. Socio-political developments such as the feminist movement created new ideas about women's roles which influenced clinical theory and practice. Connections began to be made between women's subordinate social position and their psychiatric status (for example, Chesler 1972). This 'first wave' of gender-sensitive clinical work was in part a reaction to the relative silence in professional practice about any link between women's psychological problems and their wider position in society.

A 'second wave' of gender-sensitive therapy and related discourse is now identifiable. Alongside mother/woman-focused theoreticians are writers who are incorporating an analysis of male psychological experience (for example, Rieker and Carmen 1984; Lerner 1988; Sayers 1988). The development of Lerner's clinical work exemplifies the movement away from an exclusive concern with female experience. In her latest book she criticizes the mother–daughter emphasis of much feminist psychoanalytic thinking, including her own: 'The territory that fits the feminist map is still the mother–child dyad, and causality regarding normal or pathological functioning still resides in this highly encapsulated unit' (Lerner 1988: 264).

While recognizing the 'central axis' mothers and daughters occupy in family emotional life, and the relative lack of attention paid to it, Lerner (ibid.: 282) argues for a systems perspective that 'does not minimize or obscure the role of fathers, the complexity of interlocking relationships, and the impact of culture and women's subordinate status'.

The purpose of this chapter is to offer a preliminary examination of the position of men and fathers in therapeutic environments in order to provide a basis from which to explore these interlocking gender relations. The background to this chapter is the growing research literature on the psychology of men, masculinity, and fatherhood (for example, Pleck and Sawyer 1974; Lamb 1981; McKee and O'Brien 1982; Lewis and O'Brien 1987).

Since the early 1970s American researchers of gender relations have shown a keen interest in the psychology of men. Social and behavioural scientists in the UK have been less explicit in their consideration of male roles although the issues have been visible in other arenas (e.g. in radio, television, and newspapers). For the UK the early 1980s were the years of the 'new man'. Many popular books about the male condition were published – the majority written by women (Ford 1984; Franks 1984; Hodson 1984; Ingham 1984; Roberts 1984). These and other writers suggested that the modern western male is undergoing a crisis of identity. The traditional norms of bread-winning, protecting, and being physically strong are seen as no longer totally appropriate for contemporary men. A different set of prescriptions and expectations are being put forward as more suitable for, and even more characteristic of, men. Put simply, the new man is one who: shares domestic and child-care duties; gives the family equal priority with work; discusses personal feelings with his partner and others; is emotionally closer to his children than his forefathers; and so on. Empirical data suggests that the prevalence of such a composite new man is actually quite low (Coverman and Sheley 1986; Lewis 1986).

Research and debate about male roles has implications for therapeutic theory and practice. In this chapter I will explore one aspect of male personal life: how adult males respond to emotional problems. The literature on this topic provides a useful interface between social research and clinical practice. I will first examine data which show that men are less likely than women to seek help about emotional concerns. It seems that this gender pattern recurs whether the problem is construed as individual, couple, or family based. I will then go on to consider some of the explanations for the phenomenon of the so-called emotionally disengaged man or peripheral father. The third part of the chapter will concentrate on therapist–male client interactions in the consulting room or clinic. The chapter will end by considering the implications of engaging men in therapy, particularly family therapies. It will be suggested that therapists need to be sensitive to the consequences of this process, especially for women, and may have to utilize imaginative therapeutic strategies in this regard. It will be argued here that in order fully to comprehend gender and power in families, the experiences of superordinate as well as subordinate groups and individuals have to be studied. Finding out more about the specificity of men's relationships will illuminate psychological and social processes which maintain and recreate power differentials in families and other intimate systems.

Seeking help

A starting point for many clinicians working with 'families' which include fathers is the realization that a majority of such men, for whatever reason, tend to be absent from consultations. Clinical opinion and experience is that when there are relationship problems in families (either conjugal or parental) it is mothers rather than fathers, wives rather than husbands, who make the initial approach to an agency for help. The man or father has been described as 'disengaged' in the literature on individual psychotherapy (Kirschner *et al.* 1982; Solomon 1982; Scher *et al.* 1987), marital counselling (Brannen and Collard 1982), and family therapy (Atkins and Lansky 1986; Heubeck *et al.* 1986), although we do not know whether the man himself would concur with such a description. Empirical data does align with clinical opinion but the material is rather patchy.

Marital problems

Five recent small-scale studies of marital counselling in the UK all point to the finding that women do indeed tend to make the first agency contact, are more likely than men to come along for the first session, and are more likely to continue with counselling afterwards (Brannen and Collard 1982; Heisler 1984; Gaunt 1985; Hunt 1985; Timms and Blampied 1985). In Brannen and Collard's London study, for instance, two-thirds of first contacts to formal agencies were made by wives. They found that men were also less involved in informal lay referral networks such as those involving friends and kin.

Family problems

Systematic data on gender patterns of attendance to agencies who deal with family issues and take a family approach are sparse. Published UK material on this question is limited and although there is more American research, the measures used are rather restrictive, usually based on therapist impression rather than actuarial session by session data (Gurman and Kniskern 1981). One example is the work by Berg and Rosenblum (1977) who analysed sixty family therapists' views about fathers in treatment. The therapists reported that about 30 per cent of families turned up to the first interview without father and that in general fathers were more resistant than mothers about coming back to the clinic. Time conflict between work and therapy was the most frequently stated reason why fathers were unable to attend sessions. As mentioned above, family therapists from both Europe and the USA have commented on the relative absence of men from family sessions. Indeed, a crucial task of early sessions is how to engage the reluctant father (Gurman and Kniskern 1981).

Individual problems

Routine social surveys provide us with much more comprehensive data about individual consultative and help-seeking behaviour. At an individual level men on average utilize physical and mental health-care services at a lower rate than women. For instance, analysis of the 1980 General Household Survey shows that adult men between 16 and 55 years are more likely than comparable women to report good physical health, fewer days of restricted activity due to illness, and fewer physician visits (Cunningham-Burley 1986). Identical self-report gender differences have been found in other studies (Verbrugge 1985) despite the context of a real higher prevalence of physical disease and higher mortality rate amongst men (McIntyre 1985; Bayliss *et al.* 1986).

As far as psychiatric morbidity statistics are concerned, it seems that fewer adult men than women present with psychiatric symptoms at the primary care level (Goldberg and Huxley 1980). However, in the UK at least, when men do present, they are more likely than women to be referred on to a psychiatrist and to be admitted as an in-patient (ibid.: 133). Some of the explanations for this gendered pattern of help seeking and referral will be explored later in the chapter but several writers have suggested that men's easier passage from community to hospital might be because when they present to the general practitioner their problems are at a more serious stage of development (for example, Horwitz 1977). Patterns of psychiatric diagnosis also vary by gender of patient. In the UK gender differences are most apparent for the depressive/neurotic categories which are female dominated and the drug-dependence syndromes which include more men than women (Williams 1984).

It seems, then, that the ideology of the new man or involved father, important in many clinicians' philosophies and training, is not reflected in male help-seeking behaviour nor, as will be seen, in the interactions between professionals and clients in the clinic. Recently, clinicians have been trying to understand *why* men are underepresented in the help-seeking and -giving settings and *how* fathers :an be more effectively *engaged* in therapy. Before these areas are ex- plored let us consider why we should bother to engage men and 'athers in this way at all. Possible reasons include:

(1) Adoption of a preventive approach to male emotional and physical ill-health which would emphasize the therapeutic advantages for men of earlier problem recognition and appropriate help-seeking action.
(2) Conceptual assumptions underlying a particular therapeutic intervention, as is the case with the systemic approach of family therapy which necessitates male involvement, if males are in the presenting system. With this approach a 'problem' is not seen to reside within one person but is instead understood in terms of how all individuals within a system inter-relate.
(3) Therapists might want to respond to women and mothers' requests often voiced in the first session, for more sharing, understanding, and/or less abuse from their male partners.

Why men don't present

There are many potential explanations of male patterns of help seeking. I want to begin with those which concentrate on individual psychological processing and then move on to arguments that are centred more around social and institutional considerations.

Problem recognition

Some American and UK evidence suggests that men are less likely than women to interpret symptoms associated with mild depression and low general well-being as signs of emotional problems and as a consequence are less likely to obtain professional help voluntarily for their difficulties (Kessler *et al.* 1981; Briscoe 1982). Briscoe points out that an identical affect state might have typically 'masculine' and 'feminine' *interpretations*. In her London study she found, for example, that women tended to perceive the affect state of 'not having recently felt particularly excited or interested in something' as indicative of 'things going badly' whereas male subjects were more likely to see this situation as 'a normal state of affairs'. So the process by which an individual begins to recognize or label an emotional problem as being an emotional problem might well be influenced by gender. Symptomatic men may feel the same level of malaise or unhappiness as comparable women but may process these sensations through different sets or schemas in which the criterion for problem recognition is set at a different level. Certainly there is psychophysiological work suggesting that men tend to be less attentive to certain bodily states and changes than women (Pennebaker 1982). Thus it may well be that this difference in 'internal attentiveness' carries over to interactions with others so that, in a familial context, men are slower than women in perceiving indicators of relationship difficulties.

Expressive differences

Where men do recognize familial or marital problems, expressive norms associated with conventional masculinity can, at least in western cultures, inhibit *articulation*, especially in the public domain (Solomon and Levy 1982).

Writers who subscribe to this view argue that the existence of familial difficulties is suggestive of a degree of personal weakness and so is more appropriately communicated to outsiders by female family members. Men's reluctance to attend hospitals, even in the face of possible heart attacks, and the instrumental role of wives in engineering admission give some support to this argument (Finlayson and McEwen 1977). As Richman reminds us, the first commandment of ('old') masculinity is: 'Thou shalt not cry or expose feelings of emotion, fear, weakness, symptoms, empathy or involvement before thy neighbour' (Richman 1982: 103). Jourard's (1971) work on self-disclosure also highlights social constraints on male expression of affect. He found that in general American men had lower levels of personal self-disclosure than women.

As far as the public disclosure of child-related problems is concerned, there is some evidence that both mothers and fathers accept the normative prescription of mother as child-care expert and specialist in dealing with health professionals (Kerr and McKee 1981; Graham 1984).

It seems that the mother both receives (Gluck *et al.* 1980) and transmits the emotional atmosphere of the family and, moreover, is reinforced in this position by the feedback she receives from others outside the home. In the majority of families there is, of course, a material basis to this transaction since women take on the main responsibility for child care and, some would argue, also for adult care:

> As the principal carer, the mother acts not only as the home nurse, home doctor and home tutor, she is also the person in contact with the professionals who perform these roles in the public domain. Typically it is mother who seeks out health professionals; she is the one, too, who is sought out by them.
>
> (Graham 1984: 164)

The mother might, therefore, indeed be the more reliable informant about emotional family issues. Kerr and McKee (1981) show that fathers tend to attend child-health clinics only when requested to do so by their wives or when there is a 'serious' developmental issue to consider such as immunization. Social Services involvement, for instance in cases of child abuse, may also result in fathers being compelled to attend a therapeutic setting. It might be that fathers are only seen as necessary, both by themselves and others, when family distress is exceptionally high.

Institutional factors

Further factors which influence the involvement of fathers in clinical milieux are the nature of the therapeutic institutions and the therapists they contain. A clinic might seem, to the eyes of both potential clients of each sex and the therapists themselves, a woman's place located in woman's time. Just as research on the family takes place in men's working hours and often excludes fathers, so too does therapy with the family. Also, therapists and other health workers might share the societal belief of some of their male clients that expressing concerns about fatherhood or husbandhood is indicative of weakness and femininity. Even if therapists do not consciously hold this belief, Atkins and Lansky suggest that male clients might, through the course of treatment, project these feelings on to the therapists and so create in turn quite a debilitating institutional countertransference for fathers.

> Shared social values surrounding masculinity can generate conflicts around a man's more 'feminized' past, rendering a father anxious and/or hostile toward a treatment situation he sees as passive, or as inflicting passivity or powerlessness, or as dominated by women or by 'affected, panty-waisted men'. The mental health system then becomes the inheritor, through projection, of shared inner conflicts surrounding masculinity and femininity, activity and passivity, and power and weakness.
>
> (Atkins and Lansky 1986: 183)

Other researchers into gender issues in psychotherapy have noticed the 'discomfort' some therapists feel when treating men and indeed the 'deficiencies in fledgling male therapist's appreciation of emotional issues' (Kirschner *et al.* 1982: 271).

In an interesting article, Brearley (1986), a past cricket captain of England and now a psychoanalyst, describes some of the dilemmas of being a male therapist and of working with male clients. He feels that being a male therapist is difficult as the qualities of a good therapist

– that is, to be able to 'to receive, listen, wait and to remain in the dark' (Brearley 1986: 9) – do not come easily to men. Of his patients, he comments that the men 'tend to be more cut off from their feelings', and 'experience less conscious misery, or are vaguely miserable but unable to say or know why' (ibid.: 3).

Although the gender of a clinician or therapist has always been considered a potent dimension in the therapeutic relationship, systematic research into this area is only a recent development and has been especially pronounced in the USA. We know very little about gender and therapeutic relationships elsewhere. Data from the USA indicate that male psychotherapists are more involved in marital, family, and group therapy than their female counterparts. By contrast, female psychotherapists spend a larger part of their therapy time doing individual work when compared to their male colleagues (see Dryden 1984). There is growing evidence that a male therapist in the early stages of family therapy can facilitate whole-family engagement (Heubeck *et al.* 1986). In this situation a father might feel that he is not entering into women's territory, but that he is 'in with a chance' and that he might even have an ally who can understand him.

Whatever the characteristics associated with fathers' lack of involvement with the helping professions, there is certainly a current concern to engage the peripheral father. This motivation might originate from the philosophical assumptions underlying a particular intervention, as is the case of family therapy. From a systems perspective it is important to decode the meaning and message of paternal distancing. As Lerner (1988: 270) remarks:

> Distance and disengagement have no less impact on family relationships than do their flip sides of overinvolvement and fusion. It is imperative that we carefully examine our tendency to render men to the position of the peripheral 'other' in the domestic sphere, just as women have been so rendered in the public domain.

In addition, wider political orientations, such as a belief in shared parental responsibility for child care, may be in operation. I will now move on to the third part of this chapter which considers therapist–male client interaction in the consulting room or clinic.

Men and fathers in the consulting room

Style of therapy in couple work

Just as there are often conflicts of interest between mothers and fathers in the home, these may also occur during consultations with helping professionals. Men and women in such settings may want the same outcome – for example help with children's sleep problems or relief from chronic marital arguments – but their investment in the consultations and expectations of treatment may vary considerably. It might also be that therapy behaviour reflects strategies of power maintenance between the sexes.

Brannen and Collard (1982) found that men were less satisfied than women with a non-directive, 'ventilative' style of marital counselling, expressing a preference for more structured advice giving or goal setting. Possibly, open-ended talk takes husbands and fathers into previously 'closed' areas around, for instance, metacommunication about control and decision making: understandably, the more powerful may be resistant to forays into these fields.

Research has indicated that men who persist in counselling begin to accept the value of 'just talking' (Hunt 1985). As one of Hunt's respondents commented:

> Well, unless you are actually expressing feelings regularly, the words don't come easy to describe how you feel when you are asked 'how do you feel . . . .?' Normally, you don't get down to it, so I didn't find it easy to say how I am feeling . . . basically because I'm not practised at it.
>
> (ibid.: 78)

The propensity of more men than women to drop out after the first session disallows any further practice at 'talk'. Moreover, the expectation of at least a degree of open talk about feelings at this session might dissuade some men from returning. A study of the first interview in UK marriage-guidance settings suggests that after this session men 'perceive their counsellors as slightly less warm and friendly' and 'feel slightly less understood' than female clients (Gaunt 1985: 25). There may be a greater fear among male clients that unfocused talk about personal matters will lead to loss of power.

Style of therapy in family work

Some of the active techniques used in structural family therapy (such as enactments of parent–child dialogue and explicit manoeuvres altering proximity) have also been favoured by fathers (Russell *et al.* 1984). In a longitudinal study of thirty-one cases, Russell and her colleagues found that mothers favoured relatively gentle interactions such as 'tracking' or positive connotation. It might be that the more active therapeutic techniques help integrate fathers back into the family system and decrease their feelings of parental incompetence and helplessness. Family-therapy clinics which require father presence before any therapeutic work can begin might have the same effect. But Russell *et al.* caution against change occurring too quickly as family members very involved in the original structure might experience blame and frustration. This family member is often the mother.

The manner in which particular family therapists align with fathers has come under criticism of late, especially from feminist therapists. Hare-Mustin (1981: 558), for instance, argues that some therapeutic manoeuvres reinstate stereotypical gender roles and may in fact create an even more 'one down' position for women:

> Minuchin (1974) sees himself as modelling the male executive function, forming alliances, most typically with the father and through competition, rule setting, and direction, demanding that the father resume control of the family and exert leadership as Minuchin leads and controls the session . . . . These illustrations reveal how the unquestioned acceptance and reinforcement of stereotypic sex roles takes place in much of family therapy, despite the possibilities inherent for change in the systems point of view.

However the creative use of a male therapist might be more likely to instigate a shift in a partner's family role, as Goldner (1985: 45) suggests: 'A male therapist telling a father to shape up can be seen as a rude awakening, a female therapist with the same message can be just another nag.' It therefore seems that the different ways in which female and male therapists operate to promote parental unity and equality is an area for future enquiry.

Over the last few years gender issues are being more openly discussed in the family-therapy literature (Hare-Mustin 1986). In particular there has been concern that some assumptions of systems thinking, for example the insistence that all actors play a part in the maintenance of dysfunctional behaviour, can have negative consequences for women in families where, for instance, men are violent or abusive (McIntyre 1985). Such an assumption, McIntyre (ibid.: 253) posits, overlooks the social dominance of men in the public sphere and fallaciously assumes equal power in the home. In the consulting room, as the interaction between the couple becomes highlighted, the woman's status is redefined from victim to 'co-conspirator'.

Conclusions and implications

By concentrating on the male actor, as I have in this chapter, it is possible that I have, using Hare-Mustin's (1986) terminology, committed an alpha error: that is, I may have exaggerated the differences between men and women. (Writers committing beta errors assume no difference between the sexes.) Instead, I hope that the ideas in this chapter raise the discussion above crude dichotomies. As the material shows, shifts in male behaviour necessarily affect women and vice versa. Moreover, there appears to be a complex gendered patterning in the way humans recognize and communicate personal and family malaise. Mild depressive symptoms and low general well-being both in the self and in others appear to activate women to 'make good' and to seek help. Individual and family stress has often escalated to quite a high level before men are prepared or forced to take restorative action. As research has shown, even at this time it is wives and mothers who are initially prime movers in encouraging men to 'talk' about emotional concerns.

However, despite initial reluctance on behalf of men, it seems possible that paternal involvement, for instance in family therapy, creates closer father–child relationships and enhances men's self-esteem as fathers (Heubeck *et al.* 1986). In addition, the resolution of traumatic family quandries associated with, for instance, physical or sexual child abuse, might be resolved more successfully and more quickly if fathers were present (Tyler 1986). Similarly, earlier recognition of bodily changes connected to heart disease might increase male life expectancy. But what are the consequences of these shifts for contemporary wives and mothers?

It could be argued that since in the current sex-gender system, the emotional arena seems to be a female specialism, male encroachment might have some negative consequences for women. An incompetent father often means a more competent mother, a stronger father–child relationship might mean a less intimate mother–child bond. Given the continued discriminatory character of the work-place, which in many ways operates to discourage maternal advancement, any transformation of men into competent parents and emotionally sensitive partners begs the question: What areas are left in which women can excel and from which they can derive meaning? A challenge for the future is to discover creative ways of allowing women and men equal access to public and private life. The next task for a gender-sensitive therapy?

Note

1. This chapter is an adapted version of 'Men and fathers in therapy', *Journal of Family Therapy* Vol. 10 (1988).

References

Atkins, R. and Lansky, M. (1986) 'The father in family therapy: psychoanalytic perspectives', in M.E. Lamb (ed.) *The Father's Role: Applied Perspectives*, New York: Wiley.

Bayliss, R., Clarke, C., and Whitefield, A. (1986) 'The female life span', *Journal of the Royal College of Physicians in London* 20(4): 290–3.

Berg, B. and Rosenblum, N. (1977) 'Fathers in family therapy: a survey of family therapists', *Journal of Marriage and Family Counselling* 3: 850–91.

Brannen, J. and Collard, J. (1982) *Marriages in Trouble*, London: Tavistock.

Brearley, M. (1986) 'Counsellors and clients: men or women', *Marriage Guidance* 22(2): 3–9.

Briscoe, M. (1982) 'Sex differences in psychological well-being', *Psychological Medicine* Monograph Supplement *1*, Cambridge University Press.

Chesler, P. (1972) *Women and Madness*, New York: Avon Books.

Coverman, S. and Sheley, J.F. (1986) 'Change in men's housework and child-care time 1965–1975', *Journal of Marriage and the Family* 48(5): 413–22.

Cunningham-Burley, S. (1986) 'Marital status and health', paper presented to First Congress of the European Society of Medical Sociology, Groningen, June.

Dryden, W. (1984) *Individual Therapy in Britain*, London: Harper & Row.

Finlayson, A. and McEwen, J. (1977) *Coronary Heart Disease and Patterns of Living*, London: Croom Helm.

Ford, A. (1984) *Men*, London: Weidenfeld & Nicolson.

Franks, H. (1984) *Goodbye Tarzan*, London: Allen & Unwin.

Gaunt, S. (1985) 'The first interview, in marriage guidance', *National Marriage Guidance Council, Rugby Research Paper* 2.

Gluck, N., Donefer, E., and Milea, K. (1980) 'Women in families', in E. Carter and M. McGoldrick (eds.) *The Family Life Cycle*, London and New York: Gardner Press.

Goldberg, D. and Huxley, P. (1980) *Mental Illness in the Community*, London: Tavistock Publications.

Goldner, V. (1985) 'Feminism and family therapy', *Family Process* 24 (March): 31–47.

Graham, H. (1984) *Women, Health and the Family*, London: Wheatsheaf Books.

Gurman, A. and Kniskern, D. (1981) *Handbook of Family Therapy*, New York: Brunner Mazel.

Hare-Mustin, R.T. (1981) 'A feminist approach to family therapy', in E. Howell and M. Bayes (eds.) *Women and Mental Health*, New York: Basic Books.

Hare-Mustin, R.T. (1986) 'The problem of gender in family therapy theory', *Family Process* 26(1): 15–27.

Heisler, J. (1984) *The NMGC Client*, Rugby: National Marriage Guidance Council.

Heubeck, R., Watson, J., and Russell, G. (1986) 'Father involvement and responsibility in family therapy', in M.E. Lamb (ed.) *The Father's Role: Applied Perspectives*, New York: Wiley.

Hodson, P. (1984) *Men: An Investigation into the Emotional Male*, London: Basic Books.

Horwitz, A. (1977) 'The pathways into psychiatric treatment: some differences between men and women', *Journal of Health and Social Behaviour* 18: 169–78.

Hunt, P. (1985) 'Clients' responses to marriage counselling', *National Marriage Guidance Council, Rugby, Research Report* 3.

Ingham, M. (1984) *Men: The Male Myth Exposed*, London: Century Publishing.

Jourard, S. (1971) *The Transparent Self*, New York: Van Nostrand.

Kerr, M. and McKee, L. (1981) 'The father's role in child health care', *Health Visitor* 54(2): 47–51.

Kessler, R., Brown, R., and Bronnan, C. (1981) 'Sex differences in psychiatric help-seeking: evidence from four large-scale surveys', *Journal of Health and Social Behaviour* 22 (March): 49–64.

Kirschner, L.A., Hauser, S.T., and Genack, A. (1982) 'Research on gender and psychotherapy', in M.T. Notman and C.C. Nadelson (eds.) *The Woman Patient*, New York: Plenum Press.

Lamb, M.E. (1981) *The Role of the Father in Child Development*, 2nd edn., New York: Wiley.

Lerner, H. (1988) *Women in Therapy*, London: Jason Aronson.

Lewis, C. (1986) *Becoming a Father*, Milton Keynes: Open University Press.

Lewis, C. and O'Brien, M. (1987) *Reassessing Fatherhood: New Observations on Fathers and the Modern Family*, London and New York: Sage Publications.

MacIntyre, S. (1985) 'Marriage is good for your health: or is it?', lecture to the Royal Philosophical Society of Glasgow, 11 December.

McIntyre, D. (1985) 'Domestic violence: a case of the disappearing victim', *Australian Journal of Family Therapy* 5(4): 249–58.

McKee, L. and O'Brien, M. (eds.) (1982) *The Father Figure*, London: Tavistock Publications.

Pennebaker, J.W. (1982) *The Psychology of Physical Symptoms*, London: Longmans.

Pleck, J. and Sawyer, J. (1974) *Men and Masculinity*, NJ: Prentice-Hall.

Richman, J. (1982) 'Men's experiences of pregnancy and childbirth', in L. McKee and M. O'Brien (eds.) *The Father Figure*, London: Tavistock Publications.

Rieker, P. and Carmen, E. (1984) *The Gender Gap in Psychotherapy*, New York: Plenum Press.

Roberts, Y. (1984) *Man Enough*, London: Chatto & Windus.

Russell, C.S., Atilano, R.B., Anderson, S.A., Jurich, A.P., and Bergen, L.P. (1984) 'Intervention strategies: predicting family therapy outcome', *Journal of Marital and Family Therapy* 10: 241–51.

Sayers, J. (1988) 'Feminist Therapy–Forgetting the Father?', paper presented to British Psychological Society Annual Conference.

Scher, M., Stevens, M., Good, G., and Eichenfield, G. (1987) *Handbook of Counselling and Psychotherapy with Men*, London: Sage.

Solomon, K. (1982) 'Individual psychotherapy and changing masculine roles: dimensions of gender-role psychotherapy', in K. Solomon and N. Levy (eds.) *Men in Transition: Theory and Therapy*, New York: Plenum.

Solomon, K. and Levy, N. (eds.) (1982) *Men in Transition: Theory and Therapy*, New York: Plenum.

Timms, N. and Blampied, A. (1985) *Intervention in Marriage*, Social Services Monograph, Sheffield University: Joint Unit for Social Services Research.

Tyler, A. (1986) 'The abusing father', in M.E. Lamb (ed.) *The Father's Role: Applied Prospectives*, New York: Wiley.

Verbrugge, L. (1985) 'Gender and health: an update on hypothesis and evidence', *Journal of Health and Social Behaviour* 26 September: 156–82.

Williams, J. (1984) 'Women and mental illness', in J. Nicholson and H. Beloff (eds.) *Psychology Survey*, Leicester: British Psychological Society.

Chapter eleven

Masculinity and family work

Barry Mason and Ed Mason

> Everything I know about men you could fit on the end of a pin and still have room for the Lord's prayer.
>
> (Cher, American actress and singer, 1988)

There can be few men in the helping professions who have not been challenged in recent years, directly and/or indirectly, by the ideas of feminism and the gay-liberation movement, to re-examine traditional ideas about what it means to be a man in relation to women and vice versa. It is our impression that in general men have not taken up the challenge. When we were first asked to participate in the conference that led to this book and began to think about how we as men worked with men and women professionally, we realized that we had hardly begun to tackle a number of problematic aspects of traditional male behaviour in our work.

This chapter asserts that aspects of this socially and psychologically constructed masculinity are deeply problematic and argues that we need to find ways of addressing these issues when working with individuals, couples, families, and colleagues. It goes on to suggest a number of ways in which we might challenge and reframe aspects of traditional male behaviour. This is not to say that men are to blame for all the problems that may be referred to us, but simply to suggest that too little attention has been given to these issues by men as opposed to the increasing amount of work that women have devoted to the subject. A friend of the authors possesses several bookshelves full of books and articles on feminism and/or gender issues. Only a small number are by men. This is not because she only collects work written by women but because men do not appear to write on the subject very much. If it is to be effective, family therapy must be concerned with challenging rules (both within the family and in the wider network) which are thought to contribute to the maintenance of a problem. If men do not write about gender issues, one can hypothesize that this is because they do not identify these issues as being particularly important.

The invitation

We were rather surprised to be asked to run a workshop at a conference on feminism and family therapy and at times felt uncomfortable participating in a conference that overwhelmingly comprised women. However, we believe that this is an area in which men have a part to play. We believe that patriarchy damages men's quality of life as well as women's, that it constrains men rather than enabling them to develop.

The invitation challenged and frightened us in a way that was different from being invited to do any other type of workshop. Normally, we would be nervous but would be reassured by the expertise we possessed; with this workshop we felt we had a very fragile framework to hold on to. We found ourselves going out of our way to say that we had no expertise. We wondered what we were setting ourselves up for. We felt locked in a non-therapeutic double bind – damned if we did participate, and damned if we did not.

Why a men-only workshop?

We chose to run a men-only workshop at the conference. In our experience of discussions of gender and sexism in mixed groups, women tend to get angry and men tend to feel guilty. We believe that if men are to have any real motivation for changing gender relationships it has to be based on more than simply guilt about how oppressive they have been. Men need to be convinced that, as men, they will actually benefit and we hoped that we would be able to identify some of these benefits during the workshop. We were also aware that, as men, we often rely on women's skills in understanding and nurturing relationships and we felt that by excluding women from the group we would be obliged to take responsibility for these issues ourselves.

Theoretical considerations

Although a systems-theory approach in relation to gender issues has come under attack recently (for example, MacLeod and Saraga 1988), we see it as useful in helping to move away from the notion of blame which is ultimately an unhelpful concept. Some writers (for example, Treacher and Carpenter 1984) have noted that if all family therapy does is move the locus of a problem from the individual to the family then it will have failed. Similarly, if all we do is to move 'to the other side of the net' and blame men for the problems that are presented to family therapists, we will not achieve a great deal. One could compare it to moving furniture from one room to another in the same house rather than moving to a different house. With its notion of there being no beginning or end, that behaviour needs to be addressed in terms of circularity, systems theory has been criticized as being biased against women. We acknowledge that this can be a valid interpretation if systems theory is viewed in an absolute sense. However, systems theory leads one to believe that no such thing as absolute truth exists; there are only different perceptions of reality. It therefore follows that systems theory itself cannot be absolute. It is only more or less useful. An Australian family therapist, Liz Roberts, has worked extensively with couples where the man has been violent towards the woman. She makes it clear during her first session with the couple that she does not condone violence, and has found that she can resist the temptation to ally with the woman by maintaining a systems perspective: 'Because of my gender and conditioning, I often find myself instinctively wanting to protect the woman being mindful of framing her actions in a positive light. Therapeutically with rigid family systems, this has proven ineffective and counterproductive.' (Roberts 1988: 5).

We have found that concentrating on responsibility is a more effective way of addressing gender issues than apportioning blame. Unless men take more responsibility for the part they play in private, public and professional relationships with women, there will be no substantial movement of any sort. For men, self-blame can be an easier option than an examination of the issues in terms of responsibility.

Do men have a problem?

We believe that there is a wealth of evidence (Gilligan 1982; Miller 1983) to suggest that the way men have learnt to behave significantly contributes to major difficulties in relationships. For example, the continuing need for refuges for battered women suggests that intimate relationships in our society often involve men being violent to their female partners.

In addition, women seem to be profoundly dissatisfied with the quality of their relationships with men. In Hite's (1987) recent survey of 4,500 women in the USA, 98 per cent said that the biggest problem in their current relationship was a lack of emotional closeness. The most commonly expressed complaint was that 'he doesn't listen' (77 per cent of respondents). Some 91 per cent of the women who were separated or divorced said that they and not their partners made the decision to separate. Finally, the sexual abuse of children is overwhelmingly committed by men. Less than 10 per cent of the abusers are women (Wynne 1987). It may also be true that some of the abuse by women is committed with a man and/or may be for pornography aimed at a male market.

'Real men'

Our society promotes all sorts of expectations about how men and women should behave which have very little to do with biological *sex*, and as we grow up we internalize many of these expectations. These sets of *gender* expectations are at least as important as biology to our experience of what it means to be male or female and there is a good deal of evidence (Chodorow 1978; Arcana 1983) to show that these physical, social, and psychological patterns are laid down at a very early age. Men are expected to be strong, active, and fearless, battling it out in the world to provide for their families. They develop physical, technical, and intellectual skills for solving practical problems and their 'proper' domain seems to be in the public world, whether it is the battlefield, the work-place, the sports arena, or simply the public house. Men's other equally human capabilities tend to be underdeveloped if not totally neglected. Many men lack domestic skills, such as cooking, homemaking, and child-care skills, primarily because these are seen as womanly pursuits. Many men give an impression of being emotionally illiterate, unable to identify and communicate their own feelings and needs. They rely on women, and women's conditioning contributes to the maintenance of this pattern.

Women may not be biologically more sensitive, empathic, nurturing, and affirming than men. They may simply develop these skills because they are expected to do so.

'New men'

While men who work in the 'helping' professions are not stereotypical macho heroes and may appear to be more emotionally in touch, better listeners and more sensitive than many men, we have not escaped this socialization. The women attending the conference were in no doubt that the world of family therapy was a profoundly sexist one. Men in the helping professions are probably just more subtle about sexism. An increasing number of men are challenged by feminist ideas and are struggling to break away from the more restrictive aspects of male socialization. They, like us, wish to improve their understanding of their emotions and be able to express them in a way that is not oppressive of others. They also want to sustain emotional relationships with men as well as with women, develop a less performance-orientated and more fulfilling sexuality, develop domestic skills, and become more involved with their children. However, gender socialization goes very deep and such changes are not easy to make. It takes enormous effort to exercise choice about how we behave and relate to our colleagues, friends, lovers, and families.

Looking to women for change

Women and men respond to emotional distress in different ways. When therapists see a couple, it is very often the woman who appears more 'in touch' with her feelings, more capable of talking about them, and more willing to get involved in therapeutic work. Marianne Walters has argued powerfully that this phenomenon leads therapists to join with the woman, relying on her capacity to change to bring about change in the relationship. All family therapists must be familiar with the problem of men who do not really believe that what is happening in the relationship has anything to do with them, and with the men who we, as therapists, are constantly afraid of driving away if we challenge them too strongly. Therapists, male and female, are often too ready to accept that the man cannot be engaged in work and thus only seek to work with the woman. It is easier to label men as 'unworkable with' than to spend time to think how one could do something different to engage the man. By doing this one faces the danger of giving the woman a subtle message that the man is not worth staying with. There is also a danger that the therapist may take up cues from the woman that the therapist should ally herself/himself with her. It can also lead to the woman being labelled as the only person needing help. In some respects, the attempted solution to the problem can thus serve to maintain it.

Some practice considerations for the male therapist

A number of points need to be borne in mind. In the first place, the therapist needs to accept that addressing gender issues is valid when problems are presented to him, so long as any intervention fits the context.

Second, blaming the man is an easy 'cop-out' and leads to defensiveness and withdrawal rather than possibilities for change. Any male therapist can play the 'right on' game by challenging sexist behaviour in a client in such a way as to ensure that he does not come back for the next interview. Third, change in men is threatening at times not only to men but to women as well, however much the latter may want it. It is useful to hold on to the idea of 'what people lose if things get better'. Finally, neutrality seems to be getting a rather bad press lately (Walters 1987; Treacher 1988). The original Milan team defined neutrality as 'a specific pragmatic effect that [the therapist's] other total behaviour during the session exerts on the family and not his intrapsychic disposition' (Palazzoli *et al.* 1980: 11). They state that if you were to ask the family at the end of the session whose side the therapist had supported, family members would have remained 'puzzled and uncertain' (ibid.). Some writers (such as MacKinnon and James 1987) have suggested that such a neutral stance can be seen as a bias against women.

We would suggest, however, that a misunderstanding about neutrality has developed whereby it is seen in absolute terms in the absence of one of the most important concepts in family therapy, that of context. A neutral position in a private clinic in Milan differs from that in a Social Services department in an inner-city area. Rather than considering a single form of neutrality we should be thinking in terms of *neutralities*. One of the authors (Mason 1986) has given a working definition of neutrality as 'challenging belief systems without taking sides'. The issue does not concern sitting on the fence, it is not, as Hoffman and Penn (1987) have pointed out, non-positional; it is multi-positional. We believe that neutral approaches are as important when working with gender issues as much as when working with any other issues a therapist may encounter. If male therapists who have been using a neutral approach have not been addressing gender issues, the reason, we suggest, has more to do with the therapist than with the notion of neutrality. Interestingly, Roberts (1988) has found that losing her neutrality in working with marital violence renders her less effective.

Some examples of a neutral approach

A man in individual therapy work said that his wife did not appreciate his needs. After discussing what he meant by this, the therapist asked him which of his wife's needs he felt he needed to take more account of. The question itself completely surprised him.

In an interview with a husband and wife, the latter was asked whether she thought men should be traditional in their roles around the house or whether she preferred a more modern approach. She stated that she preferred a modern approach. The husband was then asked whether he thought his wife thought him traditional or modern with regard to his doing domestic chores about the house.

During an interview with a family, disagreements were being discussed and the family was asked 'If there were to be disagreements over what men and women did in your house, what would they be?' A similar approach could include questions such as: 'Are there disagreements in your house about what women do and men do? What are they? Who would most want the situation to change? In what way? Do you want your children to be similar or different to you in the way they see their role in relation to the opposite sex.' If the answer is 'similar', one can explore what that means and then ask, 'If he/she were to be different, in what way would you like that to be?'

The mother in a reconstituted family where the first husband had gone to prison for sexually abusing two of the children was asked: 'I know from interviewing other families in similar circumstances that some women feel they cannot fully trust a man again. Is that the case with you?' 'Yes.' 'Does that mean that you will always retain some suspicion about whether your new husband will abuse the children or do you feel you won't be suspicious?' 'I will be a bit suspicious.' (To the husband) 'Were you aware of that?' 'She hadn't said it but I knew.' It is often useful to include oneself as a male therapist in such a discussion but one must take care that this does not place the woman in a problematic position and by default ally oneself with the man.

During a discussion with a couple about how members of the family showed they were upset, the woman said that she cried when she was upset and the man said that he found it difficult to cry. The woman was asked, 'Do you think that your husband finds it difficult to cry because he finds it difficult to let go, because he thinks it is not manly, or for some other reason?' The woman replied that she thought it was mainly because her husband would think it unmanly. He agreed with her. His wife was then asked whether she thought it unmanly and she said no. This answer surprised the man and the discussion developed into further examination of gender issues on the relationship. The purpose of the original question was to open up the area for discussion by challenging a stereotype in as neutral a way as possible in order to keep both parties engaged. The aim was not to suggest that crying was a good or bad thing for either sex.

In all of the above examples the therapist concerned perceived from the feedback elicited that no one had felt that he had been biased against them. Those who are familiar with the technique will have noticed that circular questioning was used to help maintain neutrality. We would argue that such a technique is crucial in establishing neutrality and joining effectively with the clients. In one of our agencies, the use of a neutral approach has contributed, over three years to a 90.7 per cent turn-up rate for appointments. In the last year more gender-related questions have been slowly introduced into the interview. A feared decrease in the turn-up rate has not occurred.

Conclusions

In our introduction, we indicated that we were somewhat nervous of running a workshop at a conference on feminism and family therapy. However, we were encouraged by the supportive comments made by colleagues of both sexes prior to the conference and by the risks that the participants in the workshop took on the day of the conference. As leaders, we learned a great deal, and this learning has continued with the agreements and disagreements we have had to face while writing this chapter. In the final analysis, there are four points which we would particularly like to stress. First, we, as male therapists have progressed a little further along the road of addressing gender issues in our work than prior to the conference. We are, though, still clearly at an early stage in our development.

Our second conclusion is the realization that a systemic approach to gender issues is more useful than the easier blaming linear approach. Third, men, whether therapists or clients, are only likely to change in any significant way if traditional sexist behaviours come to be regarded by them as constraints rather than attributes. Finally, as male therapists we need to take greater responsibility for looking more closely at how we can increase the amount of time we devote to addressing gender issues in our work.

References

Arcana, J. (1983) *Every Mother's Son*, London: Women's Press.

Chodorow, N. (1978) *The Reproduction of Mothering*, Berkeley: University of California Press.

Gilligan, C. (1982) *In a Different Voice*, Cambridge, Mass.: Harvard University Press.

Hite, S. (1987) *Women and Love*, Harmondsworth: Penguin.

Hoffman, L. and Penn, P. (1987) Introduction in L. Boscolo, G. Cecchin, L. Hoffman, and P. Penn *Milan Systemic Family Therapy*, New York: Basic Books.

MacLeod, M. and Saraga, E. (1988) 'Challenging the orthodoxy: towards a feminist theory and practice', *Feminist Review* 28: 16–55.

MacKinnon, L. and James, K. (1987) 'The Milan systemic approach: theory and practice', *Australian and New Zealand Journal of Family Therapy* 8: 89–98.

Mason, B. (1986) 'Neutrality: the worker and family therapy', in

M. Marshall, M. Preston-Shoot and E. Wincott (eds.) *Skills for Social Workers in the 1980s*, Birmingham: British Association for Social Work.

Miller, S. (1983) *Men and Friendship*, London: Galloway Books.

Palazzoli, M.S., Boscolo, L., Cecchin, G., and Prata, G., (1980) 'Hypothesising, circularity and neutrality: three guidelines for the conductor of the session', *Family Process* 19: 45–57.

Roberts, E. (forthcoming) 'Ms Columbo tracking marital violence', submitted for publication.

Treacher, A. (1988) 'The Milan Method – a preliminary critique', *Journal of Family Therapy* 10: 1–8.

Treacher, A. and Carpenter, J. (eds.) (1984) *Using Family Therapy*, Oxford: Blackwell.

Walters, M. (1987) Seminar presentation, Institute of Family Therapy, London, June.

Wynne, J.M. (1987) 'Child sexual abuse in Leeds: a medical view', *FSU Quarterly* 41/42: 17–21.

Part five

Applications: Wider Systems

Chapter twelve

'The little woman' and the world of work

Gill Gorell Barnes

> As politics and diplomacy grow more savage and warlike, men seek a haven in private life in personal relations, and above all in the family; the last refuge of love and decency. Domestic life, however secure, is increasingly incapable of providing these comforts.
>
> (Lasch 1977)

Overheard outside an infant class:

> *First wife:* My husband comes home. He says, 'Hello, how are you' and then he starts reading the paper.
> *Second wife:* You're lucky: first he comes home, second he says 'How are you'. I don't take these things for granted any more.

In this chapter I will focus on the institution of marriage as a subsystem in a larger series of interconnected systems. Aspects of the relationship of marriage to other institutions which form a regular and repeated part of the pattern of the lives of a couple will also be considered. There is an extensive literature on work settings and the way in which the characteristics of these interact with non-work life. The focus here, however, is on the paradoxes posed by gender socialization; by couple intimacy and by intergenerational patterning both as they operate within the extended family and within organizations. This exploratory essay concerns an ever-changing field which is influenced by class, culture, politics, and current economics, and fluctuations in world markets, as well as by gender theory. The clinical work from which the thinking derives has been mainly with couples under 40 years of age who form the first generation who have achieved higher education and professional status within their own families. The literature review also considers some of the wider implications of the impact of work organizations in relation to family life.

As a woman therapist working with pattern organized over time, both in couples and in the work settings to which they belong, I am aware that I am working with issues that have affected and continue to affect my own life. As the daughter of a woman whose work produced the principal income for the family, I assumed that women worked *and* brought up children before I had formulated the conflicts this entailed. However, this primary assumption obviously created a particular perspective which influences the way in which I enter and re-enter the debate about men and women's roles over time at different periods in my own life.

Carter and McGoldrick (1982, 1988) have pointed out the power of vertical stressors (defined as patterns of relating and functioning that are transmitted down the generations of a family) within the family and how the greatest stress is created when these interact and amplify current stressors. In connection with any couple's relationship with the world of work, such stressors may include powerful wishes about maintaining traditions as well as wishes from a previous generation about how things might have been different, both of which are transferred into expectations or dictums about how subsequent generations should conduct themselves. There may in addition be a hidden injunction: 'Dare not have a better life than mine.' Such vertical stressors affect the way a couple experiences and handles choices about work and the impact of these requirements on their relationship. Family expectations (some of which are gender determined) as well as the traditions of the community and culture of origin will continue to create different punctuations in the *current* work/family context, and contribute to the human tension and unhappiness which then often enters *our* domain as professional women in our role as 'therapist'.

The choice of a spouse does not necessarily include thought about that spouse's work context, which may be seen primarily as the setting which provides the financial underpinning for the formation of a new family home. Few couples initially consider how a partner's work setting may influence or change them over time. They are even more unlikely to consider how that change will influence their relationship as a couple. The question 'What does *he* do?' is a common one, the question 'What will he become?' is rare. Although it remains widespread for women to continue to work following marriage, the question 'What does *she* do?' is more rarely asked, since it is still more usual to assume that *women* will cease working for a period while they bring up their children than that birth will be an event affecting both partners equally (Lewis and Cooper 1988). The home and children have long been regarded as influential factors in women's adult development, in contrast to the pulls away from the intimacies of home potentially inherent in work commitment. It is only in the last decade that children have openly been considered as a potentially desirable influence in the adult development of men within research fields such as developmental psychology.

The impact of the relationship between parents and children has more often been considered in terms of the impact of fathers on children. Only very recently (cf Lewis and O'Brien 1987) has this been approached from the point of view of its impact on men themselves, and the maintenance and development of men in terms of affect and attachment needs. This chapter considers some of the literature on the way people of both sexes adapt their way of viewing and relating to the world in interaction with the influence and requirements of the work context. The impact of occupational role, hours of work, and of the expectations of those in charge have been widely documented in other fields of reference (cf. Yogev 1982; Lewis and Cooper 1983) and deserves wider attention from those of us who work as family therapists.

Intimacy, psychological organizations, and crises

Do work settings 'allow' the development of new psychological organization in the couple, or do they maintain prior patterns of expectations arising from families of origin? This question arises frequently in therapy in the context of work/family crises. Couples present a sense of loss stemming from one or other partner's commitment to, or absorption by, a setting which their partner sees as removing them from the area of shared intimacy in marriage. Crisis confronts a spouse who no longer feels adequately connected to the person with whom they live. They experience their spouse as different from the person they first married. In order to draw attention to this change and the crisis in marital balance, a spouse may attempt a rebalancing through some 'problematic' behaviour such as displays of extreme drinking, shoplifting, an alternative sexual relationship, violence, or desertion of the home.

Julia was fighting to retrieve her husband's attention from preoccupation with Third World disasters, but her progressive attempts to engage him were meeting with increased neutrality.

Julia: I'm just very surprised you bring this detachment to our marriage. I always thought of your work as a high-minded approach, an intellectual approach. I'm just a little 'blown away' at the detachment at home. [*To the therapist*] He gets more upset by the fact that some idiot was going to be put on the board of the World Bank – than that I was having an affair. One arouses some real strong reaction, the other doesn't. I'd like to see this one react right here and fuck Tim Brown on the executive board. OK, be passionate there but *here* too. [*She acts him being angry about Tim Brown.*] Why don't you say, 'If I ever find out who you've been having an affair with I'll take my grandfather's shotgun and blast his head off.' I'd like to see some of that action here. [*Husband remains silent.*]

Following gender research by Pollak and Gilligan (1982), some of the reasons why male partners do not always respond with concern can be hypothesized. Thematic apperception tests showed men experiencing danger as more usually arising from close personal connection and intimacy (which had connotations of entrapment and betrayal), than from the pursuit of success. In partners who are distanced, therefore, such acts can be perceived as ploys in a game. For most couples who seek help, however, questions about intimacy are more open and can be explored.

Researchers have found the qualities that make up 'intimacy' in marriage hard to define (Rutter 1986). Intimacy includes protectiveness and attachment. In adult life these are frequently linked to sexuality. Traditional components of the complementarity of intimacy in marriage include women nurturing men and men giving women protection. While the value of the maintenance of these gender-determined psychological roles is under widespread debate, this arrangement is still held to be a general expectation within the overall balance of expectations of marriage, even by feminist psychotherapists (Mitchell *et al.* 1987).

In the course of becoming adult, men and women have each absorbed differences between male and female, and each psyche contains images of self and other. In an intimate relationship, unlike other daily relationships, more tightly organized by expectations of organization and role, the couple therefore has the possibility of empathizing across the boundaries of gender to the partner's needs. The psychological capacity to take on aspects of the other, transcending socially defined aspects of gender role, may be an important aspect of intimacy. However, this capacity (which may be one of the hallmarks of a successful couple relationship) may threaten, as well as be threatened by, the requirements of an expedient self posed by the demands of work settings where controlled and planned or calculated behaviour is required. Where such 'planned behaviour' also fits into intergenerational expectations of how adults conduct themselves, the possibility of the development of fluidity and spontaneity leading to a new 'intimacy' between the couple is likely to be seriously threatened.

To use the term 'bisexuality' in relation to intimacy is to float the idea of the need for fluctuation and exploratory space in long-term partnerships and marriage. As a relationship modality that is alternative to daily relationship patterning, it can allow creativity in gender-role development. When considering sexuality, Lacan defined an important distinction between 'desire' and 'need'. Need can be met, but desire contains the possibility of longer term, less 'immediately resolvable' issues which must be kept open for exploration in couple relationships. The possibility of maintaining this capacity for exploration is an important component of intimacy. It may be an essential element in an enduring partnership in which men and women may wish over time to explore aspects of self different from those defined by the expectations of previous generations (parents and grandparents) and preorganized by class and culture of origin. The intimate area of sexuality can include fluctuation and instability of gender and patterning, in which exploration and new definitions of self can take place. Lacan speaks of the unconscious 'revealing the fictional nature of the sexual category to which every human subject is nonetheless assigned' (Mitchell and Rose 1982: 29). A further thought from Lacan may be placed alongside this idea: 'the feminine stands for a refusal . . . of the *phallic* organization of sexuality – its ordering, its identity' (ibid.: 56). Many women experience such attempts at 'organization' as requiring them to be defined in a way which allows *traditional* definitions to be maintained for both sexes, and as a major source of tension in their relationship. They may instead attempt to create a definition of intimacy that belongs to them and their partner; rather than to their families of origin or the world of stereotypes. While feminist theory may be as much in danger as any other theory of creating stereotypes of male and female, certain concepts (which could hardly be discussed while I was growing up) are now generally accepted.

Gilligan (1982) has highlighted how women's sense of themselves is strongly connected to maintaining affiliation with others and a commitment to considering relationship issues as important. In caring for others and in being cared for, they therefore derive their sense of self-worth – the price they pay is the degree to which a sense of self-worth is dependent on those others, particularly when intensified by the tie of economic dependency.

Men's sense of self is seen as more strongly connected to personal achievement than to personal relationships. Gilligan (ibid.) has also shown how it is connected at an early age to a search for abstract rules or principles by which competition generated between men can be regulated through recourse to a higher order rule. This finding may contribute towards our understanding of why it is that one may find a clearer definition of masculinity from roles outside the household and from working in organizations where following 'rules' allows the achievement of leadership and reward. However, success in such fields often also involves the development of an 'expedient' self, one that is capable of repressing emotion and connectedness in the family in the interests of promotion and connectedness within the work setting.

Gilligan also highlights the fact that men and women's attitudes to closeness are so different that they may pose a fundamental paradox to the idea of intimacy in marriage (Pollack and Gilligan 1982). Men experience danger arising from close personal ties as 'cloying' (i.e. something which constrains them), whereas women see danger as arising from isolation and alienation. This study was undertaken at a particular time and in a culture which is not our own. It should therefore be noted for the purpose of extending our thinking but should not be seen as a universal truth. It does not reflect the variety of my own clinical experience, but then nor do men who are prepared to work on relationship issues necessarily reflect the stereotypes created by those in research samples.

Dedication as the organizing premiss

In an analysis of women's relationships to their husband's world of work, Finch (1983) has shown how women often reduce tension by submitting themselves to the organizing principles of their husband's work setting and the role requirements of his job. Finch looks at the variety of ways in which women are constrained by their husband's work setting and considers why they make the choices that they do and how they remain psychologically intact. A key notion posed by Callan (1975) concerns the premiss of 'dedication' – 'the logical anchor of the complex of claims and obligations linking women to their husband's employer'. Dedication represents one of the ways in which the paradox experienced by many wives, namely the assumption that they are committed to an organization from whose central operations they are excluded, is transformed into a workable reality. These premisses operate in widely different work cultures, each with their own form of organization. Studies include mining communities (Dennis *et al.* 1969), agriculture (Chamberlain 1975), and industry (Hunt 1980). Certain callings have higher 'moral' demands to which the family's needs must be accommodated: these include the police (Cain 1973), the Church (Spedding 1975), medicine (Fowlkes 1980), managers in industry (Pahl and Pahl 1971), and journalism (McPherson 1975).

Since such constraints are part of the fabric that nourishes and supports the family, the questions of how they become built into the marriage, what allows their maintenance, and in what circumstances they can be successfully transmuted into intimacy, are important. Gowler and Legge (1978: 50, 51) argued that in conventional marriage:

> The husband derives his greatest satisfaction from his job/career outside the home while the wife derives hers from within the home itself – she will support her husband's work in return for which he will provide materially for the home and take some interest in it . . . the sanction on non-compliance understood rather than spelt out.

This definition excludes the whole question of systemically defined identity and the wife's ability successfully to 'allow' her role to be organized by rules deriving from a system (the work-place) in whose operating premisses she is essentially relegated to a peripheral position. While readers of this book are unlikely to accept the definition for themselves, and while noting that it is a decade since it was formulated (ibid.), it is still true that a proportion of couples presenting in therapy comprises women with adult children who *have* lived by this definition and are no longer prepared to do so, thus creating crisis in long-established marital relationships.

It is of course when a serious bid to change this equilibrium is made that both the constraints and the conditions for non-compliance have to be spelled out so that an attempt to reach an honest new situation can be made. The more partners are used to one of them playing a supporting role, the more painful this will be. By definition we only see couples who are not working out this balance without some crisis, and there is danger in extrapolating from this clinical experience. As evidenced in wider women's literature, the role of women in emotional 'management' is often seen by them as a very successful part of their jobs as wives, and one from which they gain legitimate gratification.

When women cannot 'manage' the constraints because they experience them as a violation of the contract that they understood they could rely upon in their partnership, and therefore a violation of themselves, they may be willing to risk losing the partnership by confronting change.

Example

After twenty years of marriage Rebecca began to experience acute backache, inexplicable weeping, and a number of other somatic symptoms which she handled by taking excessive quantities of pills.

Following her university life, she had married into a closely guarded, orthodox Jewish family in north London. Women were expected to manage the house and the children, and no other woman in the family had a job. Her husband worked long hours and travelled extensively. She had become a Jewess on marrying but this fact was concealed from the wider community, as she might have been considered 'second best'. The question of how she and her husband could together create a way of life that included some of the fundamental ideas she had put aside during her marriage was the crisis she presented at the time of her second child leaving school: 'I can't live a lie any more.' The reverberations of this decision affected three generations on both sides of the family.

The precipitating factor for Rebecca was her husband's apparent inability to view her wish to start a career of her own as anything other than a whim: to be humoured but not given any serious attention.

Gender issues in relation to family life: is symmetry in family life being achieved?

Can we assume that among younger couples, greater equality/symmetry in the sharing of household tasks, and consequently an alternative balance in marriage, is developing? Although Young and Wilmot (1957) claimed that new, more symmetrical arrangements were being established in Britain, this view was challenged directly by Gavron (1966), Oakley (1974), and Land (1978) and indirectly by other studies of young 'mobile' families on a housing estate (Cohen 1977).

Gavron's study shows that it was not marriage but the birth of the first child that took women of all classes away from the work setting. Cohen's evidence suggests that in the very area in which Young and Wilmot saw change, 'career pressures kept the majority of husbands apart from their families for considerable periods of time at a stage in their families' developmental life when wives were most in need of their support' (Cohen 1977: 603).

Recent statistics (HMSO 1987) conclude, 'Women still bear the main burden of domestic management and equal sharing is more of an ideal than a reality and honoured by men more in the breach than the observance.' Two main factors, each affecting the well-being of women, are concealed within the accompanying statistics. The first compares the asymmetry in task sharing between the sexes; the second concerns the isolation this conceals in different social groups. Although studies of depression in women with young children (Brown *et al.* 1975) have hinted at the protective role of work itself, research which subsequently developed from this finding has tended to concentrate on the establishment of protective factors within communities that connect women to other adults while they bring up their children (Mills *et al.* 1984). Rowland and Perkins (1988) further developed the theme of protective factors at work, although there is not space to review their ideas in this chapter.

Finch (1983) categorically points out the maintenance of asymmetry in marital relationships, quoting a number of studies of marriage in different social classes (Edgell 1980; Bailyn 1978; Fowlkes 1980). She also includes the more complex form of asymmetry created by *women's* work patterns in which women who work none the less maintain traditional domestic roles with little redress of balance within the overall traditional gender assignment of household tasks. In her view the implicit hierarchy of family life in Britain remains one in which the husband's work is accorded top priority; the needs of the children and the family 'as a whole' come second, and any employment that the wife may undertake comes 'a very poor third'.

The series of adjustments made within the ordering of family priorities begins with the husband's accommodation to the world of work. Evidence from a number of studies supports the belief that women's employment rarely challenges this ordering of priorities but rather 'fits around' it (Platt 1976; Leonard 1980, from Finch 1983). This seems to be the case whether the man's work is professional or semi-skilled (Hope *et al.* 1976; Shimmin *et al.* 1981). In addition Finch quotes studies showing women's reluctance to move into any employment position which could challenge her husband's work (Safilios-Rothschild 1976; Poloma and Garland 1981). Even in families which overtly support a dual-career structure, the pattern tends to revert to the norm in terms of women undertaking primary responsibility for child care and domestic arrangements (Gutek *et al.* 1981; Yogev 1982; Mannheim and Schiffrin 1984). In their study of dual-career families in Britain, Lewis and Cooper (1988) conclude: 'the present findings support mounting evidence that in spite of the increasing involvement of many dual career husbands in child care, the distribution of domestic responsibility still tends to be along traditional lines irrespective of social class'.

However, it is in this concern for both the world of work and the world of home that many women see their salvation. Yogev (1982) shows how women regard 'home' duties as 'not work' but relaxation. The expressed view of the women she interviewed was that they continued to derive their primary sense of self from their intimate relationships. Some of the implications of this finding for men and women have already been touched on in this chapter. More recently, work on fathers has demonstrated that some men are revising their own self conceptions, values, and orientations to work and society - as well as to their partners – and the need for different variables in the successful organization of both work and domestic life (Rapoport and Rapoport 1976; Lamb *et al.* 1987).

Identity and work

There are obvious traditional economic reasons why the male career has been accorded primacy in western capitalist society. However, the interweaving of these reasons with the formation of the identity of men in relation to work and home is complex. The operation of market forces continues to be based on the premiss of commitment to the ideal of production; and the requirement for mobility increases as organizations become more complex as well as more international. In order to be mobile, men need to be 'disconnected' from ties which would hamper their commitment, and women have to be sufficiently dedicated to move as their husbands' jobs require. Women who choose to have children and continue to work rarely become disconnected in the same way although their struggle not to do so may be powerful in cases where they are submitted to the same pulls of loyalty as men. It would seem that psychobiological bonds have made women endure and manage dilemmas of reconciling work and ties of attachment to the home. Whether men on a wide scale will, first, become more genuinely and committedly exposed to their children and, second, experience different dimensions of attachment and commitment as a result, we do not yet know. Such a change might genuinely affect the dilemmas outlined in the following section.

Intimacy and role: families, institutions, and hierarchy

The concept of intimacy and the concept of role may be interconnected in family and institution in subtle and pervasive ways. The family organizes and sends out messages across the generations which create and confirm gender identity, and outline acceptable sets of role behaviours for its adult members. In cultures where family and business organization remains stable, the way in which the roles of men and women can be maintained, debated, and controlled is relatively clear; and from these debates certain possibilities of change, as well as certain rigidities blocking change, become less hidden.

The complications imposed on large organizations by international expectations and requirements may create apparent opportunities for change which turn out to be illusory. The confusion reated for individuals working within large organizations at times of hange often leads to a need to revert to familiar stereotypes of gender behaviour rather than to change them. In addition, multinational companies are faced by culturally determined, gender differentiated philosophies with which they cannot easily compete. The Japanese executive who works till midnight and knows that his wife will wait up to cook his dinner inspires envy and admiration as well as dismay n his British counterpart who is working to achieve similar targets, but whose wife is holding out for shared child care at 6.00 p.m.

Institutions and attachment

Large business organizations also tend to be hierarchically determined. This lends itself more readily to reconstructions of self based upon family of origin and earlier patterns of attachment. Researchers using attachment theory have noted how as a single, biologically innate, perceptual emotional system, attachment remains in force from childhood to adulthood although it does undergo changes in the object of attachment. In adult life the features which are most strongly marked include the need for ready access to the attachment figure; the desire for proximity to the attachment figure at times of stress; a sense of heightened comfort and diminished anxiety in the presence of the attachment figure, and an increase in anxiety if the person is inexplicably absent. When all is going well, attachments amplify the sense of self and are related to the individual's own capacity for autonomy and mastering challenge. It will be apparent that all these expectations characterize the relationship between adult sexual partnerships that endure over time; but it may be less apparent that they may also characterize the relationships within work settings. Where the intensity of emotional and psychological issues arising from attachment needs become more organized in relation to work settings than to those created by the couple, the partnership may come under severe stress.

Affiliation

Affiliation is also an important component of adult self-definition and satisfaction. It may be defined not as the attachment to a single person but the attachment to a group, that association with others in which shared interests and similarity of circumstances provide a basis for mutual loyalty and a sense of community (Weiss 1982). Affiliation and the amplification of a sense of self develop in interaction with one another within a defined context but the self that develops does not necessarily transfer to a different setting. Feeling competent at home may not necessarily mean feeling competent at work, and vice versa (Quinton and Rutter 1984; Rutter 1986). Questions then arise about how competence and a sense of self-esteem can be mutually fostered and developed in both the home and the work setting and whether the two can be complementary at a time of continual gender negotiation. Where marriage, with the ambiguity of gender exploration, comes to be perceived as stressful to the self developed in a work context, and work, with the institutionalized 'safety' of the gender expectations of the organization in relation to role, becomes of greater importance to a sense of personal autonomy and competence, an intimate relationship comes under severe stress.

A further complexity is that the threat is posed to a marriage under the guide of *supporting* home and family. A paradoxical dilemma is created. Work overtly protects and nurtures the home and 'nourishes' the coupledom. At the same time it also provides a series of alternative intergenerational links and loyalties and gender-determined role requirements which may become indistinguishable from, or even replace, intrafamilial influences which affect both the life of the couple and the internal world of each partner. These influences are likely to be similar in pattern to previous constructions of attachment and will be sought in order to amplify the self and create a sense of well-being and self-esteem and protect or even repair former intergenerational battles. Offices, institutions, and companies 'provide' grandfathers, fathers, brothers, approving elders, and supportive peers. However, they may also prevent the evolution of new intimacy and new models of relationship. These dilemmas apply to all large organizations where the constructs of family life are essentially divorced from the constructs of the work-place. They become particularly acute for men in large hierarchically organized companies where the goal of upward mobility through commitment to the ideals of the organization with the overt aim of accrued 'rewards' for the family is disconnected from examining the costs of achievement in terms of the development of self in interaction with the intimacies of family life. Since the need for intimacy will continue, the search will be maintained in the context of greatest safety and attachment. Following Gilligan's research (1982), it is possible to hypothesize that this meets gender needs (that have been shown to develop early in boys) for clearer rules and higher organizing principles as the means to problem resolution; rather than the preference shown by girls to resort to exploring difference of views and attempting to negotiate a resolution.

Loneliness

Loneliness within a marriage arises if the couple does not give themselves time to create and maintain a relationship which they both want rather than one which other people have defined in the past and define for them during the period of their living together. In such cases couples resort to generalized 'stereotypes' of living together. Where either partner is kept in charge of this stereotype while the other uses it as a safe base from which to explore (Bowlby 1969) and develop their own sense of self in a different setting, conflict will arise. This will be intensified, the greater the degree to which affiliation, shared interests, and similarity of circumstances providing a basis for mutual loyalty are to be found in the work setting. Where an organization is hierarchical so that upward mobility depends on adherence to the 'organizing principles' of the work system, those of the home will become subordinate. The attempt by the partner to introduce an alternative systemic balance will be viewed as threatening (i.e. of equal value but in opposition to the goals and values of the work context) or may be disqualified as belonging to the domain of the 'little woman' (i.e. within the province of one person but not as part of the couple relationship). This therefore keeps the threat within defined limits.

A continuing struggle for intimacy may be perceived as a direct threat to the successful functioning of the self in the work setting. It may be perceived as dangerous and even threatening to the survival of an expedient self, since to connect to dependence in an intimate relationship is to reconnect to earlier experiences of dependence and the potential terrors of abandonment. If either partner increasingly demands intimacy from the other in ways which are perceived as threatening this expedient self, the demand for intimacy can become reframed as an attempt to diminish effectiveness and potency. Perhaps the most unpleasant male expression for this is the American phrase 'being pussy whipped'. It is not just the more he/she nags the more she/he retreats, it is also the more he/she demands intimacy the more she/he feels a sense of impotence in relation to those demands.

Traditional gender roles and struggles to change these

Men and women still retain much of the patterning and sense of obligation of traditional gender roles, although the consciousness training of those under 30 has equipped them to struggle to change these. In marriage there may be more advantage in this potential change for one party than the other. Husbands and wives often prefer to find fault with each other rather than redefine the power given to the balance of rules which organize the marriage or which derive from other organizations to which they belong. Changes in systems other than their own marriage may not be something that they can contemplate, whether this involves an examination of the power of the extended family or of the loyalty pulls within the work context. This can make the nuclear family situation very lonely. A husband or wife may feel he/she lacks the resources that his/her partner needs. Women may feel belittled either by being constrained in the role of wife and mother as previously defined or by trying to manage a double role as working woman and mother. A working wife, discovering the limitations a family imposes on her working hours and the real constraints of trying to manage the emotional space of two working adults, may settle for management rather than change. Men may feel equally battered by the struggle to meet daily expectations at work, and come home expecting order and some form of nurturing, only to find, instead, another battle.

Such struggles are painful because they involve the less conscious levels of the earliest experiences of social patterning (Chodorow 1978) in which the expectations for boys and girls are laid down and the 'rules' for intimacy are first meshed with the complexities of family life.

How does the therapist enter?

It is often difficult to find definitions of professional self that fit into current theory. A definition of my own theoretical and clinical position would be a 'constructivist' (following Kenny and Gardner 1988), Hoffman (1988) and an aspiring practitioner of gender-aware therapy (following Jones, Chapter 3 in this volume). Within the theory of radical constructivism, 'knowledge' is understood in terms of 'fitting the constraints' within which the systems living takes place (see also Hinde 1979; Reiss 1981; Gorell Barnes 1982). There is a recognition that this definition applies equally to therapist and patient. The work of therapy is the co-creation of a consensual reality from which new meanings emerge. Concepts of 'objective' reality are challenged. I see this as an important element in the work a couple must do in struggling with the 'realities' and ideas of one another's contextually determined 'work' selves.

Within this framework of thinking, intrapsychic systems are viewed as influencing, and being influenced by, interactional systems, and therapeutic conversations include both personal and collective ideas. In exploring and defining the context of a problem, values and beliefs are made explicit and conflicts pointed out. This includes both those beliefs that are less conscious and those that are conscious but in conflict. These ideas also derive from earlier work with Robin Skynner, based on group-analytic principles developed through the work of Ffoulkes (1964) but put into practice in family and marital therapy during the 1960s (Skynner 1967a, 1968, 1987). Being open about what one knows and what one does not know, what one understands and what one is perceived by others as not understanding; being prepared to pick up discrepancies and put ideas together in a new way, have taken on the additional dimension of considering the gender determined perspectives for each partner in the dance.

Aspects of therapeutic conversations

Example

These extracts are taken from a session with a young working mother who had come for previous sessions with her husband to discuss a severe drinking problem that had begun to create deep suspicion and mistrust between them. The extracts contain many of the dilemmas that I see as part of the package of the home/work problem discussed in this chapter.

Jane had an upwardly mobile job as a trainer in youth-training schemes, a husband Jeff who was also working very competitively as a trainer in industry, and a daughter Rachel who was 2 years old. Her own mother had always worked but Jane was the first family member to receive higher education, which had been viewed as 'extravagant' by her family. Her mother saw her as moving away from the family who had lived in the same community for several generations.

Area 1: mothers, competition, and guilt

Never giving enough Jane is describing her mother's criticism of her for not bringing her a present from America.

Jane: Oh Mum, Auntie Alice told me that you were very upset that I didn't bring you back a present.
Mum: Oh no, I wasn't upset but everyone in the office asked me what you'd brought me and I had to make something up.
Jane: Yes, but Mum I didn't see anything I wanted to buy you.
Mum: Yes but *they* think it's awful that you didn't bring me anything.

Discussion: (1) The ways in which mothers undermine self-confidence and the ways in which daughters feel bad about having left their mothers behind by getting better jobs; (2) the 'hot line' from mothers to daughters in which mothers will always be able to tap into a pool of debt which is never repaid; (3) setting realistic goals for what can and cannot be done in relation to this debt.

Competition replayed through the next generation Jane describes a meal at which her mother is showing off her granddaughter to other relatives. The question, 'In what ways was your mother using Rachel that Jeff did not like?' is followed by an account of how Jane's mother shows off and makes Rachel laugh, so making Rachel, and therefore herself, the centre of attention.

Jane: Jeff switches off, it's like a chemical reaction . . . . I sometimes think I need to say to her . . . 'Look Mum, I'm going to live a lot longer than you,' because I don't think she thinks I will.

Therapist: She's rehearsing to take over your role as mum with Rachel.

Jane: Oh yes, she'd whip Rachel off tomorrow. My room's been made ready at home, she took out all the old stuff, new bed, new duvet, pink frills, the lot, that bed is there waiting for Rachel.

Discussion: (1) The hope that grandmothers may have that their relationships with their daughters will be better than that which they had with their own mothers, and the repetition of this hope with the next generation; (2) how this hope blurs boundaries between the realities of individual people in different generations; (3) how Jane experiences disappointment that she cannot be closer to her mother, when she sees her mother trying to be closer to her daughter.

Area 2: Jane's relationship with an older woman with whom she is in competition at work

Two years previously Jane had quarrelled with a woman who was a competitor at work. This had preyed on her mind:

> It's still on my mind two and a half years later and that is bad news. She makes me feel totally sick . . . I have very strong feelings about her, stronger than my mother. I thought I should try and get on with her to see if I could do it, but I can't. She was such a cow that I went to the personnel director whom I had quite a special relationship with, not physical, but special; but he didn't know how to tackle it. I had no one to protect me from her.

Discussion: (1) Rivalry and intrusiveness; the mirroring of other aspects of Jane's relationship with her mother; (2) making boundaries in one's life and in one's mind between one person and another (following which wise analysis Jane concluded that although she could not and did not wish to tell her mother to bugger off, she could certainly say so to her colleague).

Area 3: Jane's rivalry with her husband and her wish for a better relationship

'The story of the shoelace' This story, which is a moral fable of our time known to most working women with partners, is self-explanatory as an expression of the dilemma and choice of priorities in daily life.

Jane: There's a part of Jeff that feels very neglected because I'm too wrapped up in me and in my work and Rachel. The other day I heard him wake up at six, and he was trying not to disturb me. He puts his Marks and Spencer shoes on and he breaks the lace. I couldn't be bothered to get up and I felt really sorry for him. He had to put his cheap shoes on, and he had this important meeting with two top men in his firm and he's quite a poser . . . well today I noticed that he's stolen the laces from *my* shoes to that he *could* wear his other shoes and I think he was trying to tell me, look, you should have bloody got me shoelaces today . . . but he wouldn't say it.

Therapist: Would you like it if he did?

Jane: Well I'm glad he doesn't in a way because I'm frightened it would all come to a head. I can't cope with managing the home and working . . . I might have proved what I wanted to prove . . . I do feel sorry for him when he can't buy new laces . . . but I don't see it as a priority in *my* life to go and buy him new laces, because I know if it was me and my shoes, I'd go and buy some for myself.

Discussion: Competitiveness in the home and competitiveness in the work-place. Is there room to differentiate what men and women are going to do in *her* family?

Changing the parenting patterns In the previous session with Jane and Jeff, we had discussed the need to structure space differently at home.

Therapist: You need to develop ways as a couple of getting through . . . you don't have a variety of ways you can manage together through stressful periods, knowing that you have planned a time when you will get together and deal with whatever's causing it. How can you find ways not to get more lonely and upset and persecuted by the other?

This was followed by a long, very structured planning session which included: (a) timetabling Jeff's day to give him two hours to flop and play with Rachel, (b) the agreement that Jane was not to hover around anxiously in case he suddenly decided he had had enough and she had to take over, and (c) rescheduling their meals together without Rachel so that they would be able to talk.

In the following session Jane reported that Jeff had stopped moving out of bed when they rowed, so that they could stay in touch physically even if they were not speaking. In the same way he was more content just to 'flop' with Rachel, instead of feeling a need to rush around the house doing practical things while keeping 'half an eye' on her.

Jane still felt extremely reluctant to negotiate 'trade-offs', time which she could have to do something related to her work at weekends, while Jeff looked after Rachel. She said that both the grandmothers would disapprove of this, and that she was very relieved to know that I thought it was legitimate and even essential . . . providing it was not at the expense of having time together as well.

Area 5: Conflicting speeds: the timetables of growth through babies versus self-development through institutions

Therapist: I think you have needed a certain amount of time to think about yourself, your baby, and your own development, and what being a mother means. Rachel, as a developing part of yourself, is very important . . . the tension that leads to drink seems to be when you are asking yourself if you can cope with the change of speed . . . as you rev into high gear you begin to miss the pace with Rachel and begin to hit the bottle.

Jane: When I went to the child minder on the way here she had to go out for a few minutes and I was left with three boys and they came and sat on the sofa and asked me to read to them and I really enjoyed that . . . . 'What colour's that?' . . . 'What's that called?' for ten minutes. I really enjoyed that.

Therapist: Yes, but you can enjoy it without feeling bad that you don't do it all the time. Babies also thrive when their mothers feel stimulated – it's an important thing for working mothers to know, that it's not just deprivation. [*A brief discussion on infant development followed here.*]

Area 6: Working women: common issues, individual pathways

Jane: I just want everything and maybe I can't have it.

Therapist: You are a woman with a brain, and you are struggling with the problems that women with brains and families have to struggle with today . . . that means dealing with competition at work as well as within the family . . . coping with work stress in yourself as well as your husband and making more open the unacknowledged part that you are also expected to be a sympathetic wife and a good mother . . .

Jane: It's good to have another woman to talk things over with.

Therapist: Yes, I happen to be in this *job*, but I know from my own *life* what these issues are about. It's something that women today are all struggling with . . . as yet there are no solutions but through talking solutions evolve . . .

Jane: I know what you're saying . . . I was talking to my cleaning lady today before I came to you . . . I can talk to her like I can talk to you but she can't actually handle what I'm telling her, so she just tells me all about *her* problems.

Therapist: There are common women's issues which I think it is important for you as a woman to recognize, but each person has to work out their own way of dealing with it. Although it's common, you are a highly complex individual, so it wouldn't suit you to have a universal solution. What you have to work out now includes how not to have a drink whenever you are feeling caught between different aspects of these common issues.

Therapeutic conservations

Following Jones (Chapter 3, this volume), I see therapy as enabling individuals, both men and women, to make distinctions between social rules about roles and their own experience, and freeing them to evolve new social roles where personal experience requires this. I have always believed in the evolution of strategies for change rather than direct confrontations, and I see this as a 'female' tradition dating back to the sphinx, a mythical figure of mixed gender who not only asked questions but also asked them in riddles. In moving couples or individuals to the position of observer of the systems of which they are a part, I attempt to 'demystify' or 'normalize' their experience in terms of the conflicting expectations and messages of the systems of family, work, and partnership with which they interact.

However, I also point out the dangers as well as the potential benefits of change through confronting the power of work systems and creating space for difference to evolve (Papp 1984). The dangers of change include the possible loss of aspects of the functional and expedient self; the gain is usually greater fluidity. In confronting the power of the work system, I work with couples on the structure of their lives and the ways in which this needs to change to allow them the possibility of thinking differently and even if this can only be for short periods at a time. This means heightening their observation of current patterns of interaction between them and then introducing different contexts in which discussion can take place together. It may include getting rid of children for an evening or a weekend, and breaking routines which favour habit and prevent intimacy.

Negotiated tasks include strengthening the boundary round the couple and getting them to develop strategies for preventing intrusiveness; changing the way they use these together; replaying all complaints about no change as requests for specific change; negotiating trade-offs within their time together and in relation to one another's work requirements; and a number of very focused tasks which aim to change patterns of relating around habitual issues. Very detailed work may be done on changing timetables in relation to areas of work that are encroaching on time together (Cooklin and Gorell Barnes 1988).

Couples enter therapy when they are in conflict not only with each other but also with definitions of themselves that they experience as discontinuous. In defining this discontinuity, the meaning system that determines it can usefully be widened to include work settings. The reality that is constructed in relation to a work setting may include meanings that are rejected by a partner. In defining a problem-dissolving system, therefore, boundaries around the partnership may have to be planned in a new way and new meanings constructed jointly within these. This may include different gender realities in relation both to one another as a couple, and in relation to intergenerational expectations both with parents and/or children.

Acknowledgements

Many people contribute to an essay that develops over eighteen months. In particular, though, I would like to thank my partner, Alan Cooklin, for developing the ideas about relationships and institutions with me and Janice Uphill at the Tavistock Clinic for her help in making the final draft emerge.

References

Bailyn, L. (1978) 'Accommodation of work to family', in R. Rapoport and R.N. Rapoport (eds.) *Working Couples*, London: Routledge & Kegan Paul.

Bernstein, P. (1982) *Family Ties: Corporate Bonds*, New York: Doubleday.

Bhagar, R. and Chassie, M.B. (1981) 'Determinants of organizational commitment in working women: some implications for organizational integration', *Journal of Occupational Behaviour* 2: 17–30.

Billings, A.G. and Moos, R.H. (1982) 'Work stress and the stress buffering roles of work and family resources', *Journal of Occupational Behaviour* 3: 215–32.

Bowlby, J. (1969/1984) *Attachment and Loss. Vol. 1. Attachment*, Harmondsworth: Pelican Books.

Brown, G.W., Bhrocrain, M., and Harris, T. (1975) 'Social class and psychiatric disturbance among women in an urban population', *Sociology Journal* 225–54.

Cain, M. (1973) *Society and the Policeman's Role*, London: Routledge & Kegan Paul.

Callan, H. (1975) 'The premise of dedication: notes towards an ethnography of diplomats' wives', in S. Ardner (ed.) *Perceiving Women*, London: Mallaby, 87–104 (quoted in Finch 1983: 12).

Carter, E. and McGoldrick, M. (1982) *The Family Life Cycle: A Framework for Family Therapy*, Gardner Press.

Carter, E. and McGoldrick, M. (1988) *The Changing Family Life Cycle: A Framework for Family Therapy* (2nd edn.), Gardner Press.

Chamberlain, M. (1975) *Fenwomen: A Portrait of Women in an English Village*, London: Virago/Quartet Books.

Chodorow, N. (1978) *The Reproduction of Mothering: Psychoanalysis and the Sociology of Gender*, Berkeley, Calif.: University of California Press.

Cohen, G. (1977) 'Absentee husbands in families', *Journal of Marriage and the Family* 39: 595–604.

Cooklin, A. and Gorell Barnes, G. (1988) 'Sexuality and intimacy: the couple and work', printed as 'Sessualita è intimita: Coppia è lavoro', in M. Andolfi, C. Angelo and C. Saccu (eds.) *La Coppia in Crisi*, Roma: ITF.

Dennis, M., Henriques, F., and Slaughter C. (1969) *Coal is Our Life*, 2nd edn., London: Tavistock.

Edgell, S. (1980) *Middle Class Couples: A Study of Segregation, Domination and Inequality in Marriage*, London: Allen & Unwin.

EWMD (1987) 'Developing effective partnerships', European Women's Management Development Group Conference, The Economist Conference Unit, 25 St James Street, London.

Ffoulkes, S.H. (1964) *Therapeutic Group Analysis*, London: Allen & Unwin.

Finch, J. (1983) *Married to the Job: Wives' Incorporation in Men's Work*, London: Allen & Unwin.

Fowlkes, M.R. (1980) *Behind Every Successful Man: Wives of Medicine and Academe*, New York: Columbia University Press.

Gavron, H. (1966/1983) *The Captive Wife: Conflicts of Housebound Mothers*, London: Routledge & Kegan Paul.

Gilligan, C. (1982) *In a Different Voice*, Cambridge, Mass.: Harvard University Press.

Gorell Barnes, G. (1982) 'Pattern and intervention: research findings and the development of family therapy theory', in A. Bentovim, G. Gorell

Barnes, and A. Cooklin (eds.) *Family Therapy: Complementary Frameworks of Theory and Practice*, London: Academic Press.

Gorell Barnes, G. (1985) 'Systems theory and family theory', in M. Rutter and L. Hersov (eds.) *Child and Adolescent Psychiatry: Modern Approaches*, Oxford: Blackwell Scientific Publications.

Gowler, D. and Legge, K. (1978) 'Hidden and open contracts in marriage', in R. Rapoport and R.N. Rapoport (eds.) *Working Couples*, London: Routledge & Kegan Paul.

Gutek, B., Nakamura, C., and Nieva, V. (1981) 'The interdependence of work', *Journal of Occupational Behaviour* 2: 1–16.

Hinde, R.A. (1979) *Towards Understanding Relationships*, London: Academic Press.

HMSO: Office of Population Census and Surveys (1987)

Hoffman, L. (1988) 'A constructivist position for family therapy', *Irish Journal of Psychology* 1: 1–24.

Hope, E., Kennedy, M., and de Winter, A. (1976) 'Home workers in north London', in D.L. Barker and S. Allen (eds.) *Dependence and Exploitation in Work and Marriage*, London: Longman, 88–108.

Hunt, P. (1980) *Gender and Class Consciousness*, London: Macmillan.

Kenny, V. and Gardner, G. (1988) 'Constructions of self organizing systems', *Irish Journal of Psychology* 1: 1–24.

Lamb, M.E., Pleck, J.H., and Levine, J.A. (1987) 'Effects of increased paternal involvement on fathers and mothers', in C. Lewis and M. O'Brien (eds.) *Re-Assessing Fatherhood*, London: Sage Publications.

Land, H. (1975) 'The Myth of the male breadwinner', *New Society* 34 (679) (9 October): 71–3.

Land, H. (1976) 'Women: supporters or supported', in D.L. Barker and S. Allen (eds.) *Sexual Divisions in Society: Process and Change*, London: Tavistock, 108–32.

Land, H. (1978) 'Who cares for the family?' *Journal of Social Policy* 7(3): 257–84.

Lasch, C. (1977) *Haven in a Heartless World*, New York: Basic Books.

Leonard, D. (1980) *Sex and Generation: A Study of Courtship and Weddings*, London: Tavistock.

Lewis, S. and Cooper, C.L. (1983) 'The stress of continuing occupational and parental roles: a review of the literature', *Bulletin of the British Psychological Society* 36: 341–5.

Lewis, S. and Cooper, C.L. (1988) 'The transition to parenthood in dual career couples', *Psychological Medicine* 18: 477–86.

Lewis, S.C. and O'Brien, M. (1987) *Reassessing Fatherhood*, London: Sage Publications.

McPherson, M. (1975) *The Power Lovers: An Intimate Look at Politicians and Marriage*, New York: Putnam.

Mannheim, B. and Schiffrin, M. (1984) 'Family structure, job characteristics, rewards and strings as related to work role centrality of employed and self employed professional women with children', *Journal of Occupational Behaviour* 5: 83–101.

Mills, M., Puckering, C., Pound, A., and Cox, A. (1984) 'What is it about depressed mothers that influence their children's functioning?', in J.E. Stevenson (ed.) *Recent Research in Developmental Psychology*, *Journal of Child Psychology and Psychiatry* Supplement, no. 4.

Mitchell, J. and Rose, J. (eds.) (1982) *Jacques Lacan and the École Freudienne*, London: W.W. Norton.

Mitchell, J. with Baker-Miller and Chasseguet-Smirgel (1987) in 'Voices: Part 4 – What do women want?', London: Channel 4.

Oakley, A. (1974) *Housewife*, Harmondsworth: Penguin.

Pahl, J.M. and Pahl, R.E. (1971) *Managers and Their Wives*, Harmondsworth: Penguin.

Papp, P. (1984) *The Problem of Change*, New York and London: Guilford Press.

Perens, T. and Waterman, R. (1982) *In Search of Excellence*, New York: Harper & Row.

Platt, J. (1976) *The Realities of Social Research*, London: University of Sussex Press.

Pollak, S. and Gilligan, C. (1982) 'Images of violence in thematic apperception tests', *Journal of Personality and Social Psychology* 42: 159–67.

Poloma, M. and Garland, T.M. (1981) 'The myth of the egalitarian family: familial roles and the professionally employed wife', in A. Theodor (ed.) *The Professional Woman*, Cambridge, Mass.: Schenham.

Quinton, D. and Rutter, M. (1984) 'Parents with children in care: 1. Current circumstances and parents. 2. Intergenerational continuities', *Journal of Child Psychology and Psychiatry* 25: 211–31.

Rapoport, R. and Rapoport, R.N. (1976) *Dual Career Families Re-Examined*, Martin Robertson.

Reiss, D. (1981) *The Family Construction of Reality*, Cambridge, Mass.: Harvard University Press.

Rowland, L.A. and Perkins, R.E. (1988) 'You can't drink, eat or make love 8 hours a day: the value of work in psychiatry – a personal view', *Health Press D.S.* 20(3): 75–9.

Rutter, M. (1986) 'Psychosocial resilience and protective mechanisms', in S. Rolf, A. Masters, D. Cicchetti, K. Muechterlein and S. Weintraub (eds.) *Risk and Protective Factors in the Development of Psychopathology*, New York: Cambridge University Press.

Safilios-Rothschild, C. (1976) 'Dual linkages between occupational and family systems: a macro sociological analysis', in M. Bloxall and B. Neagan (eds.) *Women and the Work Place*, University of Chicago Press, 57–60.

Shimmin, S., McNally, J., and Litt, S. (1981) 'Pressures on women engaged in factory work', *Employment Gazette*, 89(8): 344–9.

Skynner, R. (1967a) 'The minimum sufficient network', first published in *Social Work Today* 2(9) 28 July 1971.

Skynner, R. (1967b) 'Indications and contra indications for conjoint family therapy', *International Journal of Social Psychiatry* XV (4).

Skynner, R. (1968) 'Conjoint family therapy', first published in *Journal of Child Psychology and Psychiatry* 10: 81–106.

Skynner, R. (1987) *Exploration with Families: Group Analysis and Family Therapy*, London: Methuen. (This collection contains the important early papers 1967a, 1967b, 1968, edited and collected by J. Schlabobersky.)
Spedding, J.V. (1975) 'Wives of the clergy', unpublished Ph.D thesis, University of Bradford; in J. Finch (ed.) (1985) *Married to the Job*, London: George Allen & Unwin.
Weiss, R. (1982) 'Attachment in adult life', in C. Murray Parkes and J. Stevenson-Hinde (eds.) *The Place of Attachment in Human Behaviour*, London and New York: Tavistock.
Yogev, S. (1982) 'Are professional women overworked: objective v. subjective perceptions of role modes', *Journal of Occupational Psychology* 55: 165–69.
Young, M. and Wilmot, P. (1957/1973) *The Symmetrical Family*, London: Routledge & Kegan Paul.

Chapter thirteen

Why a group for women only?

Maureen Clark and Annette Kilworth

The authors initially worked together as psychiatric social workers in the Department of Psychological Medicine, Basildon Hospital, Essex, a unit that treats people with acute mental illness. This involved taking referrals from general practitioners, health visitors, and psychiatrists. The authors undertook traditional social work, family therapy, marital therapy, and groupwork, within a multidisciplinary framework. Maureen still works at the unit, while Annette moved to the Rainbow Family Centre, Basildon, in August 1987. This has been the venue for the women's group since that date. Annette has also run mothers' groups and bereavement groups; Maureen is particularly interested in preventive work and was recently instrumental in setting up and running a multidisciplinary psychosexual clinic which meets outside the hospital.

Much of our individual, family, and groupwork has largely been with women, addressing what would normally be considered women's issues. We acknowledged that many of the women with whom we work would benefit from the opportunity to share their feelings and frustrations in a group setting. We were under no illusions that all would be plain sailing. However we were unprepared for the lack of comprehension we encountered from our own trusted and respected male colleagues when we proposed the formation of a women's group.

We were asked the following questions: Why a group for women only? What is so different about women? Did men not have difficulties of confidence too? Were men always able to be assertive? Did men not need time to themselves?

Apparently many men feel unhappy in their situation and need help to gain a more equal footing in the home. By starting a 'women only' group we were accused of ignoring their predicament and compounding their problems. 'Fine', we said, 'Why don't you start a men's group as well?' That comment did not satisfy and so the debate continued with no recognition of the changed emotional dimensions that would enter the group if men were also present.

Numerous team meetings and lunch breaks were spent in pursuit of a glimmer of recognition for the validity of the feminist perspective. We justified our women's group along the following lines. Psychiatry, as with other branches of medicine, is a male-dominated discipline in which the medical model prevails. Women who are suicidal, drinking, not coping with their children, or plain unhappy, are often considered to be not normal; therefore they must be mentally ill. This is a common reaction within our society. We did not believe this applied to many of the women we encountered, but that they were often required to make more adjustments in their lives than men. Women in Basildon tend to give up work when they have a baby. They tend not to have a 'real' job again. Many of the women we encounter have suffered a broken marriage. This usually requires the woman to take almost total responsibility for the children who are likely to be somewhat disturbed themselves by the breakdown.

We began to see women as the emotional pack-horse for the family, like a blob of play-doh that becomes whatever shape is required in order to fit the needs of the family. The reason for this might be that the woman and man have different concepts of the family 'group': that the man is less likely to look on himself as a member of a unit, and more as an individual.

If the above reasoning is valid, how could a group containing men be effective?

The group started in August 1987, and over the following year positive changes occurred and connections were made for the women involved. We have used some tried and tested family-therapy techniques, but within our own feminist perspective, and without losing our desire to be innovative and creative. It is now our responsibility, as group leaders, to attempt to disentangle the threads and so highlight the nature of the processes and therapeutic interactions that have brought about the changes both for the group members and in our own thinking. In this chapter we highlight the approach we have seen to be effective for the women and will consequently use again the factors that appear to have constituted what we have come to recognize as 'therapy' for women.

Our original intention in forming the group was to focus on and analyse the opposition we encountered from male colleagues. In the light of our group experience, we have revised those aims for various reasons. First, we feel it would be a retrograde step to address further the 'male predicament' since the group's concern is to provide space for women to look at their own condition, away from the pressure of feeling responsible for the men in their lives. Second, the opposition from male colleagues did not, in the final analysis, significantly influence our thinking about the group. Our single mindedness and clarity of purpose – which enabled the group to take place – has subsequently impressed both female and male colleagues.

What is the aim of the group?

As female social workers we were becoming increasingly concerned about the number of women who were coming to the attention of the psychiatric and social services, and being labelled 'disordered' or 'inadequate' in some way. We felt that many had simply lost touch with themselves. They appeared to be trying to live their lives through their families – seeking fulfilment from their children's or partner's successes, rather than their own. We drew these conclusions from the comments made to us:

> 'What's wrong with me? Why am I so miserable?'
> 'Why can't I be satisfied like everyone else?'
> 'It's me that's the problem. Everyone else seems OK.'
> 'He says it's me that's changed, not him.'
> 'I've got no more to give, I feel empty.'

The established institutions, and the services they offer, appeared to us to re-enforce the idea that it is always the women who are the problem. Unfortunately, the label of patient/client provides relief for many women and their families, who feel they are no longer required to make changes, but simply to ride out the storm and wait for the treatment to cure the 'pathology' – be it mental illness, inadequate mothering skills, or whatever.

Our group meetings take place outside the premises of the Hospital and Area Social Work Office, in a Family Centre which is comfortable and similar to a family home. We focus on the causes of the unhappiness rather than the symptoms, and on the woman's ability to do something about those causes – thus putting the responsibility to change things, and take control, back where we feel it belongs. Our aims are therefore similar to those of many family therapists, in that we attempt to broaden the options open to the women.

What do our referrers want?

The criteria for referral used by our colleagues in various professions have changed over the years. Due to the nature of the agencies in which we work, we initially felt that we needed to justify our group in terms of the benefits it could provide in relation to 'child care' or 'mental health'. Women would need to be seen as 'better mothers' or 'cured'. We no longer feel this pressure. Our referrers have noticed that the women who have attended the group have needed less of their time. We have proved our point. Nowadays there is a better understanding of the connection between nurturing the woman and therefore nurturing the child; nurturing the woman and thereby protecting her mental health. The existence of our group has provided doctors and social workers with somewhere to direct women who have asked for 'something for themselves' – which has become a legitimate request. Women no longer need to present themselves as potential child abusers or psychiatric patients in order to qualify for attention.

What do the women want?

Therapy sessions run in 10–12 week blocks roughly following school term times to ease the burden on the crèche workers. At the beginning of the term we have a brainstorming session, to elicit what the women want and expect from the group. Some of the most common suggestions include the following: 'space of our own'; 'we want to share our specific needs and similar emotions'; 'unbiased feedback and an outside view'; 'the chance to talk about problems without burdening family and friends'; 'trust'.

Our response

Our search for a theoretical basis, and our need to update ourselves on developments in feminist thinking and how it relates to family therapy, led us to attend the second annual conference on feminism and family therapy – 'Gender and Power in Families' – which was run by a group of concerned women family therapists in London in the summer of 1987. We hoped it would help us to consolidate our own ideas and enable us to find an approach that would be helpful and appropriate to the level of awareness of the women attending the group, as well as ourselves. The influence of the conference was powerful and in particular it made us aware of the 'connections' women need to make to help them sustain good mental health. One of these might be the connection between society's unrealistic expectations and what is humanly possible. In addition, we were impressed by the idea that women are often regarded by others as 'over-involved' mothers, particularly when they nurture their daughters, themselves, or other women in the same way as they nurture their sons and other male family members. The encouragement given to our sons to express their needs and learn how to get them met, should be extended to our daughters and ourselves as women.

In *The Theory and Practice of Psychotherapy*, Yalom provided guidelines, but we attempted to clarify and reshape these ideas. Emphasis was given to the validity of what the women have achieved in their lives to date, but we also steered them away from the notion of women as the masochistic server, the constant carer, with a need to please others in order to feel fulfilled. We worked from the premiss that once the women felt better about themselves, they would be better able to 'take' for themselves, and take responsibility for ensuring that their needs are met.

What sort of women attend the group?

The seriousness of the women's situations must be pointed out in order to keep the reader in touch with the complexity of our task when we describe how we tackled it, and the frequent light-hearted interactions that took place.

During our first term of meetings it was revealed that three members were seriously suicidal. Another woman had regretfully divorced her much-loved husband after thirty years of marriage as he was deeply depressed, anorexic, and in fact dying – and she could no longer bear to watch helplessly as he slowly killed himself. Four members had suffered serious and often prolonged sexual abuse, which had led one to abuse alcohol with the result that she physically handicapped her unborn son. Two members were totally unassertive and remained silent for many weeks – illustrating graphically the difficulties daily life posed for them. Others could not speak without crying. The young sons of two members, one of whom was only 8 years old, were self-mutilating. Both children were suicidal.

How we tackled group meetings

On reflection, it appears that our work with the group seems to have involved four main areas of focus, which can loosely be described as making connections with other group members and between their difficulties and what society expects of them, reframing dilemmas (turning negative situations into positive ones), giving permission (to do things differently if they wished), and, finally, broadening their options.

We initially felt that it would be extremely difficult to make connections within such an apparently diverse group of women – whose ages ranged from early 20s to late 50s. We were to be pleasantly surprised.

As well as giving each member the time and space to talk about whatever she wished – feelings, problems, and so on – we also undertook various exercises, including role playing and psychodrama, and used various art media in almost everything we did. This enabled the more introverted members to express themselves and work through their difficulties when verbal communication was impossible. It also resulted in the spontaneous and totally unexpected use of imagery that became an accepted and stimulating part of the 'essence' of the group. The women became beautiful flowers, blossoming trees reaching for the sun – despite roots embedded in 'abuse', 'drugs', and 'depression'. The play-doh models that they made of themselves were initially featureless powerless blobs; gradually these took shape and they were able to remove from themselves the offending 'blob' that represented their misery.

We, as group leaders, also set ourselves up as role models – the 'good mothers' – who would nurture them, approve of them, and give them permission to be different from us and their own mothers. We also attempted to demonstrate that conflict can be dealt with, and people can still remain intact, and even enjoy a successful outcome. Our aim was to give the women a different experience, and we were prepared to utilize anything at our disposal to achieve this – whether it was a previously recognized therapeutic tool or not.

The 'nurturing' we undertook involved exercises that looked at their 'positives' – which we insisted they each had, and that the whole group, and eventually themselves, could recognize and express. The idea that it was within their control to change their approach to life was constantly re-enforced.

To raise self-esteem and 'make connections' we looked at the socialization of women – their own upbringing – and the expectations of society as a whole that women will fulfil certain roles. Although very basic to us, some of the women had never considered their function in such general, global terms.

We acknowledged that 'taking' for themselves might be a new experience, but argued that it need not conflict with their traditional role as carers. We valued the experience and contribution of two members who were very maternal in the way they related to, and nurtured, the others. We were able to demonstrate that this was their way of asking for some caring for themselves.

Another early connection we enabled the group to make was their common feeling of 'loss' of control, self-esteem, and self-confidence. Tied up with this loss was a sense of violation. This was related to both the sexual abuse suffered, and the things that various 'others' had done to them, robbed them of, or denied them. This linked up with a discussion we had about mothers and daughters in which it became clear that they were more distressed by what their mothers had not done for them, than by what they had done. Their mothers had not taught them how to have their own needs satisfied – merely to satisfy the needs of men, and not 'rock the boat or upset anyone'.

We then looked at what they were passing on to their own daughters, how this differed from their relationships with their sons, and whether the patterns of past generations were being repeated. We used play-doh for the exercise, and asked the women to model themselves and their mothers, and place them in relation to each other on the table in front of them. We were amazed at the impact of this simple exercise and the depth of insight it gave us into the women's lives and feelings. One member made two faceless blobs, and placed one on each corner of the table as far apart as she could possible manage. She could not bear us to bring them closer together and became agitated when we tried. She did not calm down until the 'mother' blob had been placed outside the door.

Another woman set her two figures at a distance from each other, and then proceeded to move them closer. When the 'mother' figure got too close to her she screwed it up and buried it under the remaining play-doh in the dish. She then sat quietly weeping. It emerged that this woman had been sexually abused for years by her stepfather and when she told her mother about it, she had not been believed. We were able to look at this in depth in a later session, and use role playing/psychodrama to help the woman come to terms with the issue.

The woman who found it almost impossible to speak modelled a shape resembling half a coconut and placed it upside down on the table – like a dome. Gentle coaxing revealed that this was her mother. When she was asked why she had not modelled herself she lifted the dome to reveal a small round blob inside, and said, 'There I am.' She went on to explain, calmly and lucidly, that her mother was like a shell, encasing her, smothering her, and blocking out the light – but without ever touching her. She pointed out the space inside the shell she had made, which prevented it from touching the small round blob.

We saw the process of growing and gaining maturity among the women as a process of accepting what their mothers had given them, and forgiving them for what they had withheld.

The play-doh exercise was repeated but this time the women modelled themselves and their daughters and examined what they could be passing on to their daughters from their relationship with their mothers.

We felt that the mother–daughter exercise made room for things to change, and gave us the chance to give permission to the women to change and do things differently if they wished. One woman who had modelled her mother as looking over her shoulder found herself able to move her away and place her in a position and at a distance that felt more comfortable. Much to our surprise she was later able to do this in reality, and laid down ground rules concerning the times and frequency of her mother's visits. The obsession with housework that this same woman had inherited from her mother was reframed by the group as a positive sign that she cared for the family, but the group also emphasized that 'taking space' for herself was a necessity, rather than something to feel guilty about. We all gave her permission to do things differently from her mother as she grappled bravely with her obsession.

In taking a nurturing, maternal role as leaders we recognized that we were liable to have some of the anger and rejection the women felt towards their own mothers directed towards us. We were prepared for this and would have seen it as healthy. We had planned to use the experience as a means of changing the women's understanding of that relationship and putting them more in control. This sort of confrontation did not happen.

Another session focused on the dependent/independent sides of ourselves, which need not be in conflict, and the fact that no one is solely 'male' or 'female', but a satisfying mixture of both. This was undertaken in response to a member who insisted initially that all she needed was a strong man to lean on and she would be happy! In a psychodrama exercise we placed several bean-bags which represented dependency at one end of the room and asked the women to position themselves in relation to the bean-bags. Those who felt strong and independent were to stomp around at the opposite end, declaring how strong they felt, and those women who felt particularly vulnerable and dependent could curl up on the bean-bags. Others could take up positions somewhere in the middle of the room. Once the women had found the position in which they felt most comfortable, we instructed them to change position to the opposite extreme. We wanted all the women to experience all the positions. Again we were surprised at the impact this exercise was to have. Several women were unable to leave the security of the bean-bags, and one woman who had pressed herself to the wall at the 'independent' end became distressed and sobbed when she momentarily sat on a bean-bag. Others refused to curl up on the bean-bags at all. Many women were amazed at where they had placed themselves, and at their reactions when asked to try a different position in the room. All agreed they had learnt things about themselves. We went on to discuss some of the implications of the exercise. The fact that being independent at times necessitates being assertive was picked up and dealt with in another session on 'appropriate assertiveness'. The consensus was that free movement between the extremes felt most comfortable, provided one did not stay at either end of the room for too long.

We also acknowledged that independence involves taking responsibility for one's happiness and ensuring that our needs are met – including our sexual needs. This was demonstrated by a woman who moved her hands like fish swimming in the sea. She said that we are like the fish, who sometimes brush against each other, leaving a few scales behind, but then swim off in opposite directions. We cannot therefore rely on another person for happiness. One outcome of the discussion on sexual needs, and how women are entitled to ask for these to be met, was that the two women who considered they had a 'weight problem' and were not worth loving, now regularly shop together for 'pretty things', particularly underwear – to the delight of their children who, they told us, dance around the shops yelling out 'knickers' while they are in the changing rooms! As one of these women had the 'obsessional housework' problem, her gains from this friendship are twofold for her. She has less time for housework, and her sex life has improved as she is now able to initiate sexual relations for the first time.

During our interactions in the group, we attempted, however clumsily, to interpret each other's, and our own, artwork. This also allowed us to 'reframe' things for the women. The 'festering worms' which dominated the life of our 'silent' woman were reframed by the group into something potentially good that could enrich her life in the way that worms enrich the soil. We were able to point out that we all have our 'festering worms' which must be acknowledged and used rather than allowed to remain morbid and destructive thoughts. In her last painting of 'the worms' they took up only half a page. The other half contained arrows pointing away from the worms, which the woman explained represented herself moving away from the worms, and larger arrows pointing towards them, which she said represented the group reaching out to her. She had expressed this feeling in her own way, despite the fact that during many of the sessions she was plagued by the hallucinatory symptoms of psychotic mental illness.

Outcome and evaluation

During the past term, which was the second ten-week 'block' of the group, attendance was virtually 100 per cent. All but one woman were new members. At the first session the women completed a questionnaire devised largely to measure feelings of depression. The second questionnaire at the end of the term showed improvements in about half the categories for each woman.

An anonymous consumer survey form, completed by all who come to the centre, was also filled in by members of the group. All felt the group had been useful and valuable to them, and gave the following reasons:

'Realizing I am not alone.'
'The discipline of attending.'
'The chance to put on paper what I felt.'
'I was dead and empty inside, and now I have feelings.'
'I have become more positive.'
'I liked not having to stick to the programme, so that if something arose we did modelling or painting to look at it.'
'I think more of myself and make time for myself.'

We cannot be sure, of course, to what extent, if at all, the women might be protecting us by their comments. However, our own observations certainly support their positive remarks. To say we have watched the women 'bloom' is an understatement. Our request for suggestions on ways we might improve the group was not taken up, which we regretted. We feel that a test of their newly found confidence would be the ability to challenge how the group is run, and ourselves as leaders – and we plan to tackle this in the next term.

All but one member elected to return to the group the following term. The woman who left, a depressed young mother of two, had clearly benefited as she is now able to talk about herself without crying. She had made a new friend, and started to allow herself an occasional evening out – which she had not done previously. She was pleasantly surprised to find that her husband liked the person she had become, and supported her totally in her 'search for herself'. She has the option of returning to the group if she feels the need.

Negotiations for women to leave the group when they are ready are seen as positive, and something they are all working towards. However, we like to see evidence of change before that decision is reached, and the women are extremely good at recognizing signs of improvement in one another. These usually include improved posture, greater contribution to sessions, increased eye contact, wider outside interests, spontaneous laughter, a softening of attitudes towards their children, and reports of greater harmony at home. The encouragement the women offer each other in achieving these ends is often a moving and humbling experience for us. The 'breakthrough' for one particularly rigid member – who always sat bolt upright in her single chair with her arms crossed – came the day she walked in, kicked off her shoes, and flung herself unceremoniously on to the nearest bean-bag. This startling turn of events was not missed by a single woman, and from the laughter and celebration that ensued one might have been forgiven for thinking she had just conquered Everest!

We are quite happy for members to attend for two or three terms, and do not consider this unreasonable for women who have to redress the balance of a lifetime punctuated by rejection, loss, and unequal treatment. Neither do we foresee 'group dependency' as becoming a problem, as we are constantly moving the women on, guiding them through the transition, and fostering the expectation that they will 'take the plunge' towards a more rewarding life for both themselves and their families. Our faith in their ability to do so remains unshaken.

References

Ernst, S. and Goodison, L. (1981) *In Our Own Hands*, London: The Women's Press.

Yalom, I.D. (1970) *The Theory and Practice of Psychotherapy*, New York: Basic Books.

Chapter fourteen

Psychotherapy, oppression and social action: gender, race, and class in black women's depression

Sue Holland

The setting in which I work as a community clinical psychologist is an urban multiracial housing estate in west London. The life experienced by many of the women living here can be summed up by the term '3D': depression, discrimination, and deprivation. At the root of their depression and self-deprecation lies a history of abuse, exploitation, and misuse of themselves, as babies, as girls, as women, as working class women, as black women . . .

Any psychotherapeutic intervention in their depression must address not only issues of loss and guilt, anger and reparation, but also the hidden rage and desire for justice provoked by years of poverty and oppression. A psychotherapy which does not do this is merely adaptation, not emancipation, and so by default becomes, like the prescribing of tranquillizers, another weapon in an oppressive social system's armoury of social control.

Tranquillization by means of chemotherapy is, however, much more immediately effective in suppressing the expression of desires and feelings, and consequently it is used in huge quantities on our urban housing estates as well as in our prisons and hospitals (Collier 1989). The recipients of this suppressive treatment are frequently black, no doubt due to a subconscious recognition, by the usually white prescribers, of the rage and sense of injustice simmering just beneath the patient's symptoms.

It is certainly 'the method of choice' used by the majority of local general practitioners and psychiatrists (though not of the women patients' choosing). So it was within this prevalent model of chemical suppression that our neighbourhood psychotherapy – and social action – programme was set up, not by the health authority but under the relatively progressive control of the Social Services.

Using psychodynamic counselling as a tool for action, rather than as an end in itself, our programme aims to help women move from a mechanistic view of themselves as suffering from 'nerves' towards an interpretative self-exploration via individual focal psychotherapy, and then on into group experiences which help them to voice shared histories (herstories) and collective desires: 'What do we want for ourselves?' Finally, from this collective articulation of their needs and desires, the women are encouraged to address themselves to the social structure itself, which defines and limits them in terms of their gender, race, and class.

This housing estate would nowadays be described as 'multi-cultural', its tenancies held predominantly by African, Caribbean, Asian, and Irish people. But the names of its roads – South Africa Road, India Way – remind us firmly that it is Britain's imperialist history which has brought the people here. The names of its blocks of flats – Cornwallis, Rhodes, and so on – celebrate white imperialists who won fame by putting down the uprisings of oppressed peoples in other parts of the globe. Everywhere there are daily reminders of the historic racism which has justified white superiority and victory over black peoples. Black and national minority tenants receive this silent message every time they go out of their front doors. History has subjugated them and the present continues to do so.

Racism is a very coherent ideological excuse for the domination of different groups. Throughout history a white group, Europeans, has dominated. European thought is Eurocentric because over recent history it has been predominantly white European groups which have written history. When we are dealing with very personal issues in psychotherapy, we must acknowledge that this is the wider context in which we relate to each other. This is difficult to achieve because linking individual, and very personal, psychotherapeutic issues to the wider context of global imperialism is complicated. These are issues that many of us have been struggling with for years. I have been struggling with this problem in mental health for more than twenty years, partly because of where I come from, or where historically I am coming from. I am speaking as a transracial person; an Anglo Indian.

It is possible for some to say, 'I am black.' I have to say, 'I'm black and white.' I am partly a white supremacist. I *also* feel and identify as an oppressed black woman because I am transracial, coming from a colonial background. My earliest memories are of leaving India because my family had chosen to ally itself with the white supremacists, which in fact my mother represented, although the white part of her is Irish! My father has less white blood in him and is more Asian; when he was ill-mannered we used to call him a 'Bengali Babu'. During my first years in England I denied that I looked Asian; I had very black hair and slightly slanting eyes and the other kids at school called me 'Chinky Chinky'. In 1947 people were noticed for being different. I have blended through the years as I have grown greyer and

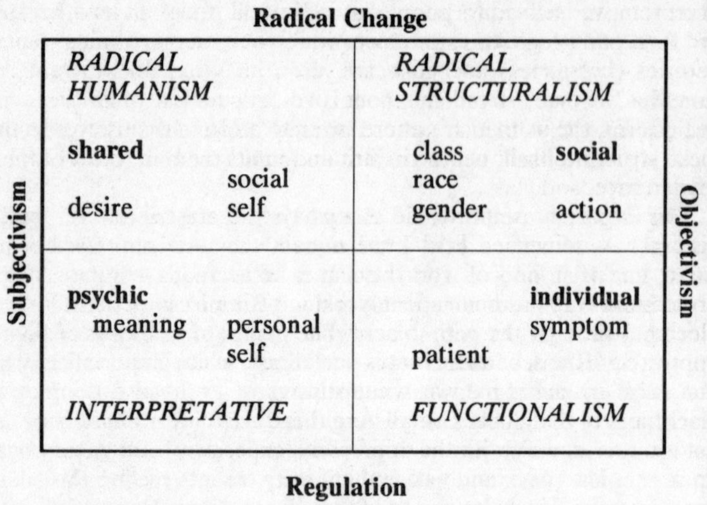

Radical Change

	RADICAL HUMANISM		*RADICAL STRUCTURALISM*	
	shared		class	**social**
		social	race	
Subjectivism	desire	self	gender	action
	psychic			**individual**
	meaning	personal		symptom
		self	patient	
	INTERPRETATIVE		*FUNCTIONALISM*	**Objectivism**

Regulation

The horizontal dimension runs between the objective and subjective poles.

Objectivism emphasizes a natural-science model; the organism, or even the machine. Things are measurable and quantifiable.
Subjectivism emphasizes the unique qualities of human experience, interpretation of meanings, and use of symbols.

The vertical dimension runs between the radical and regulative poles

Regulation suggests a relatively static or slowly evolving social situation.
Radical change implies that radical change is desirable or even inevitable.

By using this model of therapeutic intervention, depressed women can move through psychic space into social space and so into political space. 'Finding a space for oneself' thus becomes a series of options, each more socially connected than the last, in a progression from private symptom to public action.

Source: Burrell and Morgan (1979) and Whittington and Holland (1985).

Figure 14.1 Theoretical positions involved in moving from personal symptom to public action

more wan, and nowadays people say, 'Oh well, you don't look Indian', or 'You don't look this', or 'You don't look that'. Although some people say, 'You're not English, are you?', I have come to the conclusion that what we are talking about is colour sensitivity and there has been a change in British culture around colour sensitivity because there are more black people in Britain than there were in 1947 when I first arrived.

The important point for me as a psychotherapist is that this racist history has influenced how I see myself, the interest I take in my work, and what kind of work I do. It is no accident that most of my professional life has been spent working with mixed-race groups, exploring issues to do with black/white identity, and working with oppressed groups, because that is part of me. In contrast I must admit that another part of me was white supremacist – I was putting down black people and Asians as all Anglo Indians did, because they did not want to identify with the oppressed Asians. But although growing up in that kind of a family has taught me a lot, gut feeling just hasn't been enough. I have also had to look at how I could make use of existing theories and methods and work that has been done in the past.

I am not going to be an apologist for psychotherapy. I would actually be harder than most on European, white psychotherapy because I have seen its tremendous failings and it has not given me enough – although I am a clinical psychologist with psychotherapy training – because its practice and its professional institutions are both severely limited and dominated by white Eurocentric thought. Non-Europeans within these institutions are usually the focus of radical but painful conflict (Fernando 1988; Khan 1988). Suffice to say that over the last seventeen years since leaving the Tavistock Clinic with my psychotherapy training, I have worked with mostly working-class, transracial, and black people, trying to use psychotherapy in a way which would help them not only to change themselves but to change things around them. So I have had to struggle not only with psychotherapy itself, which has its limitations, but also to find other kinds of theories which would help me to achieve this.

I have set out in diagrammatic form (Figure 14.1) the framework I use when I try to talk about 'baggages of theories', because everybody carries around theories and assumptions about what is usable and useful in their work. It contains some of the material I have worked with, alongside my husband, over many years. He comes to problem intervention from a sociological background and has worked with and taught social workers. I have related that experience to my therapy and we have been interlinking some of the work that we have been doing over the years as to how we use theory in therapy, and how we can criticize theory from a sociopolitical and a psychodynamic standpoint. The diagram proposes that for practical purposes we can divide up our baggage of theory into sets of what Burrell and Morgan (1979) loosely called 'paradigms'. In its more precise form the term paradigm derives from Thomas Kuhn (1962) who used it to identify competing positions in the natural sciences.

We take two poles, a vertical pole and a horizontal pole. We mark the vertical pole at one end 'radical change'. These kinds of theories are based on the idea that radical change of society is either inevitable or desirable. It may be political change of the class structure that is emphasized, or personal change which avoids collectivism. At the other pole of the dimension we identify the more conservative approach concerned with 'regulation' and 'adaptation'.

We then introduce a horizontal dimension which distinguishes 'objective' and 'subjective' approaches. 'Objective' approaches emphasize measurement, quantification, experimentation, and hard-scientific criteria. Subjective approaches celebrate feelings, symbols, meanings, and ideas that one cannot necessarily measure and quantify.

It is important to appreciate that we all carry theoretical baggage of this kind: assumptions and paradigms of which we may not be aware. At the bottom of the vertical axis are the objective, adaptational, and regulative theories which can be summed up as 'functionalist' in character; we look at ourselves as machines that function or dysfunction and break down – there is a hiccup in the system or the machinery has gone wrong but we can adjust it slightly. It is a rather 'biologistic' theory, reminiscent of an 'engineering' stance, which in our field means describing people as symptoms or patients. Presenting problems classically include 'nerves', blood pressure, sleep disturbance; typical symptoms of a wide range of mental-health conditions.

In the present context I am referring particularly to depression in black women, since much of my work is concerned with depression in women and particularly in black and national minority (such as Irish) women. From the biologistic standpoint described above, the treatments offered would be drugs or behaviour therapy – typical 'social-engineering' solutions which get people ticking over again but we do not bother with the challenging question, 'What does it all mean?'

If we consider the subjective area on the figure then clearly we are concerned with issues of psychotherapy. Psychotherapy is implicit in the subjective approach and it certainly does ask the question, 'What does all this mean?' It consists of interpreting the meaning of depression: what is the sufferer trying to do, what is she trying to say? Being subjective, we cannot actually measure the depression, we can only listen and try to find out what is going on.

My criticism of white psychotherapy is that it is used within an institutional system which is Eurocentric, which dominates society in many ways, and which tends to offer merely regulatory, adaptational ways of getting people ticking over again. It does not make any headway towards providing an understanding of why black women feel as they do. For insights of this kind we must turn to theories of radical change. The subjective area of radical change can be identified as the philosophy of humanism: the belief that race is a fiction, except in the very general sense of the welfare and progress of the entire human race. The radicalism takes the form of consciousness-raising groups. Race awareness and the exploration of our subjective feelings towards each other: the 'groupy' movement asserts that basically we are all good and we can become 'better' if we so desire. Desire is an important word because we need to discuss not just the question of what it means but also what do we, as women, as black women or whatever, *desire*? What we really want only emerges when we get into groups.

But we cannot actually do just what we wish, and I will explain, in some examples from my work, why I honestly do not think one can achieve the most significant changes in an individual psychotherapy session. We have to face the fact that racism cannot be eradicated by individual change; it can only be eradicated by in turn eradicating imperialism. Although some readers may begin to sigh with boredom and start saying, 'Oh, God, she's a bloody Marxist!', we must face the facts that racism exists because it works, not because it is an unfortunate thing that gets in the way of you and me relating. It really works! It actually divides the world in a way which allows certain groups to enjoy tremendous power, profit, and wealth. Furthermore, it builds in its own explanation for this oppression, so a Christian can, for example, believe that although we are all God's children, one can still justify exploiting Third World countries because 'they are underdeveloped'. This attitude does not address the fact that they have not been allowed to develop, and have actually had their development distorted.

When we hear talk of culture, particularly Afro-Caribbean cultures, we must remember that because of this system of world imperialism over many generations Afro-Caribbean culture has been distorted, and that is the secret hidden in the word 'underdevelopment' (Rodney 1972). It has served as an ideological disguise for European exploitation. It has neutralized the guilt of Christians or members of whatever dominant religion has been recruited by the ruling power block. This is a crucial point because it actually gets us back into the question of depression. We must view depression not only in the Freudian sense of loss whereby the loss of a significa other is transformed into an ego loss and so becomes the core of sel deprecation (Bollas 1987), but also in terms of loss as *expropriatic* in which something is stolen from us. The difference is significan We can lose people we love, we can be let down in childhood b people leaving us because they have died or rejected us or run awa from us. That is loss as it relates to depression, and many blac women are very depressed. But in my work with them we return ove and over again to the same history of being separated from mother rejoining mothers that they did not know, leaving grandmothers the loved, finding themselves in a totally different relationship, bein sexually abused, being put into care, and so on: all the kinds of cir cumstances with which clinicians working in this field are familia That is loss, but expropriation is about what imperialism and neo colonialism does – it steals one's history; it steals all kinds of thing from black people, from people who don't belong to a white suprem acist race.

I cannot claim to have all the answers for these problems. I am stil struggling to understand these issues more fully, but what I am trying to demonstrate is the usefulness of connective and radical ways o working. For example, psychotherapy in individual work is useful tc explore questions of loss in women, whether black or white, since i is not only black women who experience loss. What I am arguing is that many black, working-class, and transracial women experience ex- treme forms of loss because of the circumstances of their lives. The health statistics show that more working-class babies and more working-class women die prematurely, so it follows that there must be more loss in working-class groups. If one differentiates among the black working-class groups, the statistics become more pronounced. In other words, more loss is experienced by some groups simply because the social system differentiates them further into subclasses. At a personal level within the family, such loss is experienced as personal loss, and in depression it is turned against oneself in the form of damaging self-hatred – 'My mother left me because I was aggressive. I was bad and aggressive and so I remain.' This process becomes a kind of damaging self-hatred. But there is also another kind of self-hatred that concerns identification. It is equally dangerous and is based on the idea that when the world was divided up globally into an oppressor group and an oppressed group, the oppressed group became identified as 'bad', taking upon themselves the negative identity found in much black self-description (Fanon 1967).

Many of the black women with whom I work present both depression and a negative black identity – 'Black women are bad and white omen will be kind to us.' This can be explored in psychotherapy ith white, black, or transracial psychotherapists, and certainly has be challenged, confronted, and changed. The weakness of one-to-ne psychotherapeutic methods lies in the fact that it is not always asy to open out the deeper sociopolitical issues, actually to look at hat is happening to so many black women. In my work in the White ity Project, which is now in its ninth year, I have tried to use focal sychotherapy with very depressed black women over a period of nonths to work on the focus of the depression and the loss in relaion to mothers and other close relatives.

In 1982 we set up an Afro-Caribbean women's history group where lepressed black women could get together and discover that, to their urprise, they have a common, shared, but hidden, history. This is onscientization (Freire 1970) and emphasizes not only the women's hared sense of suffering and loss, but also their collective strengths ind mutual interdependence in their struggle for change and emanipation. This is crucially different from the individualistic and Eurocentric notion of 'self-realization'. For example, many of the women discovered that they had at least two first names, one given by their own mothers and one by the European priest or their English friends and workmates. Thus, for example, a Nigerian 'Ibironke' would become 'Elizabeth', a Barbadian 'Carmelia' would become 'Carol'. Their names/identities had been expropriated by Europeanization. In the group we were able to reclaim our rightful names.

This might seem terribly simplistic, but many of the women with whom I work are middle aged and have not experienced the black-consciousness movement which might have given them strength. They are black, working-class, middle-aged women who have often been totally debilitated by the racism they have experienced but not understood. They have never really understood why it was happening to them and have always tried to find excuses for the white people who were doing this to them.

In a group, the women can explore these issues and look at the kind of questions I raised at the beginning of this chapter – for example, the effect of colonialism and imperialism – not necessarily using those words, but looking at the shared histories of Barbadian, Jamaican, and Guyanian women. Interestingly, we discovered that the African women in the group were much stronger (though this might be a stereotype). I put that down to the fact that tremendous struggles and victories in African countries have given them strength in spite of their difficulties. The Afro-Caribbean women do not possess this Pan-African strength.

The Afro-Caribbean women do not usually look to Africa for their roots; in general it is the young black groups and the Rastafarians who look in that direction. The African women know more clearly where they are coming from and can see the racism more clearly. In the group we talk about such matters as the effect of the educational system and the health service on black women, as well as issues of history.

Interestingly, in some of my work with women who are depressed I pick up issues such as abortions that they had against their will, and which they felt were forced upon them by a doctor. They did not have a choice, and only long after the event does this emerge in the psychotherapy sessions. Again we see the difference between expropriation and loss.

Another conscientization group was organized for women in relationships with men from other racial/cultural groups. These 'mixed-blessings' groups revealed that racism was often implicit in the sexual feelings between black and white partners and that even where this could be overcome by warmth and understanding, the pervasive influence of institutionalized racism could destroy domestic bonds, as in the machinations of the Home Office in applying immigration laws. This was tragically illustrated by an English woman whose 'good-enough' marriage to a Moroccan was destroyed by the way in which Home Office officials sowed the seeds of doubt and disgust between the couple by means of separate interrogations and innuendo. This woman, in the group, had to recall the buried feelings of love and grief she experienced for her deported husband. Other members of the group were enraged at the injustice of the Home Office. Eurocentric attitudes were re-examined in the multiracial context so that, for example, the 'arranged' marriage began to seem less fragile than the European 'romantic' marriage with its one-in-three incidence of divorce.

One distinctive feature of the project I run is that it has few rules. Although I have quite definite principles, they allow great flexibility in terms of the kinds of action that may be chosen in order to carry them through. One principle defines the need for certain kinds of movement within the spaces laid out in the map given above. Through all the shifts and diversions, I retain the notion of moving people through the different spaces. They all seem to start off as functionalists, that is to say they see themselves as machines that need a bit of adjusting; they need a tonic, or they need some tablets for their 'nerves'. Working-class people, in contrast to those from the middle class, have been taught to think like this.

Middle-class women have had a different kind of education which often allows them to move straight into the interpretative area, asking 'Where does it come from?' or 'What does it mean?'

Working-class people tend to see themselves as machines, in derivation from the labour process which is their lot; they are not supposed to 'think' and so can only react like machines; they get back to the kitchen sink to do their domestic tasks or they get back to their job, whereas a more privileged, educated, middle-class person will not suffer these restrictions. The available psychotherapy never goes beyond these working-class expectations. They might do some groupwork but clearly it is possible to do groupwork that does not countenance movement towards radical change; groupwork that is contained within functionalist assumptions.

The most difficult task is moving people into that area of the map characterized by 'radical structuralism'. In other words, how can we change structures? More specifically, 'How the hell can we change imperialism?' I am not suggesting that we can go out today and change imperialism; what I am saying is that we must always remember that this is where the battle will eventually take us if we are serious about changing this kind of oppression. We cannot remain in the area of racism and race awareness; we have really got to live it even if we cannot be there in actuality – because of our own background, our professional training, and so on. We have to know that the people we work with will eventually have to move into the sphere of conflict and political action.

The White City project was a challenge for me because I had previously worked in Battersea in a project which lasted five years before a newly elected Conservative Council closed it down. We were doing radical work and exploring some of these ideas with comrades and colleagues such as social workers and social psychologists, involved in similar community work. I learned from experience that we had to put much more time into helping, working with, and bringing out the strength and resources in the people we were seeing, so that they could help each other.

The main criticism of the Battersea Action and Counselling Centre, about which much has been published (Holland 1974; Banton *et al.* 1985; Hoggett and Lousada 1985) is that we became too distracted by the exciting experience of being in an alternative kind of work. We failed to pass on our social psychotherapeutic methods to the groups of patients, clients, or consumers, so enabling these working-class people to build on the experience, take charge of the work, and make it their own.

Because I had learnt, as I saw it, a bitter lesson, I put all my energies into the goal of activating those who could go on to help themselves and others. I worked increasingly with national minority, mixed race, and black people. Processes of self-selection and discrimination mean that, as I see it, the housing estate where I work is a place in which people become trapped. It was undergoing what we might call 'ghettoization', in contrast to Battersea's 'gentrification'. (This is now changing again as the BBC takes possession of more of the area.)

A group of women who have come through the counselling and groupwork and who now run their own project (which has become larger than mine!) has emerged out of this work. I am part of the Social Services, and they are now a voluntary organization with a Council grant. They run a project in which they take on and work with women and provide many kinds of therapeutic and preventive services for them, daring to ask the questions 'What do they want?' and 'What do we want?' They are able to take on a lot of people who will not work with me because I am too middle class, too professional, too 'straight'.

This achievement involved a move into the area of radical structuralism because they underwent many struggles with the Council simply to obtain the premises from which they operate. They address the question, 'How can we change this bit of the world to meet our needs?'; they have to face the issue of who gets what, who is allowed to speak, who does what, and so on. Their difficulty is that they lay themselves open to persecution because, unlike the tranquillized housewife, they are making demands. That is why it is so difficult to move across the boundary into radical strucuralism and why the challenge must be faced if anything significant is to be achieved by way of change. It has got to be on *our* agenda (Holland 1988).

I will cite two examples. A woman telephoned me and, from her posh accent, I thought she was English. When she came to see me, I was surprised to see a Jamaican. She turned out to have been a fairly senior secretary, and the only black in a very large firm. A new boss had forced her to leave by reason of his racist attitudes. She had not come to me because of her loss of employment, but because for many months she had been experiencing terrible panic attacks, fear, and depression. She had been prescribed many antidepressant drugs by her general practitioner although she did not really approve of such treatment. Having heard about my work she had brought herself to see me.

It turned out that the first attack had happened on a tube train on her way to the Race Relations Board to make a complaint about her ex-employer. She had had a serious attack of panic and had gone home. So naturally – almost automatically, because of the way I think – I took up the incident in terms of its meaning in relation to the social system and in relation to racism. We worked with that and with the idea that she could actually *do* something; she could actually fight such treatment. But we also had to go through some of the tremendous loss in her life and the consequences for her of taking on the system. In the past she had been hospitalized after she gave birth to her second child, her black husband having left her. She had a breakdown which sounded like very serious post-puerperal depression, in that she had wanted to kill the child. She was so disabled by the fear that she was going mad again that she could not work in any way at all.

We picked up all the issues to do with loss, her own childhood history, all of the issues relating to her identity; she identified with her white employer and did not want to hurt, question, or challenge the firm. She was able to work through all of this and to seek compensation through a Law Centre. Although she did not want to go back to the job, she did want, and did receive, reasonable compensation.

This is a brief example of the interlocking processes of loss and expropriation. She had suffered personal loss and in addition, because of racism, her job (at which she excelled) had been expropriated. The point of the psychotherapy was to disengage her neurotic hostility towards her internalized lost objects/persons from the justifiable rage at oppressive treatment by others in the external world. The guilt in respect of the former was inhibiting her from taking appropriate action towards the latter.

My second example is not uncommon. A middle-aged Barbadian woman came because she was very depressed: she had been on drugs for many years and was becoming disabled by them. She had brought up her family, now in their teens and quite able to fend for themselves. What emerged was an abortion and sterilization about which she felt very desperate and guilty. She felt she had been pressed into it by her GP. She was also concerned about a forthcoming court appearance over a divorce. She felt she could not face being seen as a black woman, pregnant, because that would imply to the white court that she was a 'slut' – a 'black whore'.

All of this had to be engaged with in terms of images and identifications as part of the normal work of psychotherapy. The social issue of abortion and sterilization could not immediately be taken up in the psychotherapy but what we could address were issues to do with loss and grief and her rejection by her mother. Later the Afro-Caribbean group was able to talk about these shared experiences: the feeling that black women are offered abortion too quickly, that they get offered sterilization too quickly. So in contrast to the struggles of white middle-class women demanding the right to abortion, here they were saying, 'Why the hell are we always aborted?!' That, of course, is a racist issue.

It will be clear that I cannot offer an answer to all of the questions raised in this chapter, but I am sure that I now have a better idea of the territory we must traverse. This makes it possible to map out some of the processes that will be involved. In so doing we become more effective in the struggle. Particularly difficult is the problem of moving from a change in insight to a change in action, and to do this in a way which puts them in charge of the process. Ironically, as I write I am aware that in giving case-studies I am guilty of expropriating some part of their lives. For this reason, and because confidentiality is all the harder to keep when involved in the social intimacies of one particular neighbourhood, my readers must contain their desire for further illustration. Perhaps one day the women themselves will feel ready to publish their own stories.

Acknowledgements

This chapter grew out of a workshop presentation at the conference on Gender and Power in Families held in London in 1987. Some of the work described in it was also presented at the London 'Pam Smith Memorial Lecture' in 1984, the Leeds Feminism and Psychotherapy conference (1987), and the Birmingham Psychotherapy and Black People in the UK conference (1988). Its timely production in 'black and white' is entirely due to the editorial help of my husband Ray.

References

Banton, R. (1985) *The Politics of Mental Health*, London and Basingstoke: Macmillan.

Bollas, C. (1987) *The Shadow of the Object: Psychoanalysis of the Unthought Known*, London: Free Association Books.

Burrell, G. and Morgan, G. (1979) *Sociological Paradigms and Organisational Analysis*, London: Heinemann.

Collier, J. (1989) *The Health Conspiracy*, London: Century.

Fanon, F. (1967) *Black Skin, White Masks*, London: MacGibbon & Kee.

Fernando, S. (1988) *Race and Culture in Psychiatry*, London: Croom Helm.

Freire, P. (1970) *Cultural Action for Freedom*, Harmondsworth: Penguin.

Hoggett, P. and Lousada, J. (1985) 'Therapeutic interventions in working class communities', *Free Associations* 1(1): 125–52.

Holland, S. (1979) 'The development of an action and counselling service in a deprived urban area', in M. Meacher (ed.) *New Methods of Mental Health Care*, Oxford: Pergamon.

Holland, S. (1985) 'Loss, rage and oppression. Neighbourhood psychotherapy with working class, black and national minority women',

Pam Smith Memorial Lecture, Polytechnic of North London.
Holland, S. and Holland, R. (1985) 'Outposts of empire and castles of skin: depressed women on an inner-city estate', in B. Richards (ed.) *Capitalism and Infancy*, London: Free Association Books.
Holland, S. (1988) 'Towards prevention', in S. Ramon and M.G. Gianichedda (eds.) *Psychiatry in Transition: The British and Italian Experiences*, London: Pluto Press.
Khan, M.M.R. (1988) *When Spring Comes: Awakenings in Psychoanalysis*, London: Chatto & Windus.
Khun, T.S. (1962) *The Structure of Scientific Revolutions*, Chicago: University of Chicago.
Rodney, W. (1972) *How Europe Underdeveloped Africa*, Louverture: Bogle.
Whittington, C. and Holland, R. (1985) 'A framework for theory in social work', *Issues in Social Work Education* 5(1): 25–50.

Name index

Subject index